D1548076

THE MAKING OF A NEW EASTERN QUESTION

BRITISH PALESTINE POLICY AND THE ORIGINS OF ISRAEL, 1917–1925

by

D. Edward Knox

The Catholic University of America Press
Washington, D.C.

Library of Congress Cataloging in Publication Data

Knox, D Edward, 1940–
  The making of a new Eastern Question.

  Includes bibliographical references.
  1. Great Britain—Foreign relations—Palestine.
2. Palestine—Foreign relations—Great Britain.
3. Great Britain—Foreign relations—1910–1936.
4. Palestine—History—1917–1948. 5. Israel—History.
I. Title.
DA47.9.I77K58   327.4105694   80-21879
ISBN 0-8132-0555-7

TABLE OF CONTENTS

Acknowledgments

To the actors themselves and to my predecessors in the field, I acknowledge an immense and grateful debt. I also owe special and more personal debts to many who gave time, effort and encouragement to bring this work to fruition. First among these is Donald N. Lammers, my mentor and friend. Others significant to me are: Alan W. Fisher, Paul R. Sweet, L. Scott Van Doren, Alan Lawson, Paul Roberts, the late Al Wakstein, Lois D. Bilsky, L. Carl Brown, Sydney Nettleton Fisher, Harry N. Howard, Helen Webster and Alma Kelsall.

And then there are the inestimable contributions of a historian father, Dr. Lloyd H. Knox, a loving mother, Harriette Belle Boice Knox, and a wife and children, Esther Zahniser, Layla and Lloyd, to make it all worthwhile.

1

EASTERN QUESTIONS

The years from 1917 to 1925 cover a crucial period, arching over that critical juncture in the path of Middle Eastern history when the Ottoman Empire was undergoing the process of final partition among other, more viable empires. Since then there has emerged a pattern of relationships bearing a close resemblance to certain late eighteenth- and nineteenth-century patterns of imperial interaction involving the Middle East. This older pattern has been known under the general title of the Eastern Question, while the newer configuration has yet to attract a name fully descriptive of its broad implications. Within this context, British policy in the Middle East in general, and in Palestine in particular, provides the focus for the transition from the wider problem of the classical Eastern Question to what may provisionally be called the New Eastern Question.

The traditional Eastern Question, usually thought of as a nineteenth-century problem in diplomacy, had roots that stretched back at least as far as the sixteenth century. By that time the flank of the entire Muslim world had been turned by the opening of direct sea communications between Europe and the rest of the world. The Ottoman middleman in world trade never fully recovered. The flow of long-distance commerce that had sustained the existence of Middle Eastern governments, merchants, and artisans was gradually choked off. By 1800 trade was reduced to merely regional significance and the area's great cities had lost their place of preeminence.

A further assault on Ottoman trade and internal control occurred as European states gradually acquired from the sultan commercial concessions, including privileges of judicial extraterritoriality. These so-called capitulations, freely given at first, later became wedges of international controversy as European governments queued up to gain commercial favors at the expense of rivals and the Ottoman state. In time European states used these concessions for the purposes of protecting minority populations from the repressive hand of the Ottoman rulers, creating, in effect, states within the state.

Throughout the seventeenth and early eighteenth centuries the Ottoman Empire complacently continued to lose momentum. Centralized administration disintegrated; provincial and local chieftains throughout the Middle East gained the allegiance of various groups in a splintering society. The military mirrored this decline of a universal Middle Eastern society. The army had become unreliable, more interested in the securing of careers by hereditary right and in trade and business than in fighting. The navy was also in a state of advanced decay.

Despite this picture of general malaise, the empire lost little territory until the overwhelming defeats inflicted by Russia between 1768 and 1774. At this point, Ottoman weakness, demonstrated beyond any realistic hope of recovery, proved to be the precise factor which allowed the empire to survive another 150 years. The delicacy of the balance of power in Europe demanded that the European states decide in concert the fate of Ottoman territory, and the solidarity necessary for that decision was not forthcoming until after that balance had been shattered in the First World War. In effect, then, maintaining the balance of power while disposing of Turkish territories "when the palsied hand of the sultan could no longer hold the reins of power" was the essence of the Eastern Question.[1]

In a series of crises—the War for Greek Liberation, the Muhammad Ali crises, the Crimean War, the Eastern crises of 1875–1878— the powers, aided and sometimes impelled by insurrections within the empire, were able to agree on minor partitions of the empire's European territory. Through these "salami-slicing" tactics, the Turks were eased out of Europe almost entirely by 1914, and the Balkan nationalities were freed for further intrigue and aggression against each other, against the parent body, and even against the interested European great powers. These adjustments in the Eastern Question only postponed solution and, in fact, made each succeeding crisis during the nineteenth century that much more potentially explosive.

Conventionally speaking, the Question reached solution with the post-World War I partition of the Ottoman Empire. The state of sultans accepted defeat in October 1918, and in April 1920 at San Remo the British and French marked out the boundaries of what would become the states of the modern Middle East. In 1923 the Treaty of Lausanne put the seal of legality on the destruction of the Ottoman Empire. Therefore, it seemed that the Eastern Question as traditionally formulated would after 1923 disturb the peace of Europe no longer. It was agreed that the Question was solved. Even today, the standard work on the classical diplomatic problem is M.S. Anderson's *The Eastern Question, 1774–1923*.[2] For many purposes this chronological limitation has been considered adequate. But for others the Question has been thought to be broader than one relating only to the political identity of the historical empire.

In fact, there is a rather bewildering absence of scholarly consensus on the definition of such a long-lasting and intractable diplomatic problem. A survey of literature on the Eastern Question reveals that the one point on which various historians have agreed is that the Question has existed and still exists quite apart from a Turkish state.[3] However, it is also clear that the term *Eastern Question* is excessively vague and that an analytical statement of the essential characteristics of its modern phases may have some use.

In its most abstract form, then, the Eastern Question may be said to have sprung from an historical situation in which powerful states confronted, and accommodated, each other in relation to a disintegrating imperial structure which was rapidly losing relative power over an area of growing strategic and economic importance. Throughout the nineteenth century, the multinational, culturally retrograde Ottoman Empire was beset from within by the clamors of rising nationalities and from without by the more ambitious and puissant of the great powers. Today that ramshackle empire is gone— though pan-Arabism is a kind of shadowy successor. At any rate, the Middle East as it emerged from the debris of Ottoman rule has not recovered the power necessary to restore within the world community the influence and initiative it last possessed in the seventeenth century. The nationalities which once found a common target in the Ottoman overlord, when they were not vying with each other, have since been freer to range themselves against one another. They have found nationalism only a partial and imperfect solution. In addition to pronounced internal weakness and the want of a new indigenous leadership, the area has retained, and perhaps even gained, a certain strategic importance for the powers. These facts have given the contending factions in the Middle East the opportunity to seek champions from outside the region. They have also provided the opportunity for the powers to seek client classes and nationalities within the region.

Thus the underlying realities of the Eastern Question have survived to the present day, though veiled and endowed with a new shape. As the old Eastern Question lost its identification with Turkey in 1923 through the legal extinction of the state of sultans, so it gained a new life with the legal creation of a new political state in the Middle East in 1947–48. Since that time the Arab-Israeli conflict has played a central role in the development of the New Eastern Question.

In the final period of Ottoman decline, various nationalities began movements that would be major factors in giving definition to this new Question. The Western assault on the East had gradually become all-encompassing and by 1914 had not only penetrated the empire economically and divided it into spheres of influence, but had fatally infected it with the germs of nationalism, self-doubt, and an overwhelming sense of intellectual and material weakness. However, it was only with the war that the empire was fully turned over to the West. The Germans intruded as allies and the British as enemies. Turks, Greeks, Arabs, Jews, Armenians, and Circassians became pawns in a Western game; their homes were destroyed, their societies shattered, their populations decimated. After the war these nationalities lacked even the protecting facade of the defunct empire, and European nations imposed their will without too much difficulty.

In the midst of this apparent military and political defeat, the Turkish nation was reborn, out of the decay and death of the Ottoman Empire, in successful revolt against the West. The Arabs, less fortunate in geography and political experience, failed in their attempts to reject imperialism and colonial control. From resentment, war fatigue, and humiliation they formed their own nationalism.

Some writers, notably the Arab historian George Antonius, have dated the beginning of Arab nationalism from the late eighteenth and early nineteenth centuries.[4] It is true that some signs of an Eastern renaissance in parts of the Ottoman Empire were observable at this time, but these early efforts all proved abortive so far as the Arabs were concerned. These stirrings were all short-lived, lacking a comprehensive doctrine and having no clear causal links with later nationalist developments. Actually, Arab nationalism was hardly known before the early twentieth century, and a doctrine of Arab nationhood was not elaborated until after World War I and the partition of the Arab portion of the Ottoman Empire into League of Nations mandates.[5]

Arab nationalism, conceived in repression and reaction, had to build its experience from the most unpromising material in cheerless and uncongenial times. Cast adrift from their ancient religious and dynastic loyalties, separated by arbitrary and unfamiliar frontiers created by alien powers, and ruled by infidel proconsuls, the Arabs could rejoice in no new faith in patriotism, liberalism, or socialism. They depended instead on traditional and narrowly-based local and ethnic nationalisms of a Central European type.[6]

The Jewish experience was very different. The Jews, while able to trace a continuous though tenuous existence in Palestine throughout the centuries of the Diaspora, joined the Arabs and the British as meaningful elements in a Middle East settlement relatively late in the world war. They made their impact, then, not as indigenous inhabitants of Palestine, for the most part, but as Zionists, nineteenth-century products of unemancipated, unassimilated Jewish communities of Central and Eastern Europe. The Zionist movement was a reaction to solutions of the Jewish problem which looked to civic emancipation alone, a rejection of the hopes of Jewish disciples of the Enlightenment, and a reaffirmation of the continuity of traditional conceptions of the nature and goal of Jewish history.[7]

Still, Zionism was a European movement led by European thinkers and writers. In 1896 Theodor Herzl, an Austrian journalist, wrote the seminal *Der Judenstaat,* in which he advanced the idea of a practical solution of the Jewish problem by colonizing Palestine or Argentina with the recognition of the international community. In August 1897, he took his ideas to Basle, Switzerland, where he had succeeded in convening the First Zionist Congress. Out of this meeting came the World Zionist Organization to oversee Zionist affairs and the famous Basle Program, which declared that the aim of the movement was "to create for the Jewish people a home in Palestine secured by public law."[8] The program went on to outline its methodology for achieving this goal, and in 1917, through the British government, the Zionists succeeded in partially fulfilling their aim by gaining international recognition of certain vague rights in Palestine. This recognition, in the form of the Balfour Declaration, was hailed with joy around the world as the Magna Charta of Jewish liberation. Zionist Jews could now claim their national inheritance in Palestine with the confidence of high expectations.

In addition to the two nationalist movements with their extreme differences in origin, history, and spirit, there was the British Empire, the third element in the triangular relationship existing in Palestine after 1917. Britain's attitudes and goals in relation to the Eastern Question, whether during the nineteenth century or the twentieth, were remarkably constant. British concerns were chiefly to preserve a balance of power in Europe by denying Turkish territory to any

European rival, and more importantly, to keep safe the routes of trade and communication to India, the true treasure of the British Empire. Methods adopted to secure these concerns were applied flexibly and creatively. At times the navy was sufficient to control affairs in the Levant and the Straits; at other times naval power would have to be used in conjunction with political influence over the Sublime Porte in an effort to keep the Ottoman Empire from lapsing into a premature coma. When these policies failed, the British reluctantly resorted to occupying selected portions of Turkish real estate to maintain their control of the routes to India. Whichever method held sway at any one time, there was a continuous thread tying them together, and that was the negative aspect of British policy. British concerns in the Middle East were not intrinsic but consisted in denying advantages of territory or influence to potentially hostile powers such as Russia and France. Even in the twentieth century Britain would continue to be guided by its compulsive need to defend the approaches to the Suez Canal, the Red Sea, and the Persian Gulf from the encroachment of European powers. The territories involved were themselves of little commercial or political importance, but it was strategically vital that no one else have them.

The British military conquest of southern Palestine in 1917, then, brought together the major elements of future conflict—the Arabs, the Zionists, and the British. The years immediately thereafter witnessed the transformation of the body of the Ottoman Empire into the modern Middle East. They also saw the forging together of the converging movements of Arab and Jewish nationalism and the intrusion of imperial necessity into the tiny geographical area of Palestine and its oriental surroundings. And it was also in these years that the Eastern Question made a transition from being the problem that haunted the nineteenth century to the one that troubles the latter part of the twentieth.

In this connection it has proved extraordinarily difficult to ascertain either the motives and goals of British policy on Palestine as set in London or the realities of the Arab-Zionist-British relations in that country. What seems to be required is a vantage point from which both policy-making and affairs in Palestine can be viewed. Fortunately, we have such a vantage point in the person of a career diplomat, administrator, and intelligence officer, Sir Gilbert Falkingham Clayton, who was intimately acquainted with the situation in Palestine from 1917 to 1925. In view of the extent to which his records will be utilized in the following chapters, his career and outlook require a brief examination.

Clayton had a distinguished career in the forefront of Middle Eastern affairs from his earliest appointment as a lieutenant of the Royal
Artillery in the Omdurman campaign in the Sudan in 1898 until his
untimely death at the age of 54 in Baghdad in 1929.[9] When war
broke out in 1914, Clayton was already thoroughly experienced in
Arab affairs and administration as a result of having spent six years
as private secretary to Sir Reginald Wingate, the sirdar of the Egyptian army and governor-general of the Sudan. Clayton had just taken
over in Cairo the dual post of Sudan agent[10] and director of intelligence for the Egyptian army, "one of the most important, demanding
and influential posts in the British Middle East."[11] In February 1916
Clayton created the famous Arab Bureau as a branch of the Department of Military Intelligence. D.G. Hogarth, an archeologist and a
commander in the Royal Naval Volunteer Reserve, acted as the bureau's immediate director. The bureau's roster included such well-
known names as T.E. Lawrence, Ronald Storrs, Kinahan Cornwallis,
Stewart Symes, Alan Dawnay, and Colonel S.N. Newcombe.

Clayton was promoted to the rank of brigadier general in 1916 and
in the following June General E.H.H. Allenby offered him the position of chief political officer (CPO) of the Egyptian Expeditionary
Force, which was on the point of setting out to capture Jerusalem.
Clayton was chief administrator of occupied Palestine from December
1917 to April 1918, when he relinquished the post to Sir Arthur
Money. He continued as CPO until mid-1919, when he followed Allenby to Egypt to serve in the crucial post of adviser to the Egyptian
Ministry of the Interior. In 1922 he succeeded Sir Wyndham Deedes
as chief secretary of the government of Palestine and negotiated on
behalf of the Colonial Office an agreement between Transjordan,
then part of the Palestine Mandate, and British government. On re-
tiring as chief secretary in 1925, he became special envoy to Ibn Saud.
In 1929, he was appointed high commissioner to Iraq, where he died
a few months later.

This man in all of his various roles was known to contemporaries
to be careful, dispassionate, impartial, and thoughtful. He had a rare
ability to operate effectively with both Arabs and Zionists, to be identified closely with the Arab movement and at the same time accepted
by the Zionist Organization. Whether dealing directly with Palestinian, Sudanese, Syrian, or Egyptian affairs, he consistently directed his
efforts toward making Britain's base in the Middle East more secure.
Though a sensitive man, responsive to the needs of those with whom
he came in contact and sympathetic to the aspirations of the people
of the Middle East, he remained a rational, highly motivated, hard-

working civil servant. Wherever he served, he maintained a clear loyalty to his government and its policy and to the strategic needs of imperial Britain.

In these crucial, formative years for Palestine, Clayton influenced, and was naturally affected by, many of the contemporaneous issues of policy. He was a key figure in the debate over the nature of the British relationship to the Middle East—the struggle between that may be called the A.T. Wilson and the T.E. Lawrence schools of thought, between the Anglo-Indians and the Anglo-Egyptians. He had roles to play in the issues of Anglo-French tension over the Middle East, postwar economic development and demobilization. He was concerned about the rise of militant Turkish nationalism and the security of the Suez Canal, the Persian Gulf, and Britain's communications with India. And he had to deal with powerful groups, such as the Zionists and Arabs, over which he had little or no direct control.

The history of British policy in Palestine from 1917 to 1925 will, then, be studied primarily from the vantage point of Sir Gilbert Clayton as a highly placed official actually in the field. He himself may not have played the most decisive role in policy-making, but all official policy formulated in London or elsewhere had to pass through his hands before it could be translated into action in Palestine.

The study will begin with 1917, when the British government developed its Zionist and Arab policies preparatory to the drive toward occupying lands of the eastern Mediterranean. The complex interplay and development of forces and events after 1917 will be examined as political options were opening and closing while the Balfour Declaration, as an instrument of British policy, moved from brilliant success toward incipient failure. This declaration, the result of intensive negotiations in London between Zionists and their supporters and the British government, will be examined in terms of its meaning and its impact on the government's Arab policy from the date of issuance to the mid-1920s. The focus will be on Palestine and on the nature and growth of the various interpretations placed on this ambiguously-worded document by enthusiasts, skeptics, and administrators seeking to use it as a guideline for action.

This chronological investigation of British policy, treated within the general framework of the beginnings of a New Eastern Question, is intended to throw light on the continuous relationship of the Middle East and the world powers. It is also expected to illuminate the workings of the British Foreign and Colonial Offices in the Middle East at this time, to identify the makers of Zionist and Arab policy, and to determine the relative influence and perspicacity of the men in the field and their superiors in Whitehall.

2

GREAT BRITAIN AND PALESTINE
IN THE WAR, 1914–1917

British policy in regard to Palestine in the war years preceding 1917 was never formulated with any precision, despite an agreement with the French in 1916 to internationalize the administration of Palestine and despite exchanges of letters with the Arabs in 1915 and 1916 over the future of Arab territory. Many individuals, offices, and departments had concrete ideas and plans for Palestine's future, but the final working out of these ideas and plans, it was generally recognized, had to be left until the larger questions arising from the war were settled. At no time was it possible to say that British policy was monolithic in its approach to Palestine. Mark Sykes, the member of Lloyd George's "garden suburb" who was responsible for the Middle East from 1916 until his death in 1919, counted at one time eighteen authorities both in London and abroad who had to be consulted before a move involving the Middle East could be made. The Sharif Husayn, a British ally whose role in the fighting against the Ottoman Empire was a subject of controversy within the British government, noted once that he saw not one government, but five.[1]

This uncertainty, vagueness, and lack of coordination was not, of course, unlimited. By 1917, as a result of the wartime need to deal with Russian, French, and Arab claims for territory in the Middle East, the British had been forced into a delineation of interests that was a good deal firmer than they really wanted. For over a century, British policy toward the Eastern Question had been governed by the overriding need to guard the approaches to India by keeping the Asian portion of the Ottoman Empire intact and keeping Arabia, Persia, and Afghanistan together as a geographical bloc which Britain had no desire to occupy but which she was determined would not be occupied by any rival. When the Ottoman Empire drifted into hostilities against the Entente powers in late October 1914, the British had to reappraise traditional policy. Their reaction in terms of tactics was immediate, but it took much longer for a new strategic policy to emerge. Two days before Britain declared war on Turkey on 3 November 1914, she recognized Kuwait's independence from the Ottoman Empire. On 5 November she formally annexed Cyprus and on 18 December established a protectorate over Egypt. Militarily, Britain reacted even more swiftly. She reinforced Egypt, bombarded the Dardanelles forts, and landed in southern Mesopotamia an expeditionary force that had been standing by in the Persian Gulf.

Despite this evident departure from a "policy of conservation," due to the fundamental change in the British-Ottoman relationship, British policy continued to be guided by the principle of denying territory to all powers capable of threatening communication with India. True, modifications were necessary. In view of the great danger of war in the West, Ottoman hostility, and British sensitivity to the Russian alliance, Constantinople, no longer vital to British interests since about 1890, was considered expendable, if the Russians desired it. On the other hand, Egypt, which had acquired the Ottoman capital's former importance in British eyes, was significantly not annexed into the empire, though that had been the first impulse of the Foreign Office, but merely included under Britain's protection. In other particulars also, the British maintained traditional lines of policy. Because of a division of opinion between the Indian government on the one hand and Lord Kitchener and the Arabists of Cairo and Khartoum on the other, even Mesopotamia remained an undecided question so far as eventual territorial acquisition went. Palestine was wanted, not for itself, but for the security of the head of the Persian Gulf and to deny France proximity to Egypt and a border with Arabia.[2] Since the Entente powers were not prepared at any time during the war to permit one power to gain exclusive control of Palestine, except for a British base in Haifa, they were all reconciled to internationalizing its administration, in effect leaving it a buffer zone. In fact the most concrete conclusion to come from war committee meetings in March 1915 was that the government's territorial desiderata should be to preserve a Muslim political entity and to maintain the security of the Arabian holy places.[3]

In reluctant pursuit of its policy of security for its own interests in the southern portion of the Ottoman Empire, the British government prior to 1917 entered into two major understandings with its French and Arab allies. The first, the Husayn-McMahon correspondence, arose from a British desire to exploit Arab dissatisfaction with Turkish rule. The second, the Sykes-Picot Agreement of May 1916, resulted from an intense French diplomatic campaign to arrive at an early definition of war aims.

In Februrary and April 1914, Abdullah, the second son of Sharif Husayn of Mecca, had approached Lord Kitchener, British agent and consul general in Cairo, and Ronald Storrs, his oriental secretary, about a modest supply of arms for the sharif to use for defense against the Turks. He had, of course, been politely refused, but the visit was momentous nevertheless. In September, Storrs, after seeking and obtaining the approval of Captain Gilbert F. Clayton, then Sudan agent and director of intelligence of the Egyptian army, reminded Kitchener in a private letter of the encounter with Abdullah. Kitchener, now secretary of state for war in London, had long cherished the idea of an Arab kingdom under British auspices, and he fell in with the suggestion by issuing an immediate order for Storrs to send a "secret and carefully chosen messenger" to Abdullah to sound out the attitude of the Arabs toward an alliance with Great Britain should the sultan be forced into war.[4]

Subsequent negotiations were protracted, formal views being exchanged over an eight-month period (14 July 1915 to 10 March 1916). In his initial letter, Sharif Husayn spelled out the Arab position to Sir Henry McMahon, the first British high commissioner for Egypt. The letter, based on the so-called Damascus Protocol drawn up by Arab nationalist groups in Syria, required that England "acknowledge the independence of the Arab countries" within certain specified boundaries, as a reward for an Arab revolt in the interests of the Entente.[5] Months later, on 24 October 1915, after the Foreign Office had begged him at the urgent request of Sir Ian Hamilton at Gallipoli to take immediate steps to split the Arabs from the Turks for military reasons, McMahon replied to Husayn.[6]

Aware of simultaneous negotiations with the French and of the need for caution, he adopted a policy of deliberate vagueness.[7] He wrote Husayn that, subject to three reservations, "Great Britain is prepared to recognize and support the independence of the Arabs in all the regions within the limits demanded by the Sharif of Mecca."[8] Among these controversial reservations were two that affected the later treatment of Palestine. The first excluded the "portions of Syria lying to the west of the districts of Damascus, Homs, Hama and Aleppo" on the grounds that they were not purely Arab, and the second excluded those regions where Britain's freedom to act alone was limited by the "interests of her ally, France."

There is a large literature on the question of whether or not Palestine was included in McMahon's limitation of Arab independence.[9] McMahon and Clayton always maintained in later years that the sharif understood and initially accepted that Palestine's future had not yet been determined.[10] Unfortunately, these official explanations came long enough after the event to cast considerable doubt on their complete veracity, and the controversy has continued to grow. Currently the weight of evidence clearly supports the British contention that Palestine was not promised to the Arabs in 1915. First, in March 1916, Foreign Secretary Sir Edward Grey proposed to the French and Russian governments that the Allies offer the Jews "an arrangement in regard to Palestine completely satisfactory to Jewish aspirations," a firm indication, even though the proposal came to nothing, that the secretary considered Palestine excluded from McMahon's promise.[11] Second, the De Bunsen Committee (named after its chairman, Sir Maurice de Bunsen), appointed in April 1915 to study British war aims in the Middle East, recommended in June that Palestine should be the subject of "special negotiations, in which both belligerents and neutrals are alike interested."[12] Thus the committee fully recognized that Britain was not free to act on Palestine without consulting French and Russian interests, and in the circumstances, a promise of Palestine to the Arabs would not have been contemplated. Third, Lord Kitchener, a staunch supporter of the idea of an Arab caliphate under Husayn and with British backing, failed to point out to the British government that the Sykes-Picot Agreement of May 1916 might contradict the pledges given Husayn. The least this indicates is that British promises regarding the Middle East were considered to be of secondary importance, tentative or speculative, and open to redefinition. Fourth, and most conclusive, in April 1918, almost two years after the beginning of the Arab uprising, events in Europe caused the British to withdraw elements from east of the Jordan in order to send reinforcements to the western front. Clayton, at the time Allenby's chief political officer, wrote Mark Sykes that he expected no difficulty with Faysal, out on the right wing of the British army, regarding the pullback of troops.[13] He pointed out that the Arab leader had "always been apprehensive of our operating east of the Jordan in case it should lead to permanent occupation." Clayton continued significantly:

> He will, therefore, regard our withdrawal as a loyal consequence of the policy which we have always laid down in our dealings with him, e.g. that we regard the country east of the Jordan as his sphere so far as he is able to make good in it.

The implication of a delineation of territories is clear. The area east of the Jordan was to be open to Faysal's influence, while cis-Jordan would remain uncommitted to the Arabs and at the disposal of Britain and her allies. This unsolicited statement, a rare instance of direct contemporary evidence on this controversial problem, came from the pen of a man who was "in daily touch with Sir Henry McMahon throughout the negotiations with King Hussein, and made the preliminary drafts of all the letters." It offers strong support for the claim Clayton made in 1923, at Sir Herbert Samuel's request, that McMahon never intended that "Palestine should be included in the general pledge given the Sherif" and that the Arab leaders understood this fact.[14]

No matter which way the evidence points, however, and there is more evidence of an inferential nature that could be added, Palestine was not specifically mentioned in their correspondence by either Husayn or McMahon.[15] But even if the Sharifians clearly understood the reservations concerning Palestine, and even if the subsequent British arguments were legally sound, it remains to be demonstrated that the people of Palestine were encouraged to draw any other inference than that they were to be included in an independent Arabia.[16] Even such an authority on the East as Lord Curzon, who was not in the government at the time of the pledges, labored under a misapprehension as he attempted to articulate British policy in 1918. At that time he declared without contradiction in the presence of several other foreign policy experts at a meeting of the Eastern Committee that

> If we deal with our commitments, there is first the general pledge to Hussein in October 1915, under which Palestine was included in the areas as to which Great Britain pledged itself that they should be Arab and independent in the future.[17]

The statement was inaccurate, but even so, to British politicians it obviously presented no significant deterrent to strengthening British interests in Palestine. The argument regarding 1915 is a very subtle one, and the ambiguity of Britain's attitude toward Palestine did not decrease as the war progressed. In fact, the situation became much more difficult when, at the end of the war, Britain appeared to have the power to dispose of Palestine as it wished, in which case, the Arab argument is, Palestine should have reverted to the area of Arab independence.[18] However, as will be seen, Britain was able to gain its way over Palestine only by using Zionism as a lever to force the French to give up their claims to the Holy Land. The Anglo-French Entente could stand—barely—the strain of fulfilling Zionism, whereas satisfying Arab aspirations might not have reconciled the French to the loss of their traditional goal.

Britain's other major commitment in the Middle East was the full-scale partition of Asiatic Turkey among Britain, France, and Russia. Talks which began in October 1915 and reached agreement in May 1916 were conducted principally by Mark Sykes, an amateur orientalist used by Kitchener as adviser on eastern affairs, for the British, and François Georges-Picot, a career diplomat, for the French.[19] Under the Sykes-Picot Agreement, as it came to be known, the British committed themselves to the complete breakup of the Ottoman Empire as the best solution of the Eastern Question. The British, in Mark Sykes's words, wanted to a see "permanent Anglo-French Entente . . . which will render Pan-Islamism innocuous and protect India and Africa from the Turco-German combine, which I believe may well survive the Hohenzollerns."[20] At the time, the British were also in favor of an "independent Arab State or Confederation of Arab States" in the areas not specifically reserved for French or British "direct or indirect administration or control," namely, southern Mesopotamia and western Syria.[21] Given the climate of ideas at the time, this interpretation of independence for the Arabs, particularly considering the vagueness of the wording, was not incompatible with the imperialist need to protect far-flung dominions in India by dividing the intervening landmass of the Middle East into zones of influence or control.

This solution of the Eastern Question was not quite the abrupt departure from traditional policy it may seem. In the spring of 1916 Clayton explained the relationship between the pledges to Husayn, the agreement with France and Russia, and the link with previous British policy. "[A]ll we want," he wrote privately, "is to keep the friendship of the various Arab chiefs . . . while at the same time, working towards maintenance of the *status quo ante bellum*, and merely eliminating Turkish domination from Arabia." A few weeks later he wrote similarly to another friend:

> to set up a great Arab State . . . was never my idea . . . . The conditions throughout Arabia, Syria and Mesopotamia did not allow of such a scheme being practical, even if anyone were so foolish as to attempt it . . . . The object we have to aim at is, I consider, to work to preserve all the various elements in the Arab territories very much in the same position as they were before the war, but minus the Turks. In this way we shall have an open field to work in.[22]

In such a world, conflicts between the McMahon promises and the Sykes-Picot articles, or even between the spirit of the two documents, must have seemed to be of secondary importance and capable of reasonable adjustment.

The agreement was achieved only after months of hard negotiation. So far as Palestine was concerned, its case was bitterly contested, the French continuing until long after the war to press the British for concessions regarding political and religious rights and the borders of the mandated area. The Russians also pressed their considerable interest in the Holy Land. However, there was no ambiguity about the status of Palestine in the agreement. Article 3 provided

> That in the brown Area [Palestine] there shall be established an international administration, the form of which is to be decided upon after consultation with Russia, and subsequently in consultation with the other Allies, and the representatives of the Shereef of Mecca.[23]

In addition, Great Britain was accorded the ports of Haifa and Acre as well as the "right to build, administer, and be sole owner of a railway" connecting Haifa to Baghdad, thus giving a minimum amount of security for the Suez Canal and communications with the Persian Gulf.

By late 1916 Britain had secured its basic interests in Palestine: it had acquired a base and denied administrative and political control to any other single power. Events, however, were moving swiftly. During the revolutionary year of 1917, Britain's initial attempts to solve the Eastern Question were quickly rendered meaningless and even dangerously out of date, and the Palestine question reached a new and more central position in British thinking.

The motivating force behind the dynamic changes in British policy in 1917 was supplied by Britain's new prime minister, David Lloyd George. Within a few days of his taking power in December 1916, preparations were begun for stepping up military activity in the Middle East and obtaining the support of Jewish world opinion for an Allied victory. Agitation for the British government to adopt a Zionist policy had begun early in the war when Herbert Samuel, then president of the Local Government Board, suggested to the foreign secretary that "the opportunity might arise" in the course of a war with the Ottoman Empire "for the fulfillment of the ancient aspiration of the Jewish people and the restoration in Palestine of a Jewish State."[24] Sir Edward Grey confessed his sympathy with the idea and said that he would do what he could if an opportunity arose. Lloyd George was also approached on the subject by Samuel, who reported that he "was very keen to see a Jewish state established there." Little came officially of these early expressions of interest largely because of Prime Minister H. H. Asquith's lack of sympathy with the Zionist ideal.[25] However, a number of influential men in government service had become converted to Zionism by 1917. Of particular importance were the outstanding and forceful personalities of Lord Robert Cecil, General Smuts, and Lord Milner. Also of importance were several men—Philip Kerr, L.S. Amery, William Ormsby-Gore, and the famous Mark Sykes—who were to be included in Lloyd George's "garden suburb," where they were well placed to reintroduce the discussion of Zionist objectives in the Cabinet whenever more pressing business crowded it out.[26]

It is unlikely that Zionism would have made the impact it did during 1917 were it not for the personalities involved. Chaim Weizmann, leader of Britain's Zionists, a Russian-born Jew whose unalterable aim was a Jewish home in Palestine under British auspices, had a peculiarly hypnotic effect upon a number of high-ranking British officials.[27] Sir Charles Webster, a junior officer on the British general staff during the war and a diplomatic historian of note, admired Weizmann's diplomatic skill in appealing not only to British strategic and political interests, but also in reinforcing each official's romantic and mystical tendencies. In a memorable passage Webster tells us how Weizmann

> adapted his arguments to the special circumstances of each statesman. To the British and Americans he could use biblical language and awake a deep emotional undertone; to other nationalities he more often talked in terms of interest. Mr. Lloyd George was told that Palestine was a little mountainous country not unlike Wales; with Lord Balfour the philosophical background of Zionism could be surveyed; for Lord Cecil the problem was placed in the setting of a new world organization; while to Lord Milner the extension of imperial power could be vividly portrayed. To me . . . he brought from many sources all the evidence that could be obtained of the importance of a Jewish National Home to the strategical position of British Empire, but he always indicated by a hundred shades and inflexions of the voice that he believed that I could also appreciate better than my superiors other more subtle and recondite arguments.[28]

This is not to overestimate the importance of Weizmann and his personality. For all his strength and skill, Weizmann could not have succeeded in imposing his vision on British policy makers without there being strong imperial reasons for taking up and using the Zionist cause. But the above does strongly indicate the powerful coupling of subject and irrational motives to existing reasons of state and empire.[29]

Lloyd George, already a most persistent "easterner," now bent on acquiring a British Palestine and on using an assumed Jewish international power, pressed for an active military program in the East to break the wartime stalemate. Although impressed by the prime minister's desire for a winter offensive, General Sir Archibald Murray, commander-in-chief of the Egyptian Expeditionary Force (EEF), timidly postponed an attack on Gaza, the gateway to Palestine, until 26 March 1917. Though the assault was a disastrous failure, the War Cabinet gained the impression that success was around the corner. On 2 April the Cabinet approved a resolute forward policy in Palestine designed to sweep the Turks out of southern Palestine and take Jerusalem. On 3 April, as he was about to leave for Egypt to become the head of the political mission attached to Murray's force, Mark Sykes received his instructions from Lloyd George and Lord Curzon, then lord president of the council. They stressed "the importance of not prejudicing the Zionist movement and the possibility of its development under British auspices."[30] Sykes was specifically enjoined by the prime minister from entering into any political pledges to the Arabs, "and particularly none in regard to Palestine." Any problems they expected would come from the French, not the Arabs, who "probably realized that there was no prospect of their being allowed any control over Palestine." With Arabs out of the running in Palestine,[31] military possession by a British army could be decisive so far as the French were concerned, and if that were not sufficient, perhaps the addition of a moral factor—Jewish opinion throughout the world—would impress the French.

Despite Murray's second failure at Gaza late in April, the War Cabinet, on 23 April, decided to adhere to an offensive policy in Palestine. The Russian revolution in March and the evaporation of the Russian army, the failure of the Nivelle offensive in France, and the fear of a renewed Turkish drive on Baghdad combined to provide cogent military reasons for an increased effort on the Palestine front. The British still had a strong army on the front, and it was felt that an impressive victory in Palestine and the conquest of Jerusalem would give a badly needed lift to the morale of the British public. The spring of 1917 was thus the turning point for the Zionists. The impending British invasion of Palestine combined with the decline of power in Russia opened the way to sharpened diplomatic conflict between Britain and France over the domination of Palestine. In appreciation of this fact, the British began moving from a position of tolerant interest in Zionism to one approaching commitment.[32]

British policy then seemed to lose its cohesion and consistency so far as Palestine was concerned. In April 1917, the Treaty of Saint-

Jean de Maurienne was being concluded by Great Britain, France, and Italy; its provisions called for an international administration for Palestine, in confirmation of the 1916 agreement.[33] At the same time the uncertainties over Russia in 1917 led to an official review of the 1916 agreement. On 12 April a Committee on Territorial Terms of Peace was set up under the chairmanship of Lord Curzon. The committee concluded on 28 April that the agreement had to be modified so that Palestine and Mesopotamia would be placed in the definite and exclusive control of Great Britain.[34] So the mercurial British prime minister had indeed broken the logjam in the East, but he had also created conflicting lines of policy.

The 1916 agreement continued to hold official sway while attempts to subvert it came from all sides. In July, Commander D.G. Hogarth, director of Cairo's Arab Bureau under Clayton, wrote to London urging its revision in favor of strengthening Britain's position in Palestine and Arabia.[35] One month later, on 14 August, Sykes, now wholly caught up by his Zionist zeal, proposed to scrap the whole agreement and "get Great Britain appointed trustee of the powers for the administration of Palestine."[36] The Anglo-French Entente was still the cornerstone of his scheme, but it was to be cemented to an alliance of Jews, Arabs, and Armenians. The French, alerted by Sykes on 6 April 1917 to British ambitions for a protectorate in Palestine, were of the opinion that London considered the 1916 agreement dead.[37] The agreement, however, clung tenaciously to life until the armistice with Turkey and even afterward.

The road to the Balfour Declaration had been cleared with surprising speed in the spring of 1917. The Sykes-Picot Agreement and the promises to the Arabs were of small importance in view of a fast-changing international picture and the new administration in London. On 25 April 1917, Lord Robert Cecil told Weizmann that if the Zionists were to ask for a British Palestine, it would strengthen Britain's hand in future negotiations. On 18 July the Zionists submitted to the government the invited draft declaration of British sympathy for Zionist aspirations.[38] After much official discussion, at times very heated, and several succeeding drafts, the British government gave the Zionists their promise in the form of a letter from Foreign Secretary Balfour to Lord Rothschild. The statement authorized by the Cabinet amounted to only one sentence:

> His Majesty's Government view with favour the establishment in Palestine of a national home for the Jewish people, and will use their best endeavours to facilitate the achievement of this object, it being clearly understood that nothing shall be done which may prejudice the civil and

religious rights of existing non-Jewish communities in Palestine, or the rights and political status enjoyed by Jews in any other country.[39]

Ambiguously and vaguely, the Cabinet looked forward to the eventual emergence of a Jewish "home," whatever that might mean, but definitely did not promise to take on the responsibility for bringing it about. On 31 October 1917, the day the declaration was approved, Balfour addressed himself in the Cabinet to the problem of the unfamiliar term *national home*. He said he understood it to mean

> some form of British, American, or other protectorate, under which full facilities would be given to the Jews to work out their own salvation and to build up, by means of education, agriculture, and industry, a real centre of national culture and focus of national life. It did not necessarily involve the early establishment of an independent Jewish state, which was a matter for gradual development in accordance with the ordinary laws of political evolution.[40]

Personally, Balfour hoped the Jews would establish at state, as he confided to Colonel Richard Meinertzhagen in February 1918, adding, "It is up to them now; we have given them their great opportunity."[41] On the other hand, Balfour was not ready to predict where this opportunity would lead. According to Sir Maurice Hankey, Balfour thought the Jewish national home "might turn out to be anything from a religious and cultural centre, a kind of Jewish Vatican, to a Jewish State; time alone would show."[42]

In later years, Lloyd George explained that the Jews—because of their genius, resourcefulness, tenacity, and wealth—were being given the chance to redeem Palestine from the wilderness. In an echo of mid-Victorian British imperialism, he characterized the Balfour Declaration as "not an expropriating but an enabling clause. It is only a charter of equality for the Jews."[43]

Thus the British Cabinet looked favorably toward a Jewish establishment in the eastern Mediterranean and had promised to view it with favor. Exactly how far did this promise go? In February 1918, Balfour summarized British wartime obligations to the Jews in one sentence: "We are bound only by the limited assurances given to Lord Rothschild in Mr. Balfour's letter."[44] Later in the year, as we shall see, it became apparent that several in the Cabinet, including Lloyd George, assumed that a great deal of freedom was still theirs in finding a solution to the Palestine question. These assumptions were probably fostered by the set of circumstances which were the immediate occasion of the Balfour Declaration.

The Cabinet was much less concerned in October 1917 about using the Zionists as a makeweight to French claims to an area flanking the Suez Canal than they were about a presumptive Zionist power in the rest of the world.[45] In a Foreign Office memorandum on 24 October, Sir Ronald Graham urged a swift decision by the government on the Zionist movement on the overoptimistic grounds that a Zionist declaration could switch Russian Jews from an anti-Allied position to one powerfully in Britain's favor.[46] Balfour also rested his argument for the declaration on its propaganda value in Russia and America rather than on long-range possibilities regarding the British or Zionist positions in the Middle East. And finally, the Cabinet was moved to urgent action because of the mistaken belief that the Germans were on the brink of making a strong play for Zionist sympathies.[47]

In these circumstances the declaration was a political document, not a legal one. The Zionists and the British wanted the declaration for different reasons, and although they understood each other's aims and the reasons for a studied vagueness in the wording of the document, they had come to no agreed interpretation. For the British, whatever individual hopes and beliefs might be, the declaration amounted to "limited assurances," while to the Zionists it was the legal fulfillment of the Basle Program of 1897, of "a home in Palestine secured by public law."

In the Cabinet, only Lord Curzon recognized the possible danger in the lack of practical thought regarding the nature of the obligation the government was assuming, the chances of its successful realization, and the wisdom of using language that suggested so much where there was so much confusion of interpretation.[48] Only he questioned what was to become of Palestine's existing inhabitants. Curzon's lack of success in persuading the Cabinet to give closer study to his serious objections suggests that the Cabinet, stampeded by events, was relying on the passage of time to indicate the direction of policy, that it was meeting a crisis with limited action and would react in the future as needs arose. There is also the suggestion, implied by Curzon's failure to press his arguments and the failure of the Cabinet to meet them, that the Cabinet was in tacit agreement with him that Zionist chances of realizing the national home ideal were slim and belonged at best to the distant future, and that in view of this, a collision with the indigenous inhabitants was unlikely and scarcely worth considering.

In late October, Allenby began his Palestine campaign. He took Beersheba on 31 October, captured Gaza, and then rolled up the coastal plain. On 11 December 1917, he entered liberated Jerusalem. The time of groping for solution from afar was at an end; it was now necessary to grapple with real military, political, and human problems at first hand. The flexibility the British had managed to retain since 1914 was about to meet the harsh realities of occupation needs.

The possibilities were enormous. One fact was certain, and that was that Great Britain was going to have the major voice in the disposal of Palestine. Negatively speaking, there was no chance whatsoever of French control and none for a combination of French and British. Outright British control was a possible solution, but not so likely as some form of international administration, or of Turkish or Arab administration under British supervision. The extent of flexibility in British policy is well illustrated in Lord Robert Cecil's report of a conversation with U.S. Ambassador Page on 20 December 1917. Cecil explained that the government's Zionist policy amounted to allowing full facilities for Jewish emigration to Palestine and for their establishment there. Details had not been worked out, but it had been agreed with the French that Palestine would be internationalized. Cecil professed himself personally in favor of putting it under American protection; failing that, he saw "no insuperable objection to leaving the country under the Turkish flag provided real securities for its inhabitants were obtained. . . ." On 27 December, Balfour, for whom Cecil had been sitting in, signed the report without comment and had it sent to the British ambassador in Washington.[49]

In any case, it was understood that the Zionists, as a reliable client class, would be protected in some undefined manner best left to the future and Jewish enterprise. The British speculatively considered the Americans in an imperial role in the Middle East, but never pursued the idea much beyond the wishful stage. In all, the British had in November 1917 good reason to believe that their future in Palestine was free from mortgage.

3

THE INVASION OF PALESTINE, 1917

The sources for British policy in the Middle East, apart from the seat of government in London, were the two great centers of British power bracketing the area, the government of India at Delhi and the British Agency at Cairo. Each of these widely separated capitals developed policies adapted to its special geographical and political needs and over a period of time built up vested interests in its particular method of dealing with the peoples of the Middle East. The differences between the two were deepened by the Great Syrian Desert, cutting north to south across the Middle East from the Taurus Mountains of Anatolia to the Arabian Peninsula, conveniently dividing the Arab provinces of the Ottoman Empire into two distinct regions. The western region, from Syria to the Yemen, fell under the direction of Cairo, while the eastern, from Kurdistan through Mesopotamia, Kuwait, the Persian Gulf, the Aden, looked to Delhi. Thus the Anglo-Indians and the Anglo-Egyptians had their respective spheres of influence in which they could carry out operations virtually without reference to each other.

The Anglo-Indian approach to the Middle East rested on a firm foundation of tradition. The vital British routes to India had been secured and maintained through the years by means of layered historic and diplomatic ties with the countless small and large shaykhdoms, fiefdoms, and sultanates ranging from the borders of India through Afghanistan, Persia, the Persian Gulf, the Arabian Peninsula and Aden. Policed and controlled by a small but dedicated band of political officers, these areas were free to administer their own internal affairs so long as they enjoyed good relations with the British, rejected foreign encroachment, and served as the quiescent occupants of the strategic routes of communication to India.

Cairo had other preoccupations. Less sensitive to the Russian and German spectres threatening the overland route to the Persian Gulf and India and more conscious of the reasons behind an Egyptian-Sudanese base—the guarding of the Suez all-water route to the East—the Anglo-Egyptians were concerned with extending control along the coasts of the eastern Mediterranean and the Red Sea. Holding this divergent view and lacking a patchwork of Arabian relationships to maintain and defend, Cairo in 1914 was more open than Delhi to the establishment of a vigorous and aggressive policy toward the disaffected elements of the Ottoman Empire. The Indian government, indeed, never ceased to consider the encouraging of Arab nationalist hopes and the organizing of native energies as anything other than sentimental folly.

In times of peace these differences had their utility. In war, each policy hampered the application of the other. Despite numerous attempts to harmonize and coordinate Middle Eastern policies, including the formation of interdepartmental committees in London, progress in this direction was uncertain and halting. Not until 1921, on the demand of Winston Churchill as incoming colonial secretary, were the territories of the Arab Middle East united under one policy-making body.

One historian has suggested that the story of conflicting policies might have come to an early end had Gilbert Clayton, in the spring of 1917, taken A. T. Wilson's place in Mesopotamia (the government of India directed the expeditionary force there) as political officer under Sir Percy Cox, as had been intended.[1] Doubtless such a substitution of personalities would not have been without effect and some greater degree of harmony between the two points of view might have resulted. If any one man could have brought the policies of the two centers of power into alignment, Clayton certainly came closest to having the requisite characteristics. But surely the perspectives from Cairo and Delhi, determined as they were by history and geography, must be held to have been of a fundamental nature, not susceptible to significant alteration by one man, especially one in a subordinate position. The fact is that Egyptian and Indian interests could not be aligned, even though the two countries were controlled by the same crown.

A forward Arab policy for the British was not a foregone conclusion in 1914. In retrospect, the drama of the Arab revolt has distorted the total picture of Britain's tentative search for a viable alternative to its traditional policy. Only gradually—and largely in reaction to events, opportunities, and chance—did an Arab policy emerge. Early

British military efforts at the Dardanelles and in Mesopotamia proved failures. Churchill and the armchair strategists of London on the one hand, and the government of India on the other, were discredited. A military solution to the Eastern Question having eluded the armed forces of the Entente, it was left by default to Cairo to formulate and direct a political solution.

As was mentioned above, it is difficult to overstate the importance of Clayton as a central figure in the development of British policy toward the Arab Middle East. The war had thrust the holder of the responsible but relatively obscure position of director of Egyptian military intelligence into sudden prominence. Through his work in an expanded intelligence department his recruitment of talented, articulate, and experienced men for the nascent Arab Bureau, and his wide correspondence with men in the Middle East and London, he built his post into one of the most influential in the British Middle East and became a chief spokesman for the Anglo-Egyptian school of thought. From his years of experience and his wide range of contacts in the Middle East, he knew the immense importance of Arabia in a war with the Turks, and he set out purposefully to separate the two nations.

His tasks at the outset of war were many. He had to convert his small Sudan office, in which he supervised intelligence operations in the Sudan, into the 'I' Branch of the General Staff of the Egyptian army and maintain close relations between the army and the Egyptian and Sudanese governments, the British Agency, and Allied and friendly diplomats, the Suez Canal Company, and the staff of the naval commander-in-chief. He also had to establish personal contacts with Middle Eastern notables and to build up a system of military, geographical, and political intelligence. He responded to the challenge of his position, becoming something of a father figure to whom practically everyone went for balanced advice.

T. E. Lawrence, the most celebrated member of the Arab Bureau in later years, has drawn a favorable portrait of the man who discovered him and made brilliant use of his unorthodox talents.

> We were not many; [he said] and nearly all of us rallied round Clayton . . . . Clayton made the perfect leader for such a band of wild men as we were. He was calm, detached, clear-sighted, of unconscious courage in assuming responsibility. He gave an open run to his subordinates. His own views were general, like his knowledge; and he worked by influence rather than by loud direction. It was not easy to descry his influence. He was like water, or permeating oil, creeping silently and insistently through everything. It was not possible to say where Clayton was and was not, and how much really belonged to him. He never visibly led; but

his ideas were abreast of those who did: he impressed men by his sobriety, and by a certain quiet and stately moderation of hope. In practical matters he was loose, irregular, untidy, a man with whom independent men could bear.[2]

Clayton had a tremendous capacity for work. He needed it, since he seemed perpetually to be short-staffed. And yet, as one who knew him from the beginning of the war once said, "the files never barricaded him against the world."[3] He was a very patient listener, this anonymous observer went on, "[f]or he understood the East; he knew that for an Intelligence officer 'haste is from the devil,' and he never failed in courtesy as he never failed in understanding."

Clayton's character made a deep impression on the men he worked with. One of his associates, H. Charles Woods, emphasized Clayton's freedom from "official prejudices" and his forthrightness in dealing with difficult questions. "He was extremely modest and quiet," Woods added; "he knew whom he could trust; and he was not afraid to express his opinion. In fact, he was a far bigger man than appeared at first sight."[4] Another colleague has recalled that the picture that was clearest in his mind was "from the early days of the War: the Director of Intelligence at his desk listening, always listening impassively, and watching with those quiet, vigilant eyes that seemed to be looking into your mind." The same writer noted that "again and again one could find him listening patiently to the news—often prolix—of the appreciations—often fantastic—of the situation brought by a refugee from Turkey, an old Sheikh from the Libyan desert, or a travelled merchant from a Red Seaport."[5]

Perhaps the best indication of his superb personal skill was in his handling of the always individualistic and at times difficult members of the Arab Bureau, who worked, as Robert O. Collins, Clayton's editor, put it, "[b]ehind the shield of Clayton's leadership."[6] Imaginative, articulate, and impulsive men required a man with the gifts to orchestrate their abilities. According to our anonymous observer,

> He was a delightful chief: quiet, never fussy, never despondent in the blackest days, afraid of no responsibility, and ready to accept any suggestion from subordinates which his instinctive good sense approved. He was an admirable judge of men, for he had never allowed military formalism to blunt his appreciation of values.[7]

Wyndham Deedes, a member of the Arab Bureau who eventually achieved the rank of brigadier general and served later as the first civil secretary of the government of Palestine, thought Clayton an "ideal 'chief', letting his subordinates have a free hand, taking the

responsibility for mistakes and giving them the credit for success."
For Deedes, Clayton's most outstanding qualities were his "wisdom
and imperturbability." Throughout Clayton's career in the troubled Middle East,

> he was ever the same, cool and collected, and he had the capacity of
> communicating his calm to others. His wisdom was based on a profound
> knowledge of men and affairs in the East. Not a great talker, he was a
> tireless listener to the endless irrelevancies in which the Easterner de-
> lights to indulge. He had a singular understanding of the native mind,
> and was always on the side of a 'liberal' policy.[8]

The balance and sense of perspective cultivated by Clayton enabled
him to play his many parts with deceptive ease. "Although seemingly
casual and even lazy," B. H. Liddell Hart has noted, "he had a knack
of keeping touch with all relevant matters, together with a capacity
to smile at troubles that often helped to allay them."[9] Clayton's
espousal of the unorthodox and flexible often created friction with
the more staid members of the headquarters staff, but Clayton never
faltered in giving understanding and support to the men of his 'machine.' Liddell Hart stressed the importance of his sense of humor,
which "was of no less value in dealing with his variegated subordinates
than in composing the differences between superiors, and which was
especially called on to protect one of the former [T. E. Lawrence, in
this case] from the frequent wrath of senior officers whose sense of
dignity had quenched their sense of humor."

Clayton's activity against the Turks had begun, as related in the
previous chapter, even before the formal opening of hostilities when
Ronald Storrs went to him for support for the idea of taking advantage of Arab unrest.

> I had recourse (like so many of my betters after me) to the calm, friendly
> wisdom of Captain G. H. [sic] Clayton, the 'Bertie' of Khartum, of Cairo,
> of Palestine and Mesopotamia. His balanced advice could no more be
> hustled by a crisis than could his beautiful deliberate handwriting: his
> character as an officer and a man was, when he left Jerusalem, to be well
> summed up by Sir Herbert Samuel in the last watchword of Marcus
> Aurelius, Aequanimitas .... the time and the place and the keys of the
> necessary knowledge adding to his natural abilities that element of for-
> tune without which none can achieve. Bertie approved my thesis. Fur-
> ther, he actively condoned my proposed irregularity of urging it upon
> Lord Kitchener in a private letter; which I accordingly dispatched.[10]

Almost two years elapsed before the efforts of Clayton and the
highly placed officials who supported him—High Commissioner

McMahon, Sir Reginald Wingate of the Sudan, and Sir John Maxwell, general officer commanding in Egypt—bore fruit. One member of the Arab Bureau proclaimed the outbreak of open rebellion in the Hijaz in June 1916 a great triumph for Clayton.[11] McMahon was generous in his praise of Clayton, acknowledging his familiarity with the country and people, his quiet firmness and steady good nature, but in particular emphasizing Clayton's value in the "collection, formation, and supervision of the 'Arab bureau,' in my negotiations with the Arabs and in the subsequent incidents of the Arab revolt."[12] Much has been obscured in the history of the Arab revolt, perhaps nothing so much as the vital part Clayton played while others were securing glory. "The credit for his work has been claimed by some, and assigned, by the uninformed, to others," McMahon explained. "Such must ever be the lot of loyal and un-self-seeking men like Sir Gilbert Clayton."

To men like Clayton and Wingate in the Middle East and Kitchener in London, the Arab revolt was not merely a wartime development to be exploited and then discarded, but a positive instrument of great potential worth to the British Empire. Any danger in a scheme for a pan-Arab union or confederation backed by Great Britain would be adequately provided for, wrote Wingate in November 1915.

> If the embryonic Arab state comes to nothing, all our promises vanish and we are absolved from them—if the Arab state becomes a reality, we have quite sufficient safeguards to control it and although eventually it might act towards its 'Allied' creators as Bulgaria has acted towards Russia—I think it is in our power to erect such barriers as would effectively prevent its becoming the menace which the Indian Government appears to fear.[13]

Clayton agreed with Wingate's argument, ridiculing India's fear of a strong and united Arab state on the road to India as a fantasy dreamed up in ignorance of the Arabs and Arabia.[14] Clayton's and Wingate's assumption throughout the revolt was that the Arab state would need considerable support for years to come from its British creators and that they could avoid producing a 'Frankenstein' monster or even a Bulgaria. A grateful Arab state would perform the task of the old Ottoman Empire, holding the reins of government over an unruly people and denying other powers proximity to the path to India.

As a policy of gaining the active assistance of the Arabs in the British war effort gathered momentum, the need was felt for a central organization for the compilation and dissemination of information and advice. On Asquith's order, an interdepartmental conference in London in 1916, at which the Foreign, War, and India Offices were represented, established the Arab Bureau. From February 1916 to the end of 1920 the bureau operated as a Foreign Office institution. Its functions were to coordinate British political activity in the Middle East, to keep the various government officers informed of enemy policy, and secondarily, to supervise propaganda in favor of Britain and the Allies among non-Indian Muslims "without clashing with the susceptibilities of Indian Moslems and the Entente Powers."[15] In the Middle East the bureau, an arm of Clayton's military intelligence apparatus, was also regarded as a means of spreading the unconventional ideas of its mentors to the Committee for Imperial Defence in London and the government of India at Delhi.[16]

Clayton's influence continued to mount during 1916. In April, at the age of forty-one, he was promoted to the rank of brigadier general and awarded by the French the order of Officier de la Legion d'Honneur.[17] On a visit to London in the summer, he left the authorities there favorably impressed with the Arab movement and with himself. While there, he reported to Wingate on 7 August, he had delivered the burden of the message he had been presenting in Cairo.

Do not forget that Germany would sacrifice much (indeed almost anything) to keep her hold on Turkey—Berlin to Baghdad, Basra, Persia, Afghanistan, India, is the key-note of German Welt-Politik . . . Granted the above, our Arab policy is one of the big cards—if not the biggest in our hand and our main weapon against the habitual Moslem sympathy for the Turk.[18]

By this time, military operations against the Turks in the Hijaz had expanded, and toward the end of the year, Clayton was appointed to the General Staff, in charge of the Hijaz. His chief in this matter was Wingate, still in the Sudan but soon to be moved to Cairo, but it was Clayton who was running the show.[19] When the Arabs, rallied by Lawrence, had consolidated themselves in the western peninsula and the British, impelled by Lloyd George, prepared to take the offensive in Palestine, Clayton was the logical choice to accompany the army north. He was ideally situated to maintain liaison with the Arabs on the army's right flank, to advise the army on political matters affecting the area, and to serve as the British representative to the Anglo-French political mission in the Middle East.

Earlier, in April 1917, Sykes and Georges Picot had traveled to the Middle East to pioneer the setting-up of the political mission, which had been decided on with the French back in the last days of December 1916.[20] The mission was to begin operating when the EEF entered Palestine. The upsetting of the timetable due to Murray's second failure before Gaza gave Clayton his opportunity to take Sykes's place alongside Picot when the projected fall offensive was to begin. In June General Edmund H. H. Allenby learned, to his initial dismay, that he was being relieved of command of the Third Army in France and that he was expected to present Jerusalem to the British nation as a Christmas gift.[21] According to Robert O. Collins, Allenby offered Clayton the post of political officer because he required an officer with "knowledge, experience, and the ability to reconcile the manifold conflicts of a land where Muslim, Jew, and Christian combined their deep spiritual interests with suspicion, if not hostility, toward their religious rivals."[22] Whether or not the offer was in Allenby's power is questionable, for we find Sykes promising Clayton in July that he would get him established as chief political officer (CPO) as soon as he could.[23] From the uninhibited correspondence carried on by Sykes and Clayton, it seems that the two had discovered a bond of sympathy and thought that would serve British policy well in the days ahead.

Clayton's position with EEF was a powerful one. As the Foreign Office link with the army, he was to "always be consulted in the first instance where matters of policy were involved.[24] And Lee Stack, acting governor-general of the Sudan and sirdar of the Egyptian army from 1917 to 1919, pointed out that his work in Palestine would be "imperially more important than what you would be doing for the Soudan in Egypt."[25] His instructions were those given to Sykes in April by the prime minister and Lord Curzon: to keep a free hand in Palestine until it was actually occupied.[26] In July, Sykes added his colorful advice.

> For policy there is only one possible policy, the Entente first and last, and the Arab nation the child of the Entente. Get your Englishmen to stand up to the Arabs on this and never let them accept flattery of the 'you very good man, him very bad man' kind . . . . Ten years tutelage under the Entente and the Arabs will be a nation. Complete independence means Persia, poverty, and chaos.[27]

Clayton, certainly, was in complete agreement with Sykes's advice and instructions. His attitude clearly was that the Ottoman Empire must be broken and replaced by firm British control. His position may be summed up as recognizing the Suez Canal as the "vital cord of our Empire" and Egypt as the "keystone of our whole Near Eastern fabric."[28] Beyond the Egyptian bastion was the Arab world and, as he had said a year earlier, "our Arab policy is one of the big cards— if not the biggest in our hand and our main weapon . . . ."

Elie Kedourie has accused Clayton, and others of like mind, of sentimentalism in their approach to the Arab world, faulting Clayton for assuming that nationalism of any stripe was bound to be liberal, wholesome and advantageous. For Kedourie, Clayton's espousal of (in Clayton's words) "a general recognition of [Arab] aspirations by England and the promise of a fair measure of self-government in the various countries concerned under the guidance and with the help and support of England"[29] was the kind of Arabophile thinking that later led to the complete destruction of Great Britain's position in the Middle East.

But what was the alternative to the "liberal imperialist" infection that caused this calamity? In Kedourie's opinion, the Sykes-Picot Agreement of 1916 had held the promise of being the cornerstone of the British empire's future position in the Middle East. However, the officials of Cairo and Khartoum, motivated by sentimental or utilitarian Arabophilia, had persistently worked out of mistaken assumptions toward revising this "workman-like device of reconciliation."[30] Had they held firm, told the natives what to expect, and not excited ambitions that could not be fulfilled, then this unfairly maligned agreement would not have had to be put aside. It was a matter of will and "the will to impose an order . . . was not manifest. . . ."[31] This alternative of resolute imperialism and responsibility was doomed late in the war, according to Kedourie, because of the weakness of "English statesmen [who] allowed themselves to believe that to satisfy the lust for power of discontented and ambitious men was virtuous and excellent."[32]

Pehaps. But is a policy leading to a "fair measure of self-government" any more sentimental than a cherished regard for a vanished empire? Is it really possible to argue that England and Europe could have remained politically powerful had they kept their resolution? This is to ascribe to men more control over their own fate and that of nations than is reasonable or possible. Clayton, it must be remembered, while not above criticism, was working within a very narrowly circumscribed framework. This "politic and well-informed" British official, as Kedourie acknowledged Clayton to be,[33] confronted a multiplicity of harsh realities that left no viable alternative to some shade of gradual approach toward self-government. The Middle East was scarcely unique in this respect; the trend was worldwide. Events rendered the agreement of 1916 obsolete by 1917, thus illustrating Professor Geoffrey Barraclough's statement that "ultimately nationalism was a response not to policies but to facts."[34]

In August 1917 Clayton first gave evidence of uneasiness about the effect of Zionism on the Arab movement. He asked Sykes for definite information on a line of policy to follow, a plea that was to become a refrain. He advised against issuing a pronouncement on the Jewish question, arguing that it would prove divisive, vitiating the war effort.

> It will not help matters if the Arabs—already somewhat distracted between pro-Sherifians and those who fear Meccan domination, as also between pro-French and anti-French—are given yet another bone of contention in the shape of Zionism in Palestine as against the interests of the Moslems resident there. The more politics can be kept in the background, the more likely are the Arabs to concentrate on the expulsion of the Turks from Syria, which, if successful, will do more than anything to promote Arab unity and national feeling.[35]

This rather mild warning failed to take effect. His Majesty's Government neither sought, nor took any interest in, the views of Zionism held by its officials in the Middle East.

When the pronouncement, the Balfour Declaration, was issued in November, it cleared up little of the confusion its prospect had caused. The officials on the spot, who had not been consulted, were not comforted by the vagueness of the policy they were presumably to follow. They had no insight into the minds of the Cabinet members, no instructions as to how much weight to assign to the various ambiguities of the declaration, and no certainty of backing for any specific measures they might carry out. Under these circumstances, it is hardly surprising that their instinct was to hold fast to the status quo, plead military necessity, and wait for guidance.

On 28 November, after the publication of the declaration, Clayton renewed his warning in a telegram to Sykes. He reported that the declaration had made a profound impression on both Muslims and Christians, who viewed with dismay the prospect of "seeing Palestine, and eventually Syria, in [the] hands of Jews, whose superior intelligence and commercial abilities [are] feared by all alike."[36] Sykes may have been disturbed by the message this time, for a few days later he passed the warning on to the Zionists, cautioning them of the need "to look through Arab glasses."[37]

Allenby's rout of the Turks at Gaza and Beersheba late in October and his pursuit of them eventually encompassed the liberation of Jerusalem on 9 December. Ronald Storrs, shortly to be governor of Jerusalem for several years, has described the reception which British troops met with when they entered the city.

> They were indeed welcomed by the inhabitants, in something near an ecstasy of hope and joy. For these were the days when the trace of a great fear was yet in men's eyes, and the gulp of relief still at their throats: when for friendship with the Allies, true or suspected, whole

families of Christians had been exiled, at an hour's notice, into the interior of Asia Minor, a Moslem Kadi hanged at the Jaffa Gate, and a young Jewish girl tortured to suicide.[38]

On 11 December, Allenby entered the city officially, accompanied by his staff. Clayton described the entry as taking place "to the accompaniment of lively artillery and musketry fire within three or four miles."[39] In seven languages, Allenby had martial law proclaimed, promising the population that it could pursue its lawful business and that the holy places of all religions would be maintained and protected.[40] This proclamation, drafted by Mark Sykes, established the status quo as a doctrine, which proved "a strong tower of defense against the encroachments from all quarters."[41] Clayton wrote to Sykes that the situation pointed to an "avoidance, for the present, of all possible commitments both political and administrative. The less we tie our own hands and compromise the local population at this juncture the better."[42]

A military administration was set up, called the Occupied Enemy Territory Administration (OETA), in which Palestine was qualified with an (S) for south. Later, after Syria was conquered, there were added an OETA (West) administered by the French and an OETA (East) run by the Arabs. Clayton was appointed chief administrative officer of OETA(S). To Storrs, whose admiration for Clayton was unbounded, it seemed that no problem was insoluble given Clayton's "unruffled equanimity and sympathy."[43]

And there were many problems. The resumption of normal life had to be arranged and an orderly administrative machinery recreated.

But the Turk, when he struck his flag and the Camp in which he had bivouacked rather than settled for four hundred years, carried with him in his retreat money, records, registers, drugs and surgical instruments, much furniture, all food and, generally, everything that could be of the smallest use to the City or to its liberator . . . . Throughout those early days in Jerusalem my chief, my nightmare anxiety, was the scarcity of food amounting almost to famine. One morning early in January I became aware of a crying and a screaming beneath my office window. I looked out on a crowd of veiled Arab women, some of whom tore their garments apart to reveal the bones almost piercing their skin. And the sight in the hospital of the children's limbs swollen with emptiness was not good; nor was the dread lest we should have delivered Jerusalem only to starve her to death.[44]

The sensitive and erudite Storrs continued his catalogue of problems facing the administration and the decimated population of Jerusalem. He worried that the "foul state" of conditions left by the Turks put the city in danger of typhus and cerebrospinal meningitis epidemics. Into March 1918 "fear of pestilence" necessitated a public order requiring that old clothing and mattresses be disinfected before sale. Transporation was precarious and slow, the roads almost impassable and the rail line torn up. Stores were empty. When the sun set, the city went to bed, for few could afford lamps. "The fellah was a shivering bundle of rags" and noisome beggars swarmed, assaulting the senses on all sides. The malodorous prison and its miserable inmates called for sympathy, as did the thousands of refugees who had to be cared for. Storrs at one point began to prepare a list of the unemployed, but abandoned it when found that it contained nearly ninety percent of the population.[45] Deedes, Clayton's assistant administrator, wrote to his mother comparing the British in Palestine to a fanciful Japanese occupation of an English county. In such a situation, how were they to gather the reins of government? "Currency, taxation of all sorts, trade, commerce, municipal affairs, relief, justice, police, gendarmerie, finance and as many other questions as you like to add. Hence," Deedes explained, "my excuse for not writing!"[46] For the military administrators of this stricken country, the larger problems of Zionism and French and Italian ambitions had to be thrust into the background until those more immediate problems could be sorted out.

The Zionists were fully aware of the importance of consolidating their claim to Palestine. In a letter to the Foreign Office, Weizmann marshalled his reasons for sending a commission to Palestine as soon as possible. The first was that it would clearly indicate to the Jews that the Balfour Declaration was being followed up, thus heightening the propaganda effect, "especially in Russia."[47] The second was to expedite relief work in Palestine. And the third was to take the opportunity of arranging complicated questions with both Arabs and French before difficulties became insurmountable.

Through Sykes, the Zionists pressed for permission to announce in the press that they were sending a commission to Palestine to assist the military authorities with problems connected with Jewish settlements and to devote attention to the question of relief.[48] Clayton, however, objected strongly both to the sending of a commission and to press announcements concerning it.[49] A few days later, he rejected Sykes's suggestion that an invitation to Faysal to visit Jerusalem might produce a useful political effect.[50] In both cases he argued that such intrusions would be unwarranted complications of the local political situation.

Sykes had earlier attempted to allay Clayton's fears by reminding him that the second clause of the Balfour Declaration safeguarded Arab interests and by informing him of the firm intention of the Zionists to pay scrupulous attention to Arab rights and interests in land matters.[51] He pushed his scheme for an Arab-Jewish-Armenian entente[52] with spirit, enjoining Clayton to impress on the Arabs the far-sightedness of the Armenians in their absolute determination to stick to the Zionists.

This project of Sykes's, a vision of contradictory interests combining into strong unity, was the stuff of dreams. Sykes—a caricaturist, a wanderer through the East, and a religious romantic—had charmed his way into a position of influence where his undisciplined, eclectic mind helped hasten the Middle East into the modern age. A true free spirit, he turned to seriousness too late and died young in February 1919, leaving a tangled legacy of infant nationalities struggling without the reconciling touch of their idealistic mentor. Nevakivi had the measure of him when he said, "The trouble with Sykes indeed was that he wanted everything at the same time."[53]

Clayton, a realist and administrator, careful and thorough, was everything Sykes was not. He saw the advantages that could accrue to Sykes's combination and agreed to try to bring it off, but he thought there was no real chance of success even if it were done slowly and cautiously. He explained in a long letter to Sykes, in which he mustered his criticisms of Zionism, that it was a matter of undoing in a few weeks the traditional sentiment of centuries.[54] The future, he thought, was shrouded from view and in consequence an opportunist policy should be followed. In the foreground were the immediate objectives of winning the war and stopping Drang nach Osten for all time; the restructuring of the Middle East would be more difficult and to force matters now would not be wise. In addition to traditional antipathies, Clayton pointed out to Sykes the shortcomings of a program of arriving at an Arab-Jewish entente through public declarations and committees. Basically, it was a matter of the Arab not believing "that the Jew with whom he had to do will act up to the high-flown sentiments which may be expressed at Committee meetings." He seriously questioned whether the value of Zionist power in international matters was worth putting at risk the British stake in the Middle East.

> I am not fully aware of the weight which Zionists carry, especially in America and Russia, and of the consequent necessity of giving them everything for which they ask, but I must point out that, by pushing them as hard as we appear to be doing, we are risking the possibility of

Arab unity becoming something like an accomplished fact and being ranged against us.

Perhaps he could have stated his objection with greater forcefulness, but his foresight was, nevertheless, soundly based and carefully presented.[55]

The caution Clayton then expressed to Sykes over the possibility of alienating sentiment in Christian countries by a "wholesale pro-Zionist policy" was, on the other hand, a gross misreading of the climate of opinion in the West, and in particular of the Bible readers of the British government.[56] Lloyd George, Balfour, Smuts, and Sykes were all very much aware of the historic Jewish connection with the land of Palestine and eager to see the connection renewed, so long as it furthered British interests.

Finally, and indirectly, Clayton alerted Sykes to a situation which he feared might add another complication and modify the intelligence picture of the Middle East. He referred to indications that the severe depths into which the prestige of Islam had fallen, due to Ottoman reverses, the capture of Jerusalem, and the weakness of the temporal head of Islam, had produced a reaction of a militant revivalist nature in central Arabia. As yet the strength of the movement could not be estimated with accuracy, but it was engaging the serious attention of the Arab Bureau in Cairo. Clayton was suggesting to Sykes the difficulty of predicting, much less controlling, the direction of Arab affairs in the vast, anarchic areas of the Middle East. He was trying to tell Sykes that the peoples of the Middle East might not fit into a tidy plan of a nationalist alliance of Jews, Armenians, and Arabs, especially when British control of the interested parties was only rudimentary at best. As an argument, this was well worth considering. However, Clayton's careful prose seemed to lack emphasis, and as a result was not calculated to make an impression on the self-confident and forceful Mark Sykes.

Two days after writing his letter to Sykes, Clayton telegraphed to the Foreign Office that propaganda along the lines suggested by Sykes was going forward, but that not much success was expected. He repeated his arguments for caution. "Mecca," he said, "dislikes Jews and Armenians and wishes to have nothing to do with them, while Arabs of Syria and Palestine fear a repetition of the story of Jacob and Esau."[57]

On 19 December, Clayton wrote to the Foreign Office in a more optimistic vein. The Arabs of Cairo appeared to be impressed with arguments for cooperation, though still nervous about the speed of

Zionist progress.[58] On the other hand, on the same day, Wyndham Deedes, a devout Christian and staunch pro-Zionist, wrote to General Allenby that an anti-Arab feeling was noticeable in the Jewish community in Palestine, an emotion which was "reciprocated and recently rather accentuated, as you are aware, by the Balfour pronouncement."[59]

Late in December, Clayton, increasingly worried by the mood of the population in Palestine—Jews elated by Zionist prospects, Arabs anxious about the possibility of a Jewish government of Palestine—requested official reassurance to calm both elation and fear.[60] However, his request lacked sufficient punch, lost as it was in the midst of a report covering local economic matters, the sympathy of the Palestinian Muslims for Husayn in the Hijaz, and Picot's pretentious activities on behalf of a French protectorate of Latin Christianity in the East.

By the end of 1917, then, it was clear that the Zionist question was fully upon the British authorities, and that friction of an intensity as yet undetermined was inevitable. To meet the problem, the authorities of the EEF had adopted a policy of adhering to the status quo so far as was convenient and putting a damper on political enthusiasm of any stripe. They pled the necessities of war, the dereliction of a war-torn population requiring strenuous relief measures, occupation tradition, established international agreements, and the peace conference to come. Even so, uneasiness spread.

1917 had truly been a watershed in the history of the Middle East. The early military failures were forgotten in the exciting development of the Arab movement and in the captures of Baghdad in March and Jerusalem in December. The Russians left the war, dislocating the map of the Middle East and causing the idea of internationalizing Palestine to collapse. The Americans entered the war, complicating Entente diplomacy and the pursuit of war aims. Lloyd George's emphasis on the Eastern theater led to the invasion of Palestine and his desire for a British Palestine to an alliance with the Zionists. The Sykes-Picot Agreement no longer covered the realities of the Middle East; there was widespread talk of its abandonment. The Zionists had obtained international recognition of their aspirations and begun to work toward their fulfillment in Palestine. Palestine was no longer a distant object about which rational policy could be discussed in comfort. It was now a responsibility.

In coming to grips with the realities discovered there by the military authorities, the British on all levels were coming to realize that all was not neatly ordered. Clayton in Cairo and Curzon in London had warned of the practical difficulties of adding a Zionist policy to an Arab policy, but neither had followed through. After all, these were conjectural difficulties until occupation took place; perhaps all would yet be well. In particular, Clayton's initial handling of his newly acquired administrative duties appeared sure. Allenby had learned that he was reliable.[61] In all, as the year closed, it presented a mixed picture of solid accomplishments and grave uncertainties. Optimism still reigned; flexibility had been retained. But underneath a certain unease was discernible.

4

PALESTINE CONQUERED, EARLY 1918

The conquest of southern Palestine had thrust that tiny area into the midst of the deepest currents affecting the modern world. For the first time since the Crusades, a force alien to Eastern culture held dominion in the land sacred to three faiths. The dynamic new world emerging in Europe hit war-weakened Palestine with disintegrating strength. The clash of civilizations that was to restructure the Eastern question resounded in that moment of brief victory as Jerusalem fell to the new crusaders.

At about this time there took place two events that were to have far-reaching consequences on Britain's position in the Middle East. The first was the Bolshevik publication and exploitation in late 1917 of the secret agreements of the Allied powers. The second was the statement of Allied war aims by Lloyd George and Woodrow Wilson, occasioned in part by the embarrassment of the Russian disclosures.

Since the publication of the Balfour Declaration had already put a severe strain on the Arab temper and since officials on the spot, Clayton among them, were pointing out the need for some new statement of assurance, the Foreign Office decided to send Lieutenant Commander D. G. Hogarth to Husayn in the Hijaz. Hogarth, an Oxford archeologist and the director of the Arab Bureau under Clayton, was highly thought of by British officials in the Middle East as a scholar and administrator. Lawrence, one of his students, had described him in *Seven Pillars of Wisdom* as follows:

> Not a wild man, but *Mentor* to all of us was Hogarth, our father confessor and adviser, who brought us the parallels and lessons of history, and moderation, and courage. To the outsiders he was peacemaker . . .

and made us favoured and listened to, for his weighty judgement. He had a delicate sense of value, and would present clearly to us the forces hidden behind the lousy rags and festering skins which we knew as Arabs. Hogarth was our referee, and our untiring historian, who gave us his great knowledge and careful wisdom even in the smallest things, because he believed in what we were making.[1]

In the message provided by the Foreign Office for the man now styled King of the Hijaz, Hogarth tried to reconcile the promises to the Arabs with the Balfour Declaration and, indirectly, to counter the effect of the new Russian diplomacy. The difficulty of this attempt to adjust conflicting policies is amply illustrated in the text of the explanation.

(1) The Entente Powers are determined that the Arab race shall be given full opportunity of once again forming a nation in the world. This can only be achieved by the Arabs themselves uniting, and Great Britain and her Allies will pursue a policy with this ultimate unity in view.

(2) So far as Palestine is concerned we are determined that no people shall be subject to another but

(a) in view of the fact there are in Palestine shrines, Wakfs and Holy Places, sacred in some cases to Moslems alone, Jews alone, to Christians alone, and in others to two or all three, and inasmuch as these places are of interest to vast masses of people outside Palestine and Arabia, there must be a special regime to deal with these places approved of by the world.
(b) As regards the Mosque of Omar [sic] it shall be considered as a Moslem concern alone and shall not be subjected directly or indirectly to any non-Moslem authority.

(3) Since the Jewish opinion of the world is in favour of a return of Jews to Palestine and inasmuch as this opinion must remain a constant factor, and further as His Majesty's Government view with favour the realisation of the aspiration, His Majesty's Government are determined that in so far as is compatible with the freedom of the existing population both economic and political, no obstacle should be put in the way of the realisation of this ideal.

In this connexion the friendship of world Jewry to the Arab cause is equivalent to support in all states where Jews have a political influence. The leaders of the movement are determined to bring about the success of Zionism by friendship and cooperation with the Arabs, and such an offer is not one to be lightly thrown aside.[2]

Despite the apparent ambiguities, several things were made clear. The British considered Palestine a "special" case, requiring special administration. In addition, the government was "determined" (a strong word) that nothing should obstruct "a return of Jews to Palestine." It was much less clear what the realization of the ideal of Zionism meant to the Foreign Office, since the government had stated with equal determination that "no people shall be subject to another."

Significantly, the phrase in the Balfour Declaration which protected the "civil and religious rights of existing non-Jewish communities in Palestine" acquired from Hogarth and the Foreign Office an official gloss which seemingly expanded Arab security. Jewish aspirations were to be favored "so far as is compatible with the freedom of the existing population, both economic and political." The vacuity of "civil" rights promised to Palestinian Arabs moved to the firmer ground of the more conventional "economic and political" freedom. Finally, the plain meaning of the section on Jerusalem's Haram ash-Sharif, which was not to be "subjected directly or indirectly to any non-Moslem authority," would lead the reader to believe that political control over the area would be invested in an international administration, but might, at least eventually, be Arab.

Husayn's response was to assent cordially to the first two paragraphs and to agree "enthusiastically" with the third section of the Foreign Office formula. According to Hogarth's report, Husayn said he "welcomed Jews to all Arab lands." Hogarth explained quite explicitly:

> The king would not accept an independent Jewish State in Palestine, nor was I instructed to warn him that such a State was contemplated by Great Britain. He probably knows nothing of the actual or possible economy of Palestine, and his ready assent to Jewish settlement there is not worth very much. But I think he appreciates the financial advantage of Arab cooperation with the Jews.[3]

Something considerably less than a Jewish state, then, was foreshadowed in the Hogarth message. But the government did advance somewhat its understanding of its Zionist policy. It defined its attitude toward the means by which a "national home" was to be established in Palestine: through the colonial movement of a "return of the Jews" to Palestine.

This was not a step backward from the Balfour promise, but a concrete measure explained to an Arab leader in support of a policy of sympathy for Zionist aspirations. That the Arabs were also encouraged and assured was not, in Foreign Office minds, a contradiction in the letter of the promises to both peoples. Only in retrospect can the seeds of conflict be seen.

At the same time that Husayn was being reassured, the Allies were embarking on a wholesale restatement of war aims that was to culminate in further specific statements later in the year. The Bolshevik revolution and the American entry into the war had totally undercut the methods and aims of traditional diplomacy. Within a month of Lenin's takeover, the Soviet government had not only begun negotiating a separate people's peace with the Germans at Brest-Litovsk and publishing secret Allied agreements, but it had released an appeal to the Muslim workers of Russia and the Middle East to revolt against European imperialism.[4] The idealism of Woodrow Wilson was scarcely less revolutionary in its effect on diplomacy as he attempted to articulate the demands of a new age.

But it was Lloyd George who gave the first official Allied response to the Soviet challenge, in a speech to delegates of the Trade Union Congress at Caxton Hall on 5 January 1918. According to Arno J. Mayer, the British prime minister's "prodigious political instincts readily enable him to detect stirrings and strivings which might eventually find expression in new power configurations. He sought to control these new-fledged forces by dealing them the deathblow of partial recognition."[5] On the Middle East, Lloyd George declared that Arabia, Armenia, Mesopotamia, Syria, and Palestine were "entitled to a recognition of their separate national conditions." He refused to be more specific about these areas, but he did say that the principles of the consent of the governed or the right of self-determination which would form the basis for the reorganization of Europe would apply equally to the Middle East.[6]

Three days later, in a speech that completely overshadowed Lloyd George's, Wilson enunciated his famous Fourteen Points. Point 12 called for "an absolutely unmolested opportunity of autonomous development" for the nationalities under Turkish rule.[7] This was certainly an expression of the principle of self-determination, though the precise term was not used. Point 12 was also, as Laurence Evans has pointed out, a declaration in "unmistakable terms that the United States considered the Middle East to be within the sphere of American interests and that the solution of its problems would not be left to the determination of the powers that had, up to now, considered the Middle East to be their exclusive concern."[8] The wording of Wilson's points may have been vague, the purpose may have been largely propagandistic, but the Fourteen Points held out to the peoples of the Middle East the hope of American intervention in the imperialist schemes of the European powers.

Word of these developments quickly reached the Middle East. It traveled fastest in the already conquered portion of the southern

Levant, raising expectations and causing administrative complications. Some of the problems caused by policies and declarations regarding the nationalities of the Ottoman Empire were rooted in the political and cultural history of the Middle East. Words and phrases full of meaning for European or American spokesmen tended to fall on bewildered but excited ears in the Middle East. Palestine, for instance, was only a vague geographic description for an area considered part of Syria; administratively, under the Ottomans, it was composed of an independent sanjak of Jerusalem in the south, the sanjaks of Acre and Balqa within the vilayet or province of Beirut in the north, and the vilayet of Syria east of the Jordan River.

The population of Palestine at this time was overwhelmingly Arab. According to the 1922 census carried out by the government of Palestine, the Arabs amounted to eighty-eight percent of a total population of 752,000. Approximately eleven percent, or 84,000, were Jews.[9] However, the Palestinian community had for hundreds of years been used to a Turkish system of administration and law whereby it was divided into religious communities or millets. Each millet—a Turkish word meaning nation—organized its own internal affairs, paying taxes to the central government and maintaining public order. The millets formed a mosaic of clear colors, not mixing, easily identifiable, related not to territory, as in Europe, but to religion. In 1917 and 1918 the Arabs were just beginning to feel themselves something different from mere members of a Muslim society. And when the Turkish empire was destroyed in the war, the Arabs had no recognized spokesmen to turn to as the millets had. Traditionally, the area of Palestine was governed by an aristocracy, the "effendi" class of the Ottoman Empire. The Muslim Arab population was mostly agricultural, the Christians and Jews predominantly urban. With the arrival of the British, the rural Arabs being without authoritative leadership, the responsibility devolved upon prominent Palestinian families, such as the Husaynis and the Nashashibis.

Thus the Arabs, though forming a single cultural group, were not otherwise a unified community. Divided by religious loyalties, economic statuses, and living patterns, the Arabs toward the end of the war presented a picture of a society in transition, with all of the incoherency and disintegration that term implies. The concepts of nationality, self-determination, independence, Arabism, and Zionism only added a heady emotional brew to an already distraught community.

The military administration, presided over by Generals Allenby and Clayton, had few of the necessary tools with which to meet this extraordinary situation. Taking the *Manual of Military Law* as its text, the administration laid down, subject to modifications necessitated by military requirements, three principles:

(1) To maintain the administrative services to at least the same extent as they had been kept up before our occupation.

(2) To recognise the validity of the civil and penal laws in force before our occupation, as well as the rights, and rights on action of enemy subjects;

(3) To collect the taxes, dues, and tolls payable to the state in accordance with the old fiscal laws, regulations, and assessments.[10]

The territory under occupation, which corresponded roughly to the Ottoman independent Sanjak of Jerusalem, was further divided into four districts, using decentralized Turkish administrative units. Military governors were appointed to each district with direct responsibility to the central administration. They were directed to retain the existing local administrative machinery if possible and to keep interference with the local population to a minimum.

As chief administrative officer of southern Palestine and adviser to Allenby on political matters, Clayton was more than busy. He had to deal with a great variety of people, all of whom were prepared to make endless trouble if not handled properly.

> It was Clayton who had to reconcile the people of Palestine to the introduction of Egyptian money and the demonetization of all their hoarded Turkish paper; to persuade the straining Army Transport to bear additional burdens, not only for the benefit of starving civilians, but even for the purpose of restarting local trade; to restrain over-enthusiastic Zionists from compromising their prospects by unwise speech-making; to maintain relations with semi-independent Arab tribes beyond Jordan; to soothe the susceptibilities of multitudinous and querulous ecclesiastics of three faiths and a dozen churches; to maintain liaison with the Allied missions, and entertain Turkish deserters of high rank.[11]

Clayton succeeded in keeping peace between the administration and the numerous conflicting elements it dealt with, due in part to his "quiet humour and the power of being pleasantly but definitely final." Many of the cases brought before him for judgment were exceedingly petty and disagreeable, ofter depending upon the finest of interpretations. One such, recounted by Lady Clayton, concerned a dispute over which of two Christian communities should have the privilege of washing certain dirty windows in the Church of the Nativity in Bethlehem. Clayton inquired as to the length of time since they had last been cleaned. "Forty years," he was told. "Well then, let it remain another year," Clayton replied. The subject was not brought up again.[12]

Not every situation lent itself to such expeditious treatment. Early in Clayton's "reign," Sykes noted that a "whole crop of weeds" was growing where nothing should have been coming up but assets for the British.[13] He cited Arab unrest over Zionism, French jealousy of the dominant British position in Palestine, Syrian-Hijazi friction, Franco-Italian jealousy, "Zionist anticipation undirected or controlled running to suspicion and chauvinism," and what he called the "Cairo Fashoda spirit." The division of authority in both London and Palestine was allowing these problems to assume formidable proportions, he thought, and therefore reorganization and centralization would speed the process of identifying and solving them as they arose. He suggested that someone in London be placed in charge of Arab affairs under the secretary of state for foreign affairs, that a clean break be made between policy in Egypt and policy in Arabia and Palestine, and that General Clayton be put in complete political charge of the Hijaz and full control of political organizations dealing with Arabian and Palestinian affairs.

Lord Hardinge of Penshurst, the permanent undersecretary at the Foreign Office and a former viceroy of India (1910–1916), concurred with Sykes's recommendations, adding that Sykes himself should be the person lent to the Foreign Office to take care of Palestinian and Hijazi affairs. No admirer of Sir Mark's, Hardinge noted carefully in a letter to Lord Robert Cecil that Sykes's papers and questions would be passed through him as supervising undersecretary.[14] Wingate, however, objected strongly to the proposed changes in the Middle East. He argued that the existing arrangement whereby Clayton maintained close touch with both Allenby and himself was keeping all parties well informed and was enabling Clayton to perform tasks for which he was "particularly well-qualified."[15] Clayton's importance as a political and intelligence coordinator was stressed over his time-consuming work as administrator and as collaborator with Picot.

Thus pressed, Sykes agreed to eliminate the idea of using Clayton to coordinate Palestinian and Hijazi matters and instead to supply Allenby with a new executive adminstrator for Palestine. Hardinge could not resist pointing out to Sykes that the main idea of his 1 January memorandum had run up against practical difficulties in the field, but he endorsed the "new scheme" anyway as the better plan.[16] The results of the reorganization were that Sykes would be the focal point in London for all matters involving the Middle East, Clayton would be relieved of his strictly administrative duties in Palestine, Egypt would continue to supervise policy in the Hijaz and would have the support of the central Arab Bureau, while Palestinian policy, completely separated from Egypt, would be controlled by Clayton, who would have a branch of the Arab Bureau under him. Because of Wingate's desire to be at the center of Middle East activities, Sykes's attempt to center political responsibility for the area in Clayton, and thus to bypass Wingate, was deferred until September.

Clayton was pleased with the new arrangement, whereby his workload was reduced. He pronounced it soundly based.[17] He continued to serve as chief administrator until 16 April 1918, when he handed the job over to Major General Sir Arthur Money. Storrs, who seemed as if made for the position of military governor of Jerusalem, felt particularly bereft. Clayton's rule had been "too good to last," he thought. He would always look back on his first months in Jerusalem "with peculiar affection . . . . So long as I enjoyed the friendly understanding of Clayton and the confidence of the Commander-in-Chief, my word was law."[18]

While this administrative reorganization was going on, the stage was being set in London, Cairo, and Palestine for the setting up of a Zionist Commission to travel to the Middle East. On 14 January 1918, Dr. Chaim Weizmann, who was to lead the commission, wrote to Justice Brandeis in Washington concerning his view of what was happening in the Middle East. He was aware that the Arabs had been upset by the Balfour Declaration and by the jubilation with which Jewry had received it, but he expected that a policy of firmness such as that utilized by Mark Sykes would succeed if the British presented Zionism as a fait accompli and stressed that the declared policy of Great Britain was for a Jewish Palestine. With startling presumption, Weizmann told Brandeis that the "prejudice and lack of understanding" on the part of British officials in the Middle East would have to be faced boldly, as would the anticipated hard bargaining with the Arabs.[19]

Two days later, on 16 January, Weizmann wrote to Sykes that the commission's schedule of objectives had been revised and approved by Balfour and the director of military intelligence. Balfour had proved to favor an early establishment of a Jewish university in order to symbolize the intellectual and spiritual side of the Zionist movement. The commission was therefore to investigate the feasiblity of the project and to initiate steps toward its realization. Balfour also warned that the question of land speculation should be taken into consideration by the authorities, supposedly in conjunction with the commission, and measures taken to prevent scandal which might be disastrous for the future of the country. The secretary had also underlined the importance of the commission's appearing to be a genuine representative of the Zionist Organization. Hence, he emphasized the desirability of having French, Italian, and especially American representation.[20]

On 23 January, Sir Ronald Graham wrote the War Office on Balfour's instructions about the decision to send a commission of Zionist leaders to the East to open communications with the Arabs and other communities in Palestine. It was suggested that Captain William Ormsby-Gore, later Lord Harlech, currently serving as assistant secretary to the War Cabinet and parliamentary secretary to Lord Milner, be appointed political officer in charge of the commission, since he was the only available officer with suitable knowledge of both Arab and Zionist movements. He would work under the orders of General Allenby and might be attached to General Clayton's staff in order to act as liaison between the authorities and the commission.[21]

For the first time since Palestine was occupied, the Foreign Office on 24 January sent Clayton a general outline of policy to be used for guidance. The details were entrusted to Clayton's discretion, but he was to bear in mind that the aim of policy was "to reap the full benefit of our position in Palestine." Much of the outline provided instructions for the handling of problems related to religion and the interests of the various faiths. Otherwise, German influence was to be removed; the use of European personnel was to be reduced to a minimum; local officials were to be employed without favoring any one community. Instruction 7 called for the "maintenance of Zionism on right lines . . . with full facilities for the reconstruction and establishment of colonies and institutions."[22] Though the wording of this last item was vague, an implied meaning—that Zionism was to be closely controlled—seemed to Clayton to be clear. He wrote Sykes that the guidelines had been helpful and that he had already been working on similar lines.[23]

Not everyone, however, found that this outline clarified His Majesty's Government's policy on Zionism. Captain Fielding of the Arab Bureau wrote Sykes plaintively: "At present, we none of us have a notion as to what is meant by a 'home', or why, if it is only to involve increased facility for landholding, the Jews should be in such a state of joy."[24]

On 26 January 1918, Clayton informed Sykes that Picot, France's political emissary in the Middle East, was actively working to counter Britain's Zionist policy. Clayton confessed that there was little he could do about Picot's undermining of Sykes's Arab-Jew-Armenian combination, principally because it had to be remembered that Picot had been promised the "French High Commissionership of Syria (and Palestine?)." At least, that was what Picot had told Clayton "once in a burst of confidence."[25]

On 4 February, Clayton reported a "most marked and steadily increasing" pro-British attitude among Jews and Muslims throughout Palestine. There was virtually no evidence that any community aspired to independence. Arab national feeling was weak; and the Jews would be content to rest under the shadow of a great power, which for the time being they considered essential. Arabs and Jews were moving toward rapprochement, though cordiality had not yet been reached. Clayton said he had urged Lawrence to impress Faysal with the need to come to terms with the Jews. Working on Lawrence's weakness, Clayton had told him that it was his only chance of accomplishing something big and bringing the Arab movement to success. "He is inclined the other way," Clayton wrote regretfully, "and there are people in Cairo who lose no chance of putting him against [the Jews]."[26] However, on 12 February Lawrence assured Clayton that the next time he saw Faysal he would talk to him about the Jews and he promised that the "Arab attitude shall be sympathetic, for the duration of the war at least." Lawrence added, "Only please remember that he is under the old man [Husayn], and cannot involve the Arab Kingdom by himself."[27]

Clayton by now had yielded to the inevitable. The Zionist Commission, despite his objections, was coming out to the East in the near future. Adopting a wait-and-see attitude, he said he looked forward to the arrival of the commission which would bring with it a "really good class of Jew." But he also noted to Wingate that careful treatment would be required to keep its members "on right lines."[28]

On 13 February 1918, the Foreign Office took the additional step of informing Clayton directly that, subject to Allenby's authority, the commission would be initiating measures to give effect to the Balfour Declaration. The telegram continued, "It is important that everything should be done to obtain authority for commission in eyes of Jewish world and at the same time to allay Arab suspicion regarding true aims of Zionism."[29] What the Foreign Office had in mind at this time regarding Zionist objectives was all very hazy and tentative. Balfour had just assured the government that it was bound to the Zionists "only by the limited assurances given to Lord Rothschild" in his name.[30] Accordingly, Sykes, as sympathetic to Zionism as anyone in the government, had written with apparent candor to a moderate

Arab group in Cairo, the Syria Welfare Committee. After making his usual strong pitch for the mutuality of Arab-Jewish-Armenian interests, he concluded by enumerating three requirements to be fulfilled by the regime controlling Palestine after the war. The holy places must be guaranteed; Zionist colonization must be offered "honest opportunity"; and the existing population must be protected "against expropriation, exploitation or subjection."[31] In the context thus provided by Balfour and Sykes, it is clear that the sending of the commission to Palestine, though a concrete step toward Zionist goals, had not yet gone beyond the limited promise implied in the Balfour Declaration. Vagueness in government policy was still being deliberately expressed at the highest positions. George Lloyd, British representative to the Supreme War Council at Versailles, complained perceptively to Wingate about the contradictory assurances and plans issued by the Foreign Office. "Mark Sykes does not attempt," Lloyd said, "to meet my arguments, but brushes them to one side by saying that it doesn't matter what we agree to as it is ten to one that all agreements will be nullified by later events, peace conferences and the like. On the whole I should prefer to have no agreements rather than bad ones. . . ."[32]

On 3 March, shortly before the commission was to leave for Cairo, Sykes followed up his letter to the Arab committee by discussing in a private letter to Clayton the question of Palestine and its future. Looking ahead to the peace conference, where he believed President Wilson would exercise nearly complete authority, he announced that British policy should be "so to order affairs, that the general opinion of the world will be, that we shall be the most suitable Trustees to hand the country over to for development and control." According to Sykes, the three areas of concern he had identified earlier—the holy places, the Palestinian population, and Zionism—should be isolated and treated separately by different departments within the administration. This would increase the chances of Britain's being nominated trustee for the last two areas, if not the first. The department handling the people of Palestine should adopt a policy of unifying the population and making it as progressive and cohesive as possible. He accurately forecast that whoever ruled Palestine would have to "protect, support and mediate for this population vis-a-vis Zionism. It is always better for the Trustee that his ward should be healthy and solvent rather than delicate in health and encumbered as to his estates."[33]

The third of the three roles borne by the administration would be developed in discussion with Weizmann and Ormsby-Gore. Consigning the prospect of a Jewish state into the semi-distant future where it need not trouble the present, Sykes explicitly explained that the "Zionists do not desire to break out into a fully fledged republic." What they wanted was an "opportunity to colonise and develop the waste lands of Palestine and their most sanguine members regard this as an event which will take at least three generations to accomplish." Sykes had thus seen and correctly analyzed the basic problems of running Palestine while encouraging contradictory nationalisms. However, his system of parallel but entirely distinct administrative departments was to have disastrous results for the relations of the military administration with both Arabs and Jews.

Sykes expanded his thesis of preparing Palestine for the peace conference in a letter to Wingate. Exaggerating the influence of international Jewry, probably in order to ease the path of the Zionist Commission in Egypt, he advised the Egyptian high commissioner to remember "that through Zionism we have a fundamental world force behind us that has enormous influence now, and will wield a far greater influence at the peace conference." In a direct appeal to Wingate's special concern for Britain's position in the Middle East, Sykes averred that it would be through Zionist strength at the peace conference that a good position would be obtained.[34]

With the way thus prepared by Sykes, the Zionist Commission set out for Egypt on the evening of Monday, 8 March 1918. A week earlier, Weizmann had survived an attack of cold feet on the part of Mark Sykes who had had second thoughts, owing to reports of unsettled public opinion in Cairo, about the propriety of a Weizmann interview with the king. However, Balfour intervened on Weizmann's behalf and the interview took place on the day of departure. Weizmann interpreted the incident from hindsight as a pessimistic omen, "a sort of prelude or thematic overture to the future."[35]

Besides Weizmann as leader, the commission was composed of Joseph Cowen, Dr. David Eder, Leon Simon, and I.M. Sieff (secretary), as English representatives; Commendatore Levi Bianchini of Italy; Professor Sylvain Levi of France; and Major Ormsby-Gore as liaison officer. The United States did not appoint a representative since it was not at war with Turkey, and the duly appointed Russian members were unable to join the commission, apparently owing to domestic political reasons.

In one sense Sykes had done well in his work of creating the proper atmosphere in the East. For the first time, Clayton felt secure enough to give his interpretation of the Balfour Declaration in a telegram to the Foreign Office. He was looking to the Weizmann mission, he said, "to put things right by impressing upon local Jews the real sense of the British Government's declaration and the necessity for taking up a reasonable and conciliatory attitude which will calm fear of local Arabs and lead to sympathetic cooperation of the two communities." He expected the commission to be understanding of the difficulties of administering the population of Palestine and to join him in construing the Balfour Declaration in "its literal sense and emphasizing intention of the Entente to safeguard the rights of all communities."[36] He wrote Wingate on 15 March that Christians and Muslims feared and distrusted Zionism. "The local Jews are of course very cock-a-hoop," he said, "and do not fail to rub in the fact that they have HMG at their backs. This, together with the tremendous amount of Zionist advertisement which goes on in Reuters, newspapers etc., does not make things easy." He hoped the commission would adopt a "thoroughly moderate attitude."[37]

Later in March the commission reached Alexandria. Weizmann found "innumerable Arab coteries . . . . organized—if that is the right word—into separate political groups, all busy pulling wires in different directions. Wartime Cairo was one vast labyrinth of petty intrigues. . . ."[38] The commission set about its work, getting in touch with the Sephardic community in Egypt, talking with influential Arabs, and listening to the generous advice of Sir Reginald Wingate. Wingate thought the Zionists reasonable but ill-informed on the situation in Arab countries. He wrote Lord Hardinge, "I therefore recommended them to feel their way carefully and to do all in their power to show sympathy and good-will to the Arab and Moslem peoples with whom their future must lie. . . . I also warned them to be very careful in regard to their discussions on the acquisition on land . . . ."[39]

Weizmann handled the Arabs in Cairo with great skill, Ormsby-Gore reported to Sykes, telling them what they wanted to hear.[40] However, Weizmann was not very happy with the local Jewish community. Instead of providing a bridge for the commission between East and West, most of the Jews "remained as remote as the Arabs."[41] Ormsby-Gore agreed. "The rich Egyptian Jews care little for Zionism," he wrote, "and intending to remain amongst the fleshpots of Egypt are merely interested in possibilities of making money by exploiting the labours of others in Palestine."[42] These were the type of people feared by the Arabs and consequently they were the ones who must be "kept out with a strong hand."

Now at the beginning of April 1918 the commission was poised for entry into Palestine. The first hurdles had been taken: it was now up to the commission to make good among the Palestinians. The world had been intruding upon the Ottoman backwater area of Palestine for many years prior to the Zionist Commission of 1918. The indirect imperialist invasion of technology and the foreign consuls and missionaries of the nineteenth and early twentieth centuries had already given way to the crude rush of an Allied army with its stringent martial law and its promise of a new regime. Trailing political promises in its wake, the army had settled down for the time being, spreading the tentacles of military administration and Western ideas and power throughout the country. Now, in April 1918, a new intruder stood on the border, formed and nurtured by Western thought and power, and determined to achieve its objectives.

5

THE ZIONIST COMMISSION
IN PALESTINE, APRIL/JUNE 1918

After its short stay in Egypt, the commission arrived piecemeal in Palestine on or about 4 April.[1] Weizmann found the change from the uneasiness of Cairo to the highly-charged "war atmosphere" of general headquarters in Ramleh abrupt and startling. He felt that the group had arrived at an inopportune moment. Allenby's advance northward had been checked completely, and the train on which Weizmann arrived from Cairo had promptly returned to that city loaded with men and officers being rushed off to Europe to break the force of Ludendorff's spring offensive. Breakfasting at headquarters on his first morning in Palestine, he had been wedged between Generals Allenby and Bols, who "talked war" across him.

Weizmann wrote later that he was soon dismayed to learn that the Balfour Declaration, to which he had devoted so much time and effort and which had made such a stir in the outside world, had evidently not been officially brought to the attention of Allenby's officers. "They knew nothing about it," he complained, "and nothing about the sympathy shown at that time to our aims and aspirations by prominent Englishmen in every walk of life." Allenby had greeted Weizmann's credentials and letters of introduction from Lloyd George and Balfour with polite interest and the explanation that nothing could be done at present. The sensitive Zionist leader felt the commission had been received as a nuisance, "a very motley group of civilians—injected into the military organism like a foreign body."

Actually, Weizmann's impression of near-total ignorance and indifference (if not simply a post-facto rhetorical contrivance) was inaccurate. Allenby and other high-ranking officers certainly knew of the declaration, even officially, and it had received discussion in the *Arab Bulletin*, the organ of Cairo's Arab Bureau.[2] The determination of its official meaning, however, had been left by the Foreign Office to the initiative of the Zionist Organization and the commission, and as a consequence the Foreign Office had issued no authoritative statement explaining the details of Zionist aims.

Weizmann spent his first three days at Ramleh, days he felt were in the nature of a period of probation. While there he had his first conversations with General Clayton, who informed Mark Sykes that headquarters had been struck with Weizmann's intelligence and openness and that Allenby had evidently formed a high opinion of him.[3] Unfortunately, one incident that deeply impressed Weizmann was the dramatic disclosure during an early conversation with Lieutenant Colonel Wyndham Deedes that extracts from the notorious *Protocols of the Elders of Zion* were in the possession of some British officers in Palestine.[4] Deedes told Weizmann that the extracts had been brought in by members of the British military mission serving with the Russian Grand Duke Nicholas in the Caucasus. Weizmann was horrified by this knowledge. He even thought he could detect that the extracts from the *Protocols* "had been obviously selected to cater to the taste of a certain type of British reader."[5] The Zionist relationship with the military administration could hardly have started out on a worse footing. "The messianic hopes which we had read into the Balfour Declaration," Weizmann emphasized, "suffered a perceptible diminution when we came into contact with the hard realities of GHQ."[6]

Nonetheless, Clayton, who had been skeptical at first, became convinced through long talks with Weizmann that many of the administration's difficulties arising from the mutual distrust and suspicion between Arabs and Jews in Palestine would now disappear. Weizmann, however, remained personally unconvinced that there was any more than a mere "tender plant of confidence" between the military administration and the commission. Years later he described himself as having been placed between hammer and anvil:

> between the slow-moving, unimaginative, conservative and often unfriendly British administration, military or civil, and the impatient, dynamic Jewish people, which saw in the Balfour Declaration the great promise of the return to them of their own country, and contrasted it resentfully with the administrative realities in Palestine.[7]

Clayton, Deedes, and Allenby were "notable and noble exceptions," in Weizmann's view, to the men lower down in the military heirarchy, who were, "almost without exception, devoid of understanding, or vision, or even kindness." Major William Ormsby-Gore, the political officer attached to Zionist Commission, also had an unkind word for the "ineradicable tendency of the Englishman who had lived in India or the Sudan to favour quite unconsciously the Moslem both against Christian and Jew."[8] Even so, he thought things were proceeding soundly thanks to Clayton, whom he increasingly admired.

Clayton thought Ormsby-Gore's charges of prejudice against British officials unfair and untrue. He defended those against whom he thought the remarks were directed, Storrs and Pearson, the governors of Jerusalem and Jaffa respectively, in a letter to Sykes which termed the allegations "unjustified." He affirmed his personal support for Zionism, entirely apart from the fact that it was official government policy, and pronounced it "one of our strongest cards." But he pleaded for Sykes to agree with him that there was need for caution if the British were to bring that policy to a successful conclusion.[9] Thus if Weizmann was between hammer and anvil, so too were the administrators of Palestine, men caught between impatient Jew, suspicious Arab, and the ambiguous policy of His Majesty's Government.[10]

Weizmann's problems with the military administration were partly of his own making. He can hardly have expected his initial tactics of appealing to his letters of introduction from the prime minister and the foreign secretary to obtain for him a series of vigorous measures for achieving Zionist objectives. He had not come to the East expecting a favorable climate of official opinion, but rather expected that his letters, unsupported by detailed, constructive recommendations, would fail.

In addition he and other members of the commission had become sharply disillusioned with the Arabs of Palestine. The talks with Palestinians in Egypt had apparently not gone as well as they had thought at the time, and an Arab version of the discussions, passed on by Clayton, led to bitter reflections. "I am trying to maintain in my own mind an attitude of sweet reasonableness towards the Arabs," Leon Simon noted in a 7 April diary entry. "But when one. . . reads these absurd demands and . . . sees the Arabs who walk about here, it is not easy to prevent oneself from slipping into a pronounced anti-Arab frame of mind. I simply cannot see the elements of an *entente*."[11]

In casting about for a new, bold method of approach, Weizmann had decided to disregard the cautious advice of his political officer, Ormsby-Gore, in an aggressive attempt to deal with Palestinian Arabs by going over their heads and in addition to gain the leadership of the Jewish community in Palestine.[12] He therefore seized upon a minor incident and built it up into a symbolic complaint in order to jolt the military administration into action and to capture the imagination of Palestinian and world Jewry.

On 11 April, a theatrical performance at an Arab school, which Ronald Storrs attended, had provided an occasion for a rhetorical display which, on hearsay evidence, seemed to bear out the commission's complaint about inadequate official concern for generating the appropriate political atmosphere. Weizmann claimed, on the basis of extracts from two speeches by Arabs, provided by an unidentified source, that anti-Jewish sentiments had been uttered in Storr's presence and that there had been forthcoming virtually "no word to suggest that there was any discrepancy between those sentiments and the Government's policy."

This incident gained significance, Weizmann said, from the fact that it took place on the same day that the Jews of Jerusalem had welcomed the Zionist Commission to Jerusalem with a great demonstration; on that occasion, a "warm tribute of gratitude" had been paid to the British government and people for the Balfour Declaration and a hearty endorsement given to Ormsby-Gore's public insistence on the need for harmony and cooperation between Jews and Arabs in Palestine. There could not have been a stronger contrast between the spirit of the two meetings, Weizmann maintained.

> On the one side, a kind of crusade against an imaginary enemy, and expressions of an intransigent and aggressive nationalism; on the other side, absolute loyalty to Great Britain and a sincere desire for peace and friendship between different national groups.

The fault was clear. Useful negotiations with the Arabs and Syrians were impossible because no official steps had been taken "to bring home to the Arabs and Syrians the fact that H. M. Government had expressed a definite policy with regard to the future of the Jews in Palestine."

Weizmann stressed the need for the military administration to look beyond the immediate population, overwhelmingly Arab, to the Jewries of England, Russia, and America. The Jewish population might be a minority in Palestine, he said, but it represented the "organised national will of millions of Jews throughout the world; it is the advance guard of the Jewish people." It was for this reason that its views and demands were to be given consideration far beyond what mere numbers would suggest.

Since the Arabs were not in the right frame of mind to give "serious attention" to Zionist explanations, Weizmann continued,

What is necessary is that the exact meaning and scope of Mr. Balfour's declaration should be authoritatively explained to them and that it should be made perfectly clear to them that this declaration represents the considered policy of H. M. Government, and that it is their duty to conform to it.[13]

This was an unreasonably sharp demand which certainly exceeded the terms of reference of the Zionist Commission. Weizmann knew perfectly well that the declaration's exact meaning and scope were still undetermined. He elicited an equally sharp reply from the ready pen of Ronald Storrs, the alleged offending official.

Storrs firmly denied that the incident had happened in the way described by Weizmann. In his view the members of the commission had acted hastily, upon faulty evidence, and in a manner not calculated to "increase their reputation for practical statesmanship." Not only had the abuse been directed against the Turks, not the Jews, but the audience had responded spontaneously in a demonstration of loyalty to the British government, an expression of enthusiasm Storrs contrasted favorably to the situation in Egypt, where such a response would have been "utterly unthinkable." He thought the venture "at least as creditable on the part of those who know they will shortly be requested to make, as from those who hope in the near future to gain, elbow room in Palestine."

Then Storrs went over the attack. What had the Zionists themselves done to check the rumors which had caused "grave disquietude" among the Muslim and Christian people in Palestine? He recalled that a variety of enthusiastic articles on the future of Zionism, published in the British press, had wrought uneasiness and depression among the Muslims of Palestine. These feelings, he reported, had been accentuated by numerous meetings of Jews at which lectures on the subject had been delivered before "interested and demonstrative audiences."

Storrs gave specific examples of speeches by prominent Jews during February and March dealing with the delicate matter of extremist views on Jewish sovereignty over the land. Aside from these speeches, other agitation, and the usual rumors, Storrs asserted, "no kind of enlightenment or further definition of the necessarily general terms of His Majesty's Government's declarations have ever reached Arab ears." As a matter of fact, Storrs continued, the "almost certainly unwelcome details [to the Arab population of Palestine] of H. M. G.'s Zionist policy. . . have never yet been disclosed to the general public, nor, so far as I am aware, to any living soul." This was an astonishingly candid statement. It was also quite accurate.

Storrs went on. Contrary to Weizmann's demand for administrative action by the British, it was really the Zionists who should assume the responsibility of exposing to the Arabs, as accurately and conciliatorily as possible, their "real aims" and policy. Despite advice to this effect given to the Zionists when they were in Cairo, he reported, no such statements had been made. He suggested that Weizmann remedy the situation by speaking to the leaders of the various communities in Palestine, and he offered to provide a suitable occasion.[14]

A clash of this type was bound to leave scars. Storrs, despite evidence of his sincere sympathy for Zionism, was heavily criticized by Zionists both during and after his tenure in Jerusalem. More seriously, the entire British military administration was forever stained by the tarbrush of general anti-Semitism. Weizmann never forgave Storrs for his earnest defense of his actions in the theater incident. Doubting Storrs's sincerity, he claimed the governor was merely subtler than others in his approach to anti-Zionism. "He was everyone's friend" Weizmann wrote, "but try as he might he failed to gain the confidence of his Jewish community."[15]

Storrs eventually became the storm center of Jewish criticism of the military administration. He had been identified for years with the Arabs and the Arab revolt. Perhaps, as many were tempted to think, such a man could not be pro-Zionist as well. But T. E. Lawrence's portrait captured the spirit of the man in quite a different light from Weizmann's summary spotlight.

> The first of us was Ronald Storrs, . . . the most brilliant Englishman in the Near East, and subtly efficient, despite his diversion of energy in love of music and letters, of sculpture, painting, of whatever was beautiful in the world's fruit. None the less, Storrs sowed what we reaped, and was always first, and the great man among us. His shadow would have covered our work and British policy in the East like a cloak, had he been able to deny himself the world, and to prepare his mind and body with the sternness of an athlete for a great fight.[16]

Christopher Sykes has suggested that Storrs's very accomplishments and his sensitivity may have been to blame for the legends that grew up about his wickedness. Had he been less intelligent, the belief would not have gained currency that he was no obedient subordinate but the originator of the government's Middle East policy.

> He had nothing to give except this maddening British gift of fairness, and the fact that he gave it with a somewhat extravagant show of diplomatic good manners, instead of with the accustomed British gaucherie and blast of pipe-smoke, merely increased the bitterness of disillusion and convinced his former friends that he was a monster of hypocritical

intrigue . . . . Nothing was ever even faintly proved against him beyond the fact that with his anxiety to please he sometimes appeared to give promises which he could not, or as Jews (and Arabs) said, did not fulfill.

Sykes added significantly that Storrs' Palestine career added

> a curious proof that the task which the British Government undertook was beyond accomplishment. A sensitive and intelligent man was at no advantage over a stupid or oafish one—unless he took sides.[17]

So Storrs's reputation became an unintended casualty in a struggle for power.

Clayton also had been troubled by the aggressive and impatient line taken by the commission. In a very defensive letter to Balfour, he tried to explain the difficulties of the situation. The chief problem was the time it would take to switch from an Arab policy "over to Zionism all at once in the face of a considerable degree of Arab distrust and suspicion." Loyally, he was prepared to advance projects in the Zionist interest, if that indeed were government policy and despite his own close identification with Arab movement. However, he pointed out, "precipitate action" would only harm this interest and reduce the efficiency of the army. He made a strong case for the need to proceed with caution:

> Arab opinion both in Palestine and elsewhere is in no condition to support an overdose of Zionism just now. Events on the Western Front have produced a very marked effect here to our disadvantage, and great care is essential in developing a policy, which is, to say the least, somewhat startling to those other elements whom we have been at such pains to cultivate during the past three years, and to whom we are morally pledged. Moreover, Arab military cooperation is of vital importance to us at the present juncture, a fact fully realized by our enemies who are using every possible means to seduce the Arabs from their alliance with us.

He strongly urged that the Foreign Office trust the local authorities to deal with the situation and pleaded that they not be "forced into precipitate action which might well wreck our whole policy, both Arab and Zionist."[18]

Unfortunately, the Foreign Office was ignorant of Weizmann's presumptuous initiative and tended to dismiss Clayton's observations and misgivings out of hand. Sir Ronald Graham said he knew of no attempt to force the local authorities to act precipitately. Sykes was irritated by Clayton's letter: "I am uneasy about this despatch as it seems to show a sort of hesitating state of mind which is dangerous.

This idea that we have dropped the Arabs wants dealing with." But no further instructions were forthcoming and the situation in Palestine continued to develop along lines of conflict.

On 19 April, Ormsby-Gore dispatched a report, his second, on the progress of the commission.[19] He emphasized the uphill struggle the commission had faced from its arrival to dispel widespread ignorance regarding Zionist aims and policy, a lack of understanding shared by Arabs, Palestinian Jews, and the military authorities. Charitably, he explained the reigning ignorance and confusion as resulting from a combination of: (a) a dearth of information available to the authorities on Zionist activities throughout the world; (b) the circumstances which led up to the Balfour Declaration; and (c) the absence in Palestine of a "clear definition of the interpretation put upon it by the responsible Zionist leaders."

According to the report, Weizmann had not been slow in taking the initiative to attempt to dissipate the atmosphere of nervous speculation in the Arab community. On 11 April he and the major had paid a formal visit to the house of Ismail al-Husayni, of the prominent Husayni family, where they had a long conversation with their host and his cousin, Kamal al-Husayni, the holder of the double post of mufti and qadi of Jerusalem.[20]

Weizmann, adopting a bold approach, told the two notables that it was "no part of his aim to establish anything in the nature of a Jewish State or Jewish Government at the end of the war," but that, on the contrary, he and the Zionist Organization earnestly advocated the establishment in Palestine of an administration "under which Jew and Arab could work harmoniously for the development of the Country on a basis of equality and Justice." He disclaimed any intent to interfere with the holy places or the way they were run by their traditional guardians, and he assured his hosts "that expropriation or the driving out from Palestine by economic means of the Arab proprietors or Arab fellaheen was the last thing he desired." He gave a certain substance to his assurance by pointing out that the existing Jewish colonies had in the past added "not merely to the increase in numbers and prosperity of the Jewish population of the district, but also of the Arabs in those districts."

The two Arab officials, despite being favorably impressed by Weizmann's personality, showed a marked lack of enthusiasm. Their politeness, in fact, was exceeded only by their caution. According to Ormsby-Gore, they expressed their "full concurrence" with Weizmann's declared aims and their "desire to live in peace and friendship with their Jewish neighbours." But, the mufti later told Colonel

Storrs skeptically, all would be well only if the "Jews acted upon Weizmann's word." Clearly they would not depend on a Zionist pledge, but would wait for action.

At about the same time that Ormsby-Gore was reporting to London on the Zionist Commission, the new director of the Arab Bureau in Cairo, Major Kinahan Cornwallis, was analyzing the impression made by the commission on leading Syrians and Palestinians expatriated in Egypt.[21] Cornwallis, another experienced orientalist, had become director when Hogarth opened a Palestinian branch of the bureau as one of the administrative changes effected earlier in the year. The tough intelligence officer was another of the men immortalized by Lawrence, who thought him "a man rude to look upon, but apparently forged from one of those incredible metals with a melting point of thousands of degrees. So he could remain for months hotter than other men's white-heat, and yet look cold and hard."[22] In Cornwallis's estimation, the Arabs in Egypt had moved a considerable distance from a "phase of uncompromising opposition to a gradual admission that perhaps [Zionism's] aims were not as black as they had been painted, and that under certain circumstances the population might even benefit from a Jewish 'invasion'." He warned, however, that they retained a deep fear that the Jews "not only intended to assume the reins of Government in Palestine but also to expropriate or buy up during the war large tracts of land owned by Moslems and others, and gradually to force them from the country." He went on to say that although suspicion remained, there was small doubt that it would gradually disappear if the commission continued its attitude of conciliation.[23]

It is worth noting again that until the commission arrived there had been no authoritative statement explaining the details of Zionist aims.[24] In the meantime, the Major said, Arab apprehensions had been fostered "not only by their previous experience of a rather undesirable class of Jew," but also by the attitude of the local Jewish committee, which had been unable to give any satisfaction, owing to its own lack of direction as to its future course. The British officers had done what they could to allay fears, but here again they had to work from an ignorance of the complete Zionist program, which made them less than convincing.

The Zionist program absorbed by Major Cornwallis and the other British officers was the program outlined by the Zionist Commission, first in Egypt and then in Palestine, to Syrian and Palestinian Arabs. According to the memorandum by Cornwallis, Weizmann said he wanted a British Palestine, "that a Jewish Government would be fatal to his plans and that it was simply his wish to provide a home for the Jews in the Holy Land where they could live their own national life, sharing equal rights with the other inhabitants." On the land question, he had assured the Arabs of his interest only in "waste and crown lands of which there were ample for all sections of the community." He held out hope of education, which would benefit Muslims, Christians, and Jews equally. And, finally, he spoke of the inviolability of the Muslim holy places and waqf, or benevolent foundation, property and of his sympathy for the Arab revolt against Turkish oppression. He was apparently being completely frank, but by sidestepping the issue of ultimate sovereignty by falsely disclaiming plans for a Jewish government, he satisfied only the British and aroused the fears of the Arabs.

Later on, as we see the rift between the Zionists and the military administration widen, this should be remembered. The authoritative sources available to British authorities for the details of the Zionist program were Weizmann and the Zionist Commission, and the moderate program outlined above, in Major Cornwallis's memorandum, was, in the absence of more precise instructions from London, the most nearly complete official explanation that existed in the Middle East of what the Balfour Declaration meant. Given this situation, John Marlowe's judgment on the ambiguity of British policy was only fair: that it had its "propagandistic advantages for both Arabs and Jews: it had some advantages for H. M. G. in that it enabled them to adjust their policy in accordance with events. But it had no advantage for the local administration."[25]

The next opportunity for Weizmann to meet with Palestinian Arabs came on 27 April. As he had promised, Storrs arranged a dinner party on that day in order to give the Zionist Commission an opportunity to inform the leading inhabitants of the city about its intentions in Palestine. Weizmann spoke eloquently of the recognition offered Palestine's former inhabitants, the Jews, by "the greatest of Bible-loving nations."[26] He explained that the Jews were not coming to Palestine, but returning to it.

> We return in order to link up our glorious ancient traditions of the past with the future, in order to create once more a great moral and intellectual centre from which perhaps the new word will come forth to a sorely tried world. That is for us the innermost meaning of a National Home.

He invoked his idea of "close settlement" on the land and argued that the creation of conditions under which Jewish moral and material development could take place would not be "to the detriment of any of the great communities already established in this country, but on the contrary to their advantage." He promised a land "flowing with milk and honey" to be enjoyed under conditions of communal equality, and warned "solemnly" against misinterpretations or false allegations. "Do not believe," he said, "those who insinuate that we intend to take the supreme political power of this country into our hands at the end of the war." Instead, he looked forward to a long period of apprenticeship during which the supreme political authority in Palestine would be vested in "one of the civilised democratic Powers" selected by the League of Nations until the population was capable of self-government.

Weizmann expressed sympathy for and interest in the struggles of the Arabs and Armenians against the "Turanian hordes," and predicted that Palestine would become a link between East and West. He said,

I think that our people are eminently fitted to perform this honourable task. We ask only for the opportunity of free national development in Palestine, and in justice it cannot be refused. We want to cultivate the long neglected land by modern methods, and under a just economic system, avoiding the evils from which the advanced countries of Europe are only now beginning to free themselves. We want also—and here I mention what will perhaps be regarded in the future as the coping-stone of our present work—to help to make Palestine once more a fountain of knowledge and idealism through the creation of a Hebrew University, a great intellectual centre open to all, in which the ancient truths of our Prophets will obtain expression in a modern form. In all this work, whether agricultural or intellectual, we shall not be injuring our neighbours in Palestine, on the contrary we shall be helping them towards a fuller and a richer life. I would ask you not to underrate the measure of our help. Though we are few as yet in Palestine, the eyes of our scattered people in every corner of the globe are fixed on what we are doing here, and the Jewish communities of the West are not without their influence in the counsels of the Nations.

At the conclusion of Weizmann's speech and after Storr's Arabic translation, the mufti gave a brief reply. He rejoiced in the full statement of Zionist ambitions, saying that since he had complete confidence in the sincerity of Weizmann's declarations, he looked forward to loyal cooperation with the Zionists in the future development of Palestine. The mufti concluded by quoting a hadith (a non-Quranic, traditional saying of Muhammad): "Our rights are your rights and your duties our duties."

At the same time that Weizmann was having such an apparently profitable time with Palestinian notables, his private views were being aired in a far harsher tone. He had now spent three weeks in Palestine, almost exclusively conversing with and listening to the Jewish community. On 25 April he sent Brandeis an outline of his up-to-date impressions.[27] The letter was passed by Ormsby-Gore to General Clayton, who sent it on to the foreign secretary along with his own observations. Weizmann admitted that it had been impossible to verify all the statements he had heard and to disentangle the many complicated questions existing in Palestine. Nevertheless, he proceeded to pass on to the justice a clear expression of the problems he perceived he was facing, notably in his relations with the military authorities.

He described General Allenby as generous and broadminded, but primarily a soldier and only secondarily interested in political questions: he praised General Clayton and his assistant, Colonel Deedes, for their sympathy with the Zionist movement and for considering a "Jewish Palestine as the only worthy aim and possible solution." But their usefulness was limited, he said, due to imperfectly clear instructions from London and, hence, a "certain vagueness" of mind. Still other British administrators had failed to recognize "the qualitative difference" between the Jewish and Arab populations.

Weizmann's attitude of superiority was clear and was symptomatic of the Jewish-Arab relationship. The assumption of "qualitative superiority" gave structure to the Zionist belief that the Jews had a greater right to the land of Palestine than had its Arab inhabitants. This assumption may also have been Weizmann's unstated reason for deceiving the Arabs about the Zionists' ultimate goal of founding a Jewish state in Palestine, just as it was a British assumption that the aims of empire and the prerogatives of power stood higher than the rights of 700,000 Arab natives of Palestine. And it should be clear that Weizmann was knowingly being deceptive. He had stated at the commission's second meeting that "Zionism had as its ultimate political objective the creation of a Jewish Commonwealth. The methods by which such a political state was to be evolved would be clearer to us on our return from Palestine."[28]

Weizmann continued his letter to Brandeis by saying that further Zionist problems with the military administration arose from the harsh fact that fighting was still going on in Palestine. The chief object of the administration, therefore, was to avoid rendering the internal situation more difficult. According to Weizmann, the natural consequence was that the old machinery of the Turkish administration was still in effective control, exercising a "very great, if not a decisive, influence on the course of events" in Palestine. These "corrupt and cunning" Arab and Syrian officials were "anxiously watching the situation and putting obstacles in the way of the Jews, abusing British

democratic notions and trying to apply to every administrative measure the numerical standard." Yet, in spite of these and other differences with the military administration, Weizmann felt justified in
declaring that the Zionist Commission had been received with a spirit
of fairness and that there was hope of establishing "mutual understanding and confidence."

Clayton refused to accept Weizmann's remarks without comment.
In a covering letter to Balfour on 3 May, he described the statement
regarding former Turkish officials in the administration as "quite
incorrect."[29] He explained that a number of such officials had been
used when the country had first been occupied. but that the policy
of the administration had been "perfectly independent and free from
any outside influence." Furthermore, he said, "Every effort has
been made to deal fairly with all communities and to see that the
interests of no particular section suffered." He noted that the presence of the Zionist Commission itself was evidence of the support
being given to the Zionist movement and that this had "indeed been
the cause of comment by other communities, who consider that they
are at a disadvantage in not having any corresponding organisation
to push their particular interests."

So by May 1918 the Zionists were sharply at odds with the military
administration, owing largely to Weizmann's excessive demands and
complaints, and they were having small success with the Palestinians,
having shown only limited zeal in meeting and talking with their local
counterparts. Then, sometime in May, possibly between the 12th and
the 21st,[30] there occurred a significant but little-known confrontation
between Weizmann and a group of Palestinian Arabs. Apparently the
results of this meeting caused a fundamental change in Zionist strategy. The initiative for the meeting had come from two members of
the prominent Husayni family, Musa Kazim (later president of the
Arab Executive, 1920–1934) and Muhammad Amin, a Turkish army
deserter who in 1917 had recruited a force of 2,000 Palestinian Arabs
to fight alongside Faysal in Transjordan.[31] These Palestinians and
others had become worried over the issue of Sharifian subservience
to British interests and the future of Palestine as envisaged by the
Hijazis, the British, and the Zionists.[32] Amin al-Husayni had talked
with T. E. Lawrence, who added to Palestinian fears by complaining
about Palestinian unreliability in the campaign and, when queried
about the Balfour Declaration, replied that "it was a good thing to
tame the Levantines with a Jewish God."

A secret meeting was set up between Weizmann, David Eder, Leon
Simon, and Israel Sieff, all of the Zionist Commission: Kazim: Kamal:
Amin al-Husayni: Abd ar-Rauf al-Bitar, the mayor of Jaffa: and Dr.

Faris Nimr, editor of the influential Cairo daily *al-Muqqatam*. Weizmann took the lead, speaking of collaborating with the Arabs to establish a unitary Arab state under the Hashimite dynasty with the financial aid of international Jewry and the protection of Great Britain. Under his scheme, Palestine, as the spiritual home of the Jews, would eventually confederate with the Arab state.

Musa Kazim welcomed the prospect of Jewish aid, but warned the Zionists that the culture of the West was not wanted in Palestine and they would have to throw off their alien ways. He questioned Weizmann about the *Protocols* and the Zionist connection with the "Elders of Zion" and the Bolshevik movement. Weizmann explained that the Zionists were actually anti-Bolshevik, that the *Protocols* were a Russian forgery, and that the commission wanted the British to administer Palestine in trust for both Jews and Arabs.

After further discussion, Musa Kazim repeatedly affirmed to Weizmann that the Palestinians were not opposed to a Jewish national home so long as Palestinian Arab sovereignty was upheld. Further, it was important that if the Zionists dealt directly with the Hashimites, they must keep the Palestinians and Syrians fully informed and participate in the talks only as full partners. The two sides then appointed representatives to maintain contact with each other and agreed that the Zionists would not talk with the Hijazis unless Syrian or Palestinian nationalists were present.

Musa Kazim reported on the meeting to Clayton, Storrs, and Colonel Waters-Taylor, another British officer. Later, when Kazim tried to arrange a second meting, he learned to his astonishment from Storrs that Weizmann had apparently broken his word and gone to meet Faysal, the Hijazi leader, out on the right flank of the regular army, without consulting the Palestinians.

Despite the slender basis for our knowledge of the meeting, some incident of this nature almost certainly took place in May. It would be difficult to account otherwise for subsequent changes of Zionist strategy and attitude. Weizmann had never expected to have an easy time with the Palestinians, but until May he had managed to maintain a "correct" attitude toward them. However, by the time the Zionist Commission had spent seven weeks in Palestine, he had become thoroughly frustrated in his dealings with the military and with the Palestinian Arabs, even though he had had the "good will and great assistance" of Allenby and his immediate entourage. At all events, on 30 May he wrote a long and remarkable letter to Balfour in which he fully expressed his bitter feelings about "the treacherous nature of the Arab" and the hostility of the administration.[33] He described the Arab variously as "superficially clever," worshipping only power and success; as one who "screams as often as he can and blackmails as much as he can"; and as one having a "fundamental qualitative difference" from the Jew.

Weizmann also repeated the charges that the English were " 'run' by the Arabs" in an administration left over from Turkish days and the Arabs were "corrupt, inefficient, regretting the good old times when baksheesh was the only means by which matters administrative could be settled." Even worse, he argued, "The present system tends . . . to level down the Jew politically to the status of a native," whereas under the Turks the Jews had held a more privileged position because the "Turk, being himself of inferior culture, saw in the Jew a superior to himself and to the Arab." Under the Ottoman Empire, "by virtue of his intelligence and his achievements the Jew held a position in the country perhaps out of proportion to his numerical strength."

The Arabs, he complained bitterly, were considered important because of their temporary status as a war asset. What the military administration did not realize was that

> we represent an asset which, although it cannot be estimated in rifles or machine guns, is nevertheless of very great war value and of still greater peace value. In short, they do not realise that the somewhat shifty and doubtful sympathies of the Arabs represent in the long run infinitely less than the conscious and considered policy of the majority of the Jewish people, which sees in a British Palestine the realization of its hopes and aspirations, and has seen in your Declaration the beginning of this realisation.

Not only were the Jews more useful to the British, but the Palestinians did not even exist. Weizmann went on:

> The present state of affairs would necessarily tend towards the creation of an Arab Palestine if there were an Arab people in Palestine. It will not in fact produce that result because the fellah is at least four centuries behind the times, and the effendi (who, by the way, is the real gainer from the present system) is dishonest, uneducated, greedy and as unpatriotic as he is inefficient.

Weizmann's outburst to Balfour must have resulted from his realization that the two nationalisms, Arab and Jewish, were set on a collision course, with the immediate advantages of number and presence on the land going to the Arabs. By discrediting the Arab of Palestine as unreliable and shifty and pushing forward the Jew as the loyal and steady upholder of British interests in the Middle East, he could hope to build up organically a substantial Jewish community as the client of Britain. His analysis of the Arab communities of Palestine was hardly a model of objectivity, but rather was a politically motivated statement intended to destroy British confidence in the Palestinian Arabs or to lead to a concerted Zionist-British effort to circumvent the Palestinian people by the formation of a Zionist alliance with Arabs outside of Palestine. It was also probably a cri de coeur on the part of a man driven to lead the Jews toward the establishment of a state in spite of a population already settled upon the land.

Weizmann also wrote that he had taken up his frustrations with Clayton and Deedes and after consultation had been directed to the commander-in-chief. Allenby had shown sympathy, but was unable to provide satisfaction beyond suggesting that any change in the principles of policy must come from the foreign secretary.

Finally, in practical terms, Weizmann had only two requests to make: one, that the Wailing Wall be handed over to the Jews; two, that the Zionists be allowed to put into operation a land scheme which would incorporate practically the whole of southern Palestine. The land scheme, then, whose importance was "impossible to exaggerate," was the real problem between the Zionists and the administration, the cause of Weizmann's frustration and the reason for his harsh portrayal of the Arabs and, indeed, for his denial that there was in fact an Arab people in Palestine. Without land, the Jewish community, the yishuv, could not continue to grow; and without a large and prosperous Zionist settlement, there would be no chance for a Jewish state to be set up. The logical end of Zionism would be a stillbirth.

The Zionist Commission recognized, Weizmann said, that when work began on the vast areas under discussion, "all sorts of claimants" would appear; but he was confident that the claims would prove shadowy and nobody would be ousted from "properly" cultivated land. As a matter of fact, he said, there was enough land for the Jews to develop without encroaching on the "real rights of the Arab inhabitants of Palestine. And that is the essential fact. For the problem of our relations with the Palestinian Arabs is an economic problem, not a political one." Political relationships were to be developed with Faysal and an Arab kingdom, he asserted, "but with the Arabs of Palestine . . . only proper economic relations are necessary." Earlier he had written his wife in much the same vein. His speech to the notables in Jerusalem had been well received, he admitted, but he had found it difficult to trust the Arabs. "I consider," he explained to her, "that it is unnecessary to bother any more with the Arabs for the present; we have done what was asked of us, we have explained our point of view sincerely and publicly; let them take it or leave it."[34]

Thus by the end of May the Zionists, for whom Weizmann spoke, were ready to turn their backs on the Palestinians. They had come to the East expecting British prejudice, military opposition, and Arab stubbornness. Without doubt, they had created or evoked much of what they had looked for. In Palestine, Weizmann had virtually ignored the Arabs while he wooed the Zionist and non-Zionist Jews living in the country until Storrs and other British officials induced him to try to come to an understanding with non-Jewish Palestinian leaders. In short order, he found that while he met with courtesy, the native leaders of Palestine had no intention of making enough room in the land, even eventually, for the establishment of a Jewish state. In such a conflict of national wills, Weizmann was willing to alter his methods. He wrote off the Palestinians as not being truly Arab and certainly not deserving national independence. He would work for a liberal land policy for the Jews and an alliance with Arabs outside Palestine, while maintaining only economic relations with Palestinian Arabs. On 30 May, the same day he wrote Balfour, he set out for his desert meeting with Faysal, his first step on the road to a hoped-for alliance with the Sharifians.[35]

On the other hand, Clayton and the other British officials had tried to adjust their understanding of British interests and policies in the Middle East to accommodate the hard-driving Zionist leaders. Clayton had been thrown off stride by the sharp tactics of this commission, which had been accredited by the Foreign Office, and had done little beyond observing that such a sudden and complete shift in policy as the commission seemed to presage would take time and cautious handling. With conflict shaping up in occupied Palestine, he was prepared to bow to Foreign Office wishes to satisfy the Zionists, if this could be accomplished without alienating all the Arabs. By mid-May he recognized that the Zionists had to be given some small success or Weizmann would be eclipsed as the leader of pro-British Zionism. The danger then would be "to throw Zionism into the arms of America or even at worst, on to Germany. Thus the death-blow would be dealt to pro-Brisith Zionism, and at the same time, to any hope of securing Zionist influence at the Peace Conference in favour of a British Palestine."[36] To avoid this looming catastrophe, Clayton clearly took the initiative, in agreement with the new Zionist strategy, in seeking a meeting between Faysal and Weizmann.[37]

The Palestinians themselves were not considered, the only worry of the British being that unrest in Palestine might spill over the border and stir up the Syrians, Mesopotamians, and Hijazis. To obtain the desired result, Palestine would have to be isolated from the rest of the Arab world, a wedge driven between Palestine and other Arab areas, and the Zionists would have to form an understanding or alliance with the Sharifians that would keep the remainder of the Arab world at rest while the Zionists—with the British in the near background—restructured Palestine in their own image.

The fateful patterns set up in the spring of 1918 persisted. The British were determined to retain the dominant influence in Palestine or at least to exclude all other potentially hostile powers. Palestinian Arabs were suspicious of Zionist intentions and impervious to any suggestion or hint that they might eventually have to share sovereignty with Jewish colonists or in any other way suffer the eclipse of their age-old rights to their land. And the Zionists, led by Weizmann, recognized the inevitable truth of their position: that they desired—in uneasy harness with an imperial power—to hold a land already settled largely by others. The decisions adopted then—to deny that the Palestinians were a people with a right to the land they occupied, to confine relations with the Palestinians to economic transactions, and to negotiate with other Arab groups and with imperial powers—have never been altered.

There is little doubt that neither the British nor Weizmann expected their policies to harm the Palestinians. Both were motivated by a powerful and high ideal, whether it was the maintenance of an empire or the well-being of the Jewish people. On the other hand, the Palestinian Arabs, who were relatively powerless, were driven by an equally compelling ideal: to resist alien demands, to cling to their land. But the choice of the means to pursue all these ends led to the formation in Arpil-May 1918 of an unfortunate pattern of relationships that, while shifting in particulars from time to time, has yet to be broken.

6

WEIZMANN, FAYSAL AND OTTOMAN
DEFEAT, SUMMER 1918

By June 1918 the British had begun to hope that a meeting between representatives of the Arab movement and Zionism would
prove fruitful. The Sykes-Picot Agreement had stipulated that the
form of international administration for Palestine would be decided
on in consultation with a Sharifian representative. In January 1918
Hogarth talked directly with King Husayn about British intentions to
encourage Jewish colonization of Palestine under some type of "special regime" and the king responded generously without waiving his
claims of Arab sovereignty. Sykes then wrote in March to Faysal,
Husayn's son and agent, as part of a literary campaign preparing
the East for the advent of the Zionist Commission. He entreated
Faysal to recognize the Zionists as a powerful ally, even as "the great
key to Arab success."[1] With the ebullience for which he was famous
and which he thought was in accordance with Arab style, Sykes told
Faysal that Jewish "race [,] despised and weak [,] is all powerful, and
cannot be put down. Judge not the superficial side of things. Look
deep down. In the counsels of every state, in every bank, in every
enterprise there are members of this race." Despite their power,
Sykes continued, the Jews did not seek to conquer the Arabs, to settle
in millions, or to drive the Arabs out of Palestine. All they asked was
"to return to the land of their forefathers, to cultivate it, to work with
their hands, to become peasants once more. . . . to feel that in Palestine a Jew may live his life and speak his tongue as he did in ancient
times." Thus when deadlock did occur in Palestine, owing to the
irreconcilable aims of Palestinian Arabs and Zionists, the British were

already prepared to urge Weizmann to visit Faysal for direct talks. And so, at the instigation of Clayton,[2] Weizmann and Ormsby-Gore left general headquarters for Aqaba on 30 May 1918 to meet with the amir.[3]

After an arduous and roundabout trip from Palestine to the amir's camp north of Aqaba, via Suez, Aqaba, and the Wadi Arabah, Weizmann reached the Transjordanian plateau and the Arab army headquarters. He later wrote of wandering around the camp the night before his talks were scheduled to begin.

> Here I was, on the identical ground, on the identical errand, of my ancestors in the dawn of my people's history, when they came to negotiate with the ruler of the country for a right of way, that they might return to their home. . . . Dream or vision or hallucination. I was suddenly recalled from it to present-day realities by the gruff voice of a British sentry: "Sorry, sir, I'm afraid you're out of bounds."

The next morning he and the amir sat down for a two-hour conversation which, in Weizmann's later estimation, "laid the foundations of a lifelong friendship."[4] After the initial courtesies, Weizmann explained to Faysal the reasons for the Zionist mission in Palestine and the Zionist desire to cooperate with the Arabs. He went on to point out that the "Zionists did not propose to set up a Jewish Government, but wished to work if possible under British guidance in order to colonise and develop the country without encroaching on other legitimate interests."[5] Weizmann promised that this Jewish Palestine would assist in the development of an Arab kingdom and that an Arab kingdom would receive Jewish support.[6] Faysal, in turn, expressed the opinion that Jewish and Arab interests were indeed closely allied, but he carefully pointed out that he had no power to take action on political questions, as he was merely his father's agent in such matters. Personally, he accepted the possibility of future Jewish claims to territory in Palestine and again emphasized the need for close cooperation between Jews and Arabs for their mutual benefit.

The British were delighted with the interview. Colonel Joyce, who was present throughout, thought Faysal entirely sincere in welcoming Jewish cooperation and expressed the opinion that Faysal would accept a "Jewish Palestine" if it assisted Arab expansion further north. Clayton thought "nothing but good" could result from the talks while Mark Sykes exulted, "Most satisfactory" and Hardinge wired congratulations to Weizmann on the "tact and skill shown by him in arriving at an initial understanding" with the Arab amir.[7]

Weizmann's own first impression was far less enthusiastic. He thought Faysal was only indulging in "elaborate Arab courtesy." He soon changed his mind, however, and later wrote that he had had substantial evidence to believe that the amir was in earnest regarding Jewish-Arab harmony.[8] In fact, in Weizmann's mind, his exchange with Faysal marked the turning point of his tour of duty in Palestine. After his return to England, he told C. P. Scott, the liberal editor of the *Manchester Guardian*, that he had at last succeeded in blowing up "the iron wall of military routine."[9] Faysal was eulogized as "a splendid specimen of a man surrounded by the scum of the earth" and as the Arab with whom the Zionists were to establish relations. Weizmann had decisively turned his back on the Arabs of Palestine and the drudgery of reality and now threw himself energetically into the realm of high politics.

He returned to general headquarters from his desert encounter buoyed up by his hopes for an alliance with Arab parties outside Palestine. There he spoke to Stewart Symes of the Arab Bureau, who was in Ramleh on loan to Clayton for a few days. Symes kept a series of secret notes from 9 to 13 June on possible ways to harmonize the three antagonistic policies—Zionists, Syrian, and Sharifian (or Hijazi)—in a manner agreeable to the British Empire, based on Weizmann's enthusiastic idea of a grand alliance. Weizmann began by eliminating the Palestinian Arabs from the political equation, stigmatizing them as a "demoralized race with whom it was impossible to treat." He contrasted them with Faysal, "a true Prince and a man 'whom one would be proud to have as an enemy and would welcome as a friend'."[10] His liaison officer echoed this dubious judgment. In speaking of the "so-called Arabs of Palestine," Major Ormsby-Gore described the Arabic-speaking effendi of the Mediterranean littoral as really "a parasite who had subsisted for generations on successive alien civilizations from which there is no vice which he has not learnt." The bedouin Arabs of Jordan, the Hijaz, and eastern Syria were "quite different and it is with the latter that I rejoice to think that Dr. Weizmann through Sherif Faisal has begun the foundation of an entente."[11]

Then on 10 June Weizmann followed up the previous day's discussion by putting forward a suggestion which he said he had already communicated to General Clayton. He proposed that the Zionists deal directly with King Husayn as the head of the Arab movement and offer: (a) financial and, if necessary, other assistance for the establishment of the Kingdom of Hijaz, and (b) support in Europe and America for Syrian autonomy. In return the Zionists would want recognition of their aims in Palestine, or, as Symes candidly expressed it, "a free hand with the Palestinians." Weizmann was prepared to offer an immediate pledge of £40 million to aid the Sharifian kingdom. As for the Syrian side of the alliance, he recognized that Faysal lacked his father's political authority. Therefore, if the British had no objection, he wished to confer with King Husayn before going to the United States to gain President Wilson's support. With that in hand he could convene an international Jewish congress at Jerusalem in order to ask for a British protectorate over Palestine and to declare publicly "their alliance with the Sharifials and their support of the Syrians' aspiration for autonomy, with or without Sharifial suzerainty, and under British (not French) guidance."

Back in Cairo, Symes, and probably Cornwallis, analyzed the imperial advantages of such a harmony. They concluded that a "working agreement mutually advantageous and politically efficient" might be reached under two conditions: *"if our obligations to France under the Sykes-Picot agreement were finally repudiated and all idea of conserving the privileges of the Palestine Arabs abandoned."*[12] Neither condition seemed unobtainable at the time, since, as Symes added, the "latter may be taken as implied" in the Balfour Declaration, and the Sykes-Picot compact, "according to private advices from London, is already in abeyance and practically defunct."

In mid-June Clayton began a major reassessment of Palestine problems. He reported to Balfour that the Zionist Commission had succeeded in gaining the confidence of and had secured a large measure of control over the various factions of Palestinian Jewry, and that the organization of relief, the restoration of educational institutions and the rehabilitation of the Jewish colonies had made excellent progress thanks to the coordinating efforts of the commission.[13]

The commission's task of dissipating Arab distrust and apprehension, however, while partly successful in Egypt and Arabia, had met with almost total failure in Palestine itself. According to Clayton, the more advanced Arabs appreciated to some extent the progress and prosperity possible for all classes of the community under Jewish enterprise, "if wisely controlled," but the great majority regarded "any prospect of Zionist extension with fear and dislike." He spelled out the economic and social fears of various members of the Arab population: the small landowner who realized he could not hold his own against Jewish science and energy, the trader who foresaw Jewish money and modern business methods squeezing him out of the market, and the small effendi who saw his ambition for a government appointment disappointed by the predomination of the better-educated and more intelligent Jew. It was not a question of national feeling, he noticed, "for I have detected but few signs of real patriotism amongst the population of Palestine, but the classes to which

I have alluded above will spare no effort to induce in the peasantry a hostile attitude toward the Jews." Although he could offer no optimistic predictions about those Arabs whose vested interests might be harmed, Clayton did observe that local opposition would disappear in the case of most of the agricultural population, provided the Zionist program were carried out on the lines laid down by Weizmann. Even then, he suggested, there was wisdom in proceeding slowly in order "to reduce to a minimum the field for hostile propaganda among the Arabs as a whole."

On the other side of the ledger, Clayton was charged with assisting the Zionist Commission to meet its objectives, as he understood them from Weizmann. He fully realized that if the development of Zionist policy were postponed, the whole movement would suffer and, in the face of such a setback, the commission might have to depart and Weizmann withdraw as leader of pro-British Zionism. To avoid this blow to British prestige, Clayton suggested that it might be possible to place a liberal interpretation on the international principle of maintaining the status quo in occupied areas. In this way minor changes and innovations might be introduced in order to conciliate Zionist opinion while at the same time avoiding offense to the susceptibilities of the Arabs and others.

So far as practical concessions were concerned, the Hebrew university proposal posed no difficulties which could not be resolved by a direct instruction from the home government. On the other hand, the proposal regarding the acquisition of the Wailing Wall for the Jews was more troublesome. Clayton thought a property transfer might be worked out quietly for a generous sum, but that since the object of securing the site was to advertise the commission's success in Palestine, the publicity would render the transaction undesirable.[14]

Finally, the land scheme, viewed sympathetically by Clayton in the summer of 1918, proved an extremely difficult question. Land was on its way to becoming a major policy issue rather than one that could be finessed through "minor changes and innovations," and its ramifications require a detailed explanation. In retreat the Turks had left the land system in chaos by taking with them most key personnel and the official registers of landholding.[15] Not that such registers could have given more than partial help. Ever since the late nineteenth-century Turkish ban on the owning of property by foreigners, a dual set of land records had been kept. When a foreigner did buy land, he did so in the name of a citizen of the empire and the record was kept in the second set of books, the secret one. This record was hard to keep straight owing to transfers, inheritances, and other pitfalls of illegal land dealings. Also, the Ottoman land-tenure system, super-imposed on local tradition, caused confusion over which parties could exercise which rights on a given piece of land. OETA found that many landowners had been forced to borrow money at high rates of interest during the war. These people were in danger of dispossession if they had to meet their obligations immediately. So in November 1918 OETA finally closed the land registry for the time being and declared the status quo ante occupation regarding all land transactions.

There were further problems of land ownership related to the efforts of the peasants to evade Ottoman taxation and oppression which were to lead to bitterness and tragedy. Frequently, the Arab peasant allowed the title of his land to gravitate into the hands of an absentee landlord in Beirut or Damascus. The peasant, although exploited by the landlord, thus gained a measure of protection from the even harsher exploitation of the Ottoman government. To the peasant "it was incomprehensible that through the edicts of a distant government, whose authority he had hardly ever felt, the land had ceased to be his."[16] But since the British authorities had to work from surviving Ottoman records and with Western legal concepts, such indeed was often the case. This situation was to lead in time to the eviction by Zionists of thousands of Arab Palestinians from land which the latter felt was theirs by every right of occupation, tradition, and morality.

In the summer of 1918, however, OETA was still trying to find some way to satisfy the Zionists on the land issue without upsetting every other community in Palestine. Clayton reminded Balfour of Weizmann's letter of 30 May 1918. He noted that the Zionists clearly considered the Balfour Declaration to mean that Jews of Palestine were to receive increased privileges, a "measure of preferential treatment," and he pointed out that such treatment was bound to give rise to Arab discontent which might be exploited by enemy propagandists. But he suggested, while making no definite recommendation, that Weizmann's scheme might work if it were given as "military a complexion as possible" and if the leaders of the other communities were invited to participate. He asked Balfour to consider both his dispatch and the letter, trusting that the government could then decide on the limits of Zionist development and "issue general instructions which will lay down the broad lines which the present Military Administration should follow in this important question."

Two days later Clayton wrote Mark Sykes privately to say that T. E. Lawrence and Weizmann had had a very satisfactory talk and agreed on main principles, "even though they may approach them from different stand-points." "Both are looking far ahead," he said, "and both see the lines of Arab and Zionist policy converging in the not distant future."[17] Weizmann admired the ability of Lawrence and thought that he would be particularly useful in Zionist political schemes owing to the large amount of influence he attributed to Lawrence over Faysal.[18]

Based on the above conversation, Lawrence dictated on 16 June a set of secret notes setting forth his views on the situation in the Middle East. Faysal was about to invade Syria and despite his denial of ambition there would find a way of taking power there. The Turks would be beaten and then Faysal's troubles would begin, because the "effendi class, the educated class, the Christians, and the foreign elements" would turn against him. In Lawrence's scenario, the Jews could then step in, "securely established under British colours in Palestine," and offer help; then, with Anglo-Jewish advisers backing him, Faysal could "dispense with the effendis, and buy out the foreigners."[19]

According to Lawrence, Faysal believed that the British intended to keep Palestine for themselves

> under the excuse of holding the balance between conflicting religions, and [he] regards it as a cheap price to pay for the British help he has had and hopes still to have. He has no idea at all that any of us ever dreamed of giving it to the Jews.

However, a Jewish Palestine need not present an obstacle to an Arab state. Lawrence succinctly analyzed the Zionist program and its place in the total Middle East picture.

> Dr. Weizmann hopes for a completely Jewish Palestine in fifty years, and a Jewish Palestine, under a British facade, for the moment. He is fighting for his own lead among the British and American Jews: if he can offer these the spectacle of British help, and Arab willingness to allow Jewish enterprise free scope in all their provinces in Syria, he will then secure the financial backing which will make the new Judaea a reality. The capitalists will subscribe for Jews in Palestine—and you cannot govern by subscription: they will invest in a Jew-advised Syria, and that means success in Palestine.
>
> Weizmann is not yet in a position, as regards Jewry, to make good any promise he makes. In negotiating with him the Arabs would have to bear in mind that they are worth nothing to him till they have beaten the Turks, and that he is worth nothing to them unless he can make good amongst the Jews.

Weizmann did not care about the Arab military problem of ousting the Turks from Syria; he was only concerned with dealing with an Arab power holding a line from the Taurus Mountains southward. However, Lawrence argued, it was not yet time for an alliance to be consummated. Faysal did not need Jewish help to defeat the Turks "and it would be unwise on our part to permit it to be offered." Faysal's movement was a military one and he must be allowed to succeed or fail by his own strength.

Lawrence's language is extravagant but the insight is coldly cynical and crystal-clear. His scenario might have worked had it not been for the assumption, widely held among British officials in the Middle East, that French participation in the future of Syria was at an end, and had it not also been for the growing power of the movement for Syrian autonomy, which was aimed at obviating Hijazi ambitions.

On 16 June, the same day that Lawrence was dictating his notes, a Foreign Office document known as the Declaration to the Seven was being communicated to Arab leaders at army headquarters in Cairo. This was a response to the fears of certain Syrians living in Cairo, who, in a memorial handed in at the Arab Bureau in Cairo for transmission to London, expressed their desire for a "clear and comprehensive definition of Great Britain's policy with regard to the future of the Arab countries as a whole."[20] These seven Syrians, who wished to remain anonymous, also talked with sympathetic British officials, notably Osmond Walrond, who was a senior civil servant attached to the Arab Bureau and former secretary to the new secretary of state for war, Lord Milner.[21]

The document divided the Arab East into four categories. The first two, the Arabian Peninsula and the Hijaz as far north as Aqaba, were promised "complete and sovereign independence" for their inhabitants. The third category contained territories occupied by the Allied armies, including Palestine to the north of Jerusalem and Jaffa. In this area the British government promised that "the future government of those territories should be based upon the principle of the consent of the governed" and that this would "always" be British policy. As for the fourth category, the Arab lands still under Turkish rule, the declaration expressed the desire of the British government "that the oppressed peoples in those territories should obtain their freedom and independence." The declaration also promised that the government would "continue to work for the achievement of that object."[22]

The result of this statement was that the Sykes-Picot arrangement was shoved further into the background, leaving Allenby and his CPO with nothing better to work with than a few contradictory political promises, some of them vaguely worded. The 1916 agreement was not much liked in the Middle East, but it was the most concrete scheme officials had and was still nominally in force. The impact of the Declaration to the Seven on the area's inhabitants was even greater. The declaration went further than the Husayn-McMahon correspondence, it was public, and it was phrased in the seemingly clear language of idealism. "A wave of jubilation swept the Arab world as the contents of the Foreign Office statement became known," wrote Arab historian George Antonius.[23] He thought the fact that these assurances were given after the disclosure of the Sykes-Picot Agreement and the issuance of the Balfour Declaration greatly increased their significance and their effect on the minds of Arab leaders. Truly, Lloyd George's and Wilson's epoch-making statements favoring the principle of self-determination seemed to have acquired precise formulation so far as the Middle East was concerned.

The Zionists, meanwhile, as though the new declaration had never been pronounced, continued to move forward on the twin fronts of an alliance with the desert Arabs and the promotion of Weizmann as the leader of a British Palestine. On 17 June Ormsby-Gore spoke in Jaffa before a conference of Jews called together to draw up plans for a Jewish constituent assembly. As the political officer attached to the Zionist Commission, his presence there was deemed politically significant, especially since he chose to talk about the meaning of the Jewish national home. He urged patience with the British government because of the grim reality of warfare, but he also held out the promise of the "ideal of the future," a national center for Jewry all over the world to look to. He strongly urged his listeners to be guided by Weizmann, "a leader who will see you through."[24]

The situation in Palestine, however, had not improved despite the dramatic switch in Zionist-British strategy or because the British Foreign Office had disseminated a new promise. On 29 June Clayton wired the Foreign Office that the condition of Palestine was "critical" and that it was therefore "essential to avoid any political action calculated to excite unrest and suspicion." He reported that "any striking development of Zionist policy" would be dangerous and that he had talked this over with Weizmann, who was entirely of the same opinion, although undoubtedly for different reasons. Under the circumstances, they had decided, and the Foreign Office concurred, that Weizmann would be better employed developing "bigger issues" in Europe and America.[25]

By now Clayton had had time to reflect on the whole spectrum of Arab-Zionist relations and on possible international implications. On 1 July 1918, he submitted his observations on Eastern political strategy to Balfour as a continuation of his 16 June letter. He reviewed the Arab and Zionist movements as established pillars of British policy. Faysal's ambitions, supported heretofore by the British government, were for an autonomous Arab Syria with himself as ruler. One of his future requirements would be economic support, which he hoped to get from more than a single power, in order to escape a position of subservience and to give at least the outward appearance of independence. With the help of Zionism, Faysal thought he could counter unsavory international concessionaires, French political influence, and "all those forces which tend towards foreign exploitation and which are detrimental to development on national lines."[26] In addition Faysal would need political support and, according to Clayton's analysis, he recognized the international influence of Zionism "which permeates every country from which the future Syrian State may have anything to hope or to fear." And, finally, Faysal saw behind Zionism, and working through it, the British Empire "on which in the last resort" he placed his trust.

Clayton thought that Zionism, on the other hand, depended on the establishment in Palestine of a "centre of Jewish culture and sentiment, based on the soil itself, to which all Jewry will turn and which will justify its political existence by providing a bridge between East and West." He considered it vital that a Jewish Palestine be linked in "close sympathy" with its neighbors; this would be "a condition of its development, and indeed of its existence."

Within this simplified framework, the two policies were interdependent. Clayton thought it would be difficult to see how "our pledges to both parties concerned can be fulfilled in anything approaching the spirit in which they have been accepted unless the aims of Zionists and Arabs can be coordinated somewhat on the lines indicated above."

So far, Clayton's line of reasoning had not been too dissimilar from Lawrence's display in his 16 June secret notes, for the very good reason that in all probability Clayton had been the original author. But Clayton went beyond Lawrence's offhanded assurances. The first problem he saw which bore on this desirable coordination of nationalist policies was that of the Sharif Husayn, the king of the Hijaz. There was small hope of a favorable attitude from him, Clayton reasoned, unless he could be convinced that Zionism would assist his son to attain Syria. The second obstacle, opposition from vested interests in Palestine, could probably be taken care of only in a situation of increased general prosperity. A third obstacle considered was the opposition of Syrians living outside Syria. This factionalized group was united in hostility to the division of Syria, Sharifian domination, and Zionism; but, in the British view, these Syrians could not be said to represent Syrian opinion until the wishes of the actual population, still under Turkish control, could be consulted.

Finally, the logical development of this line of argument would lead to direct conflict with French imperial objectives in Syria. Clayton's unwelcome, but unavoidable, conclusion was:

> No development can take place on the lines suggested by Dr. Weizmann's interview with Sherif Faisal so long as the Sykes-Picot agreement remains in force and until a definite understanding is arrived at with the French Government that it is no longer a practical instrument.

The desired harmony of Arabs and Jews which had led Clayton to this conclusion would accomplish far more than simply easing the problems of Britain's two clients in the eastern Mediterranean. Two weeks earlier, Clayton had written to Sir Clive Wigram, the King's assistant private secretary and a man who wielded great influence in London, revealing that there were strong imperial reasons for such an Arab-Zionist alliance. It would, Clayton stressed, "create a strong pro-British buffer to the north of Egypt and the Suez Canal." Once again the continuity of traditional British interests in the Ottoman domain was underscored. Suez was paramount and other powers must be excluded from proximity by creating a "buffer."[27]

By mid-July, Weizmann seemed to have recovered from some of his earlier frustration and was working closely with the authorities in the field. On 17 July he wrote to Balfour rather hopefully on lines suggested by Lawrence and Clayton regarding the "possibility for a sincere cooperation" between the Arab and Zionist "nations, which will lead to a mutual benefit and to a consolidation of the British [position] in the Near East."[28] He had spoken with Arab experts in the Middle East about the encouraging development of the Arab movement and now the Zionist movement stood ready to help Faysal, "not as exploiters or as concessionaires," but with a sincere desire to cooperate. Indeed, the future of Zionist relations with the desert Arabs looked so attractive that Weizmann had concluded that the "so-called Arab question in Palestine would therefore assume only a purely local character, and in fact is not considered as a serious factor by all those who know the local position fully."

At this point he joined the chorus of British Middle East observers in denouncing the Sykes-Picot Agreement as being out of step with reality, obstructing the realization of Zionist and Arab aspirations, and forming a center of political intrigue, since it obscured the "true vision" and ran "counter to the principle of real self-determination as expressed in the Zionist and Arab movements."

On 2 August 1918 Clayton reported in a private letter to Wingate in Cairo that the Arab movement was not "really popular" among the people of Palestine, although it was useful as a "counter blast" to Zionism, which inevitably was greatly disliked. He still noted "little real patriotism" and thought the large majority of the more educated class "hopelessly corrupt and tainted by centuries of Turkish rule." Optimistically, he counseled no cause for worry, predicting that the future would work out well if the administration took it easy and was tactful and sympathetic.[29]

Meanwhile, in London, all was not proceeding smoothly. Balfour told the War Cabinet on 13 August of his agreement with his on-the-spot observers in the Middle East that their chief diplomatic difficulties were due to Franco-Italian jealousy and to the Sykes-Picot Agreement, "which, though still remaining as a diplomatic instrument, was historically out of date."[30] Indeed, the agreement was as dead as the policy-makers declared it to be, "although," murmured one of the agreement's authors, "the French refused to admit it."[31] The problem was to find a modification of, or substitute for, the old agreement. Unfortunately from the British point of view, this was not accomplished before Allenby and his Arab auxilaries had taken Damascus and presented a fait accompli to the policy-makers in London.

Policy on the future of Palestine remained unsettled. In the Cabinet meeting of 13 August, both the prime minister and Lord Reading suggested approaching the United States with a view to asking the Americans to undertake the responsibilities of trusteeship for Palestine.[32] In a Cabinet meeting two days later, Lord Curzon and Austen Chamberlain added themselves to the list of ministers prepared to accept the suggestion of an American trusteeship over Palestine.[33] Foreign Secretary Balfour, meanwhile, was still assuring the Italians that Palestine was eventually to be internationalized.[34] Small wonder that Hogarth complained to Clayton that there was "no one taking hold of the Near Eastern Question at present here, and no one looking ahead. Generally people are optimistic and vague."[35]

Major W. Ormsby-Gore, back in London, met with the London Zionist Political Committee at Empire House on 16 August 1918. He reported fully and optimistically on his five months abroad. He was convinced that "sooner or later" there would be a Zionist Palestine. He had gathered a very favorable impression of the existing Jewish colonies in Palestine, being amazed by the courage and determination of the settlers, and had concluded that the country could support a much larger population than he had at first imagined. There were problems to be faced, however, the chief trouble being the lack of the right type of personnel, and he counseled following a policy of moderation and "peaceful penetration" by Zionist Jews from the coastal areas toward the hills. Even though, in his view, a constellation of interests—Palestine, the Near East, the British empire, and civilization—pointed toward the creation of a Zionist Palestine, he advised that any "attempt to force the pace in the direction of a Jewish State would set back the clock."

Once again he dismissed the Arabs of Palestine with contempt. They were not even Arabs. They were only Arabic-speaking. They were a vice-ridden, demoralized, obstructive people who could be ignored by the Zionists as they went ahead handling the practical problems of the country.

On 22 August, Ormsby-Gore handed in his formal report to the Foreign Office. He explained in it that the Zionist Commission had not been able to accomplish much toward its objective of laying the foundation for the national home for the Jewish people, due to the "lack of definition on the part of the British and Allied Governments in regard to the future political status of Palestine." He pointed out that the Sykes-Picot Agreement made it extremely difficult for the military admistration to give the necessary political direction, with the result that the Zionist Commission had been compelled to look forward to submitting definite proposals to the Allied powers at the Peace Conference instead of continuing the attempt to give effect to the Balfour Declaration. "The most that could be done under the present system," he said, "was to secure that, in as far as possible, no changes should be made by the military administration in Palestine such as would be inimical to the subsequent carrying out of the policy of Zionism."

There were certain objects to be secured before the convening of a peace conference, he noted. The first was the liberation of the whole area by Allied troops and the second was "the northward progress of the Arab movement culminating in the establishment of an independent Arab capital at Damascus." He pronounced himself satisfied that neither Husayn nor Faysal was "seriously upset by the Zionist movement" nor were they desirous of including cis-Jordan Palestine in their dominions. And, in his view, a Zionist Palestine would be a help to an Arab movement centered at Damascus, rather than a hindrance. Indeed it would introduce "an element of strengh and stability which would help "to bridge the gulf between the East and West, and enable the Arabs to learn from the Jews how best to develop the country, not in the interest of concessionaires living in Paris, but of the population resident in the East."[36]

Meanwhile, Weizmann, sensing that the end of the war was approaching, decided to leave Palestine for London in order to be at the place of decision when the crucial moment came. He left near the end of September just as Allenby and the EEF were preparing for a final push northward. Dr. Eder took over the duties of heading the commission, while Vladimir Jabotinsky, a Russian Zionist, was put in charge of relations with the military authorities. Neither man was as flexible or as diplomatic as Weizmann, who worried that Jabotinsky's practice of irritating Clayton by calling on him at all hours of the day and night did not augur well for the commission's future.[37]

Early in September, Wingate informed the Foreign Office that his objections in January to the proposed changes in the organization of the EEF's intelligence services no longer existed. He and Allenby had agreed that Clayton should be appointed CPO for both Palestine and Hijaz and assume general supervision of the central Arab Bureau in Cairo as well as of its branch bureau. Thus Clayton was prepared to deal with Faysal's movement into Syria and coordinate Arab policy there with developments in Faysal's home territory of the Hijaz. Clayton was still to consult with Wingate on questions affecting general Islamic policy.[38] On 25 September, the Foreign Office approved Wingate's dispositions, and in so doing seemingly conferred approval on Clayton's attempts at long-range strategic planning.

Allenby swiftly crushed the Turks in battle in mid-September and entered Damascus before October was many days gone. By the end of the month the EEF was in the foothills of the Taurus Mountains, having taken all of Syria. On 30 October the Turks capitulated and signed an armistice at Mudros. The war in the East was over, but the political tangles that had developed during its course had yet to be straightened out. Clayton's warning that a haphazard policy would only land Britain in a muddle was about to be put to the test.[39]

In the few brief months before the Mudros armistice, the entire Palestinian situation had changed dramatically. Weizmann and Faysal had met, with the blessing of the British authorities, and had laid the foundation for an alliance or understanding that was to allow the Zionists, Sharifians, and British to ignore Palestinian appeals to the various Allied promises of self-determination. Little seemed to stand in their way. The Sykes-Picot Agreement, buried under changing circumstances, was condemned on all sides. The French would have to give way. And yet this line of thought proved naive. Although the

French had contributed only marginally to the EEF, they had lost a million more men in Europe than Britain. Their traditional interest in Syria, extending back to the days of Harun ar-Rashid, the Crusades, the alliance of Francis I with Sulayman the Magnificent, would continue to be pressed with vigor and skill. In the event, they would waive the 1916 agreement over Mosul and Palestine, but would stubbornly hold on to Syria.

The British, meanwhile, still had not come to a definite conclusion about what to do with Palestine. They displayed little eagerness to rule it themselves, speculating that the Americans might yet be persuaded to take it or that it might still be internationalized. Clayton's strategic design of a Zionist-Sharifian alliance was going forward with the eventual promise of nationalist harmony and a secure buffer for the Suez Canal. The British were accordingly pressing for a new statement on the Middle East to be issued jointly with the French, which the British hoped would replace the agreement that seemed to hang so heavily around their necks. Even Balfour, now a steady though detached champion of the Zionist cause, had his doubts about the outcome. Personally he wished to see a Jewish state in Palestine at some time in the future, as he wrote to Alfred Zimmern of the Zionist Organization in mid-September 1918. "But," he wavered, "it may prove impossible, and in any case it is not likely to be more possible if it is prematurely discussed."[40] At any rate, Balfour's statement should lay to rest the myth that the Declaration that bears his name implied that Britain would consistently and regardless of all other considerations back the establishment of a Jewish state in Palestine.

Whatever the uncertainties might be after Allenby's stunning victory, one fact stood out. The Ottoman Empire had just sustained its greatest defeat and suffered dismemberment. The part of the Eastern Question dealing with the manner of the empire's death was answered. There remained the more difficult portion of the Question: how were the empire's territories to be divided so as to avoid further bloodshed? Not only were the Western victors, who had long thought of themselves as heirs presumptive of the Ottomans, in on the kill, but client nationalities also hung on to the carcass hoping for more than a fair share. Not trusting the words of princes, the Arabs, Armenians, and Jews thought to thrust aside the great powers and themselves become the successors of the Ottomans. Certainly this was the time to settle the Eastern Question. A single power occupied the vast territories of the sultan-caliph from Alexandretta to Gaza to Basrah and the Persian Gulf. The great geopolitician Halford Mackinder wrote, "If we accept anything less than a complete solution of the Eastern Question in its largest sense we shall merely have gained a respite, and our descendants will find themselves under the necessity of marshaling their power afresh for the siege of the Heartland."[41]

Military victory, indeed, was not enough to solve this ancient political question. The long war had created a tangle of diplomatic difficulties, political concepts, strategic visions, and uplifted aspirations. Empires had disappeared, old governments had fallen and others taken their places, and a new power of world stature had risen. The relations of power would need time for sorting out and for men to take these problems into account, and in that time a new Eastern Question would slowly develop from elements of the old.

7

BETWEEN WAR AND PEACE

The occupation of Syria before the details of its administration had been worked out with the French was welcomed by Wingate, who thought it would give the British greater opportunities and flexibility. In reality it caused untold confusion.[1] Officially the Sykes-Picot Agreement formed the basis of British-French relations, although it had long since been wishfully consigned by the British to the archives as a historical document. Well before the invasion of Syria, Sykes had contended that it was "most important to get the French on the right lines as regards Syria" prior to occupation. He thought the French should be induced to associate themselves with the British in a joint declaration of such a nature that they "would be definitely committed to what virtually amounted to an abrogation of the agreement."[2] The British, however, failed to revise, modify, or abandon the 1916 agreement before the capture of Syria heavily accentuated the nationalisms, imperialisms, and idealisms in the Middle East.

The British were undecided as to how far they could go in their intended revision of the 1916 document, or how hard they dared press the French for concessions. On September 23, 1918, Balfour gave the French ambassador to Great Britain, Paul Cambon, an official declaration of arrangements that would be carried out in case of Allied occupation. The declaration was worded in such a way as to give assurance to the French, while preserving British freedom to maneuver. The British government promised to adhere to its declared policy concerning Syria: "Namely that if it should fall into the sphere of interest of any European Power, the Power should be France."[3] The declaration also provided for immediate talks in case Allenby invaded Syria and for French officers to carry out civilian duties there under the supreme authority of the commander-in-chief. Balfour observed that Cambon accepted the statement as "accurate and adequate."

On 30 September, the French succeeded in getting the British to agree further that in case of Allied occupation, a French chief political adviser to General Allenby would be appointed to act in the areas reserved to special French interest.[4] Numerous other details were worked out at the same meeting at the Foreign Office. Allenby would still be in overall command, but French rights would be protected, at least on paper. In accordance with the specific nature of this agreement, the Eastern Committee agreed on 3 October that they must make every possible effort to induce the French to consent to abrogate the 1916 agreement outside the limits of Syria proper. In the course of this discussion, the committee touched upon the subject of the northern boundary of Palestine. General Macdonough, the army's adjutant general, pointed out that the border arranged in 1916 omitted Galilee from Palestine and consequently left some Jewish colonies outside Palestine. Curzon agreed, saying that Banias, the ancient Dan of the old kingdom of Israel, was well inside the French zone. Sykes's view was that the smaller Palestine was more in accord with Zionist interests, since it would exclude the "Lebanese population of Galilee." However, he added that rectification of the 1916 border to include control of the Jordan was essential.[5]

The detailed work of border drawing was to go on for years. But for the time being, according to the September arrangement, Palestine would be administered by OETA(S). Palestine's border was extended northward into the area assigned to the French in the 1916 partition in order to include the Safad region, which contained a large number of Jews. The Arabs, with a capital at Damascus, were put in charge of OETA (East), roughly the old vilayet of Syria, a more generous share than had been planned in 1916. The Arab area included both British and French zones of influence. The French administered OETA (West), a territory shrunken from its 1916 conception, comprising the coastal regions of Syria and Lebanon.[6]

On 8 October Lord Robert Cecil sent a memorandum to the French foreign minister, Stephen Pichon, explaining that the great changes that had taken place since 1916 had so altered the situation that the provisions of the 1916 agreement were no longer wholly suitable. He suggested that new conversations, to include Italy and the United States, be held.[7] Two days later George Lloyd wrote Wingate confidently that the Sykes-Picot Agreement was very nearly defunct. He was sure Wingate would be glad to hear the news because the agreement would have created increasing difficulties in the fu-

ture.[8] On 1 November Hogarth assured Clayton that the agreement
was "considered scrapped here," and that even Cambon was admitting that talks must eventually take place.[9]

At the 30 September meeting, it had been agreed that both sides
would recommend that their governments take an early opportunity
of issuing a proclamation defining their attitudes toward the territories liberated from the Turks. On 8 November this declaration was
published and widely disseminated in the Middle East. The two Western powers claimed to be fighting selflessly for the complete emancipation of the peoples oppressed by the Turks and for the "establishment of national governments and administrations deriving their
authority from the initiative and free choice of the indigenous populations." Specifically mentioning only Syria and Mesopotamia, they
promised to encourage and assist in establishing indigenous governments "freely chosen by the population themselves."[10]

The document had every appearance of sincerity. Issued on the
eve of peace, it was not a wartime measure to insure the alliance or
interest of a party needed by the Allies. However, the British and
French in their eagerness to guard themselves against possible intervention by President Wilson were really addressing the declaration
to each other and to the United States, not to the Middle East. It was
not a policy statement, but misleading propaganda designed to cos-
meticize the worst features of naked imperialist ambition.[11] It was
also intended by the British to obviate outdated French claims to
Syria by a spurious display of devotion to self-determination.

Reaction in the Middle East took the British by surprise. Major
Hubert Young, an officer usually identified with Iraq but who was
in Damascus at the time, wrote later that "all the telegraph wires were
cut, the tram services and electric light installations put out of action
by the cutting of cables, and roughly 200,000 rounds of ball ammu-
nition fired into the air."[12] Clayton wired to the Foreign Office that
a "great procession and demonstration" had been held in Damascus
culminating in a visit to the office of the British and French liaison
officers, where the Arab notables had made speeches expressing to
the two governments their gratification over their declaration of policy. He added that the omission of Palestine had caused a great deal
of comment, but that the general impression was that the declaration
would apply to that country, thus giving Muslims and Christians relief
by means of what they considered a "check to extravagant Zionist
aspirations."[13]

For nearly a month, Clayton and the military governors of Palestine
sent requests for clarification of the 8 November declaration. Most
Palestinian Arabs were taking it for granted that the general promise

to abide by the principle of self-determination applied to Palestine. Clayton had been saying, when asked, that he knew of no interpretation of the document other than that of the text. On 3 December he inquired if he could be given the information he wanted in an unofficial message. The next day he was told by the Foreign Office that, as a matter of fact, Palestine had been deliberately excluded, but he was told also that this news was reserved for his private information.[14] The people in Palestine were thus to be encouraged by official silence to persist in their delusion that their future would be determined by themselves.

This exchange between a foreign office and its political officer in the field was certainly extraordinary. And the strain on Clayton as he had to conceal the duplicity of his government must have been immense. The British government's Arab policy seemed to merit the general criticism leveled at it by Gertrude Bell, the oriental secretary to the civil commissioner of Mesopotamia and a member of the Arab Bureau. She called it confused, unclear, and dishonest.[15]

Meanwhile, the French still insisted on the continuing validity of the May 1916 agreement.[16] They did not take the British view that the 30 September arrangement secured French rights in Syria while the 8 November joint declaration waived previous agreements on Palestine and Mesopotamia. On 25 October, Balfour, trying to counter French claims, told Cambon that the September agreement did not refer to Palestine, since that was outside the area of special French interest, and it certainly did not refer to Mesopotamia, since it covered only areas occupied by the EEF.[17] Thus, despite the increasingly urgent need for new and definite arrangements in the Middle East, the foreign offices in London and Paris continued to rest on dead center.

On 27 October, Dr. Eder, the pioneer psychiatrist and socialist whom Weizmann had left in charge of the Zionist Commission in Palestine,[18] wired Weizmann about Faysal's urgent financial needs. Faysal had incurred obligations of £200,000 a month and, since the Turks had already collected taxes, he would be without an income until the harvest season the following year. Faysal was therefore requesting a loan from Jewish sources and a financial adviser as well. Eder also reported that the "free hand" in Palestine sought by the Zionists—or, as he circumspectly put it, the "other side of policy"— would be theirs, but that the details of this policy must be formulated clearly and immediately. It would be necessary for Weizmann or someone acting on his instructions, Eder said, to see Faysal to draw up an "explicit agreement on lines of your original proposition."[19]

The Foreign Office, in ignorance of the advanced stage of the Zionist-Sharifian alliance, reacted to the news of this proposal with surprise. The Treasury was authorized to grant Faysal an immediate subsidy of £50,000 to enable him to carry on. Instructions to Allenby to enter into conversations with Faysal and Picot for a French loan were deferred until the implications of Faysal's request could be worked out. Ormsby-Gore carefully explained that the idea of a loan had been discussed by Weizmann with Faysal in June 1918 and with Colonel Lawrence in Cairo in August. According to Ormsby-Gore the motives behind the idea were Faysal's reluctance to become indebted to the French and a mutual desire for good relations between Arabs and Zionists. He did not mention the more specific hopes of the Zionists.[20] Shortly after the arrival of this cable in London, Lawrence informed the Eastern Committee that he had learned from Picot in Rome that the French intended to impose French advisers upon Faysal, but that Faysal was anxious to obtain assistance from American or British Zionists.[21]

French-British rivalry was indeed intensifying in the Middle East. The two powers were engaging in a race to sign an armistice with the Turks. Further heat was being generated by the French takeover of Lebanese and Syrian coastal towns from the Arab troops who had liberated them with Allenby's concurrence. And finally the French were irritated by the mounting strength of British efforts to revise or scrap the Sykes-Picot Agreement. The solidity of the Entente itself had come into question.[22] Hogarth was pleased with the trend of events. "Our whole attitude towards the French is hardening here," he wrote to Clayton, and as a consequence Sykes, a leading Francophile, was losing influence. "His shares are unsaleable here," Hogarth gloated, "and he has been sent out (at his own request) to get him away." Lawrence had "put the wind up everybody and done much good," but he was a man who should be used sparingly, Hogarth thought, because of his unfortunate habit of "treading too often on corns."[23]

Weizmann, too, was glad that Lawrence had arrived. He wrote Clayton on 5 November that Lawrence had been most helpful with the Eastern Committee as he had illuminated Jewish-Arab Palestinian relations to that body.[24] Lawrence, of course, had his own motives for assisting the Zionists. Just the day before, 4 November, he had submitted a memorandum for consideration by the Cabinet which strongly supported Faysal's attempt to form an Arab government in Syria.[25] Syria's borders were to extend from Alexandretta in the north to Arabia in the south, from the Mediterranean at Alexandretta to Tripoli in the west, and eastward along the Homs-Lake Huleh-Jordan River line, excluding only Lebanon and Palestine. Furthermore, Faysal would require that his foreign advisers draw their authority from the Arab government and not from their own governments. The French thus would have no place of influence in the Arab world except for Lebanon, which was largely Christian anyway and hence received little of Lawrence's attention.

As for Palestine, the Arabs were hoping that the British would keep what they had conquered. The Arabs would not, Lawrence said, approve of a Jewish state in Palestine, but would support Jewish "infiltration if it is behind a British, as opposed to an international facade." By "international" Lawrence meant French. Lawrence continued by saying that if any attempt were made to set up international control, Faysal would "press for self-determination in Palestine, and give the moral support of the Arab Government to the peasantry of Palestine, to resist expropriation."

Lawrence was playing a rather complicated game. He wanted the French out of the Middle East because he knew they would take Syria if they stayed, and Faysal's Arab government would cease to exist. To prevent this, he was backing the Zionists in Palestine, even though, as he said in his memorandum, the Arabs would not approve a Jewish state. It is noteworthy that nowhere in his comprehensive ideas for the reconstruction of the Middle East did he identify who Faysal's advisers were to be, nor did he state anywhere what the Zionist quid pro quo would be.

Lawrence was, however, still following the lines of the scenario he had sketched out in June. Lawrence, Weizmann, and Hogarth had recently come to "complete agreement on the main points of policy," Weizmann reported to Clayton, the main points being practically the same as those discussed with Faysal at Aqaba and with Clayton in Palestine.[26] The three of them had considered Eder's telegram about aid to Faysal very carefully, Weizmann wrote, and had concluded that it was "not desirable at present to advance any money to Feisal as it may seriously prejudice our good relations." He explained the reasoning behind the joint conclusion:

If we lend money to Feisal at present we lay ourselves open to a reproach that we are attempting to put him and his friends under an obligation. We are very anxious to help Feisal with advisers both financial and technical and at some not distant future we shall be glad to give him such financial help as may be found necessary and possible but we would only like to do it with the consent of His Majesty's Government and after we have arrived at a clear and frank arrangement with Feisal, an arrangement which must be approved of by General Allenby, yourself, and the Government here.

Cecil had suggested that Weizmann see Faysal again soon to discuss a scheme of cooperation. In the meantime, the British government would continue to look after Faysal's financial needs. Weizmann protested at length that the Zionists were not meeting Faysal's request only out of a desire to eschew even the appearance of taking advantage of Faysal's financial plight to lay hands on the newly created Arab government. Weizmann had pointed out to his fellow Zionists, he said, that the "fundamental principle on which co-operation with Feisal must be established is that whatever we do there must be done in the same spirit and under the same conditions as we do things for ourselves." The same fundamental principle would not of course be extended to the hapless Palestinians.

On 9 November, the Foreign Office sent to Clayton and Allenby a comprehensive and ambitious list of proposals drawn up by the Zionist Organization. The Foreign Office had so far not taken a stand on the list and was now soliciting the views of its officials. The Zionist Organization asked that the Zionist Commission in Palestine be continued for the period of military occupation and be officially appointed as advisory body to the administration in all matters affecting the Jewish population. It also asked that the commission be allowed to continue to work at organizing the Jewish population and that the authorities be instructed to assist them; that Hebrew be recognized as the language of the Jewish people in Palestine; that the commission be allowed to proceed with the development of the site of the Hebrew university; that the commission be empowered to take measures toward settling Jewish soldiers who took part in the Palestine campaign; and that a representative of the commission be sent to Damascus to establish permanent contact with the Arab government.[27]

In addition to these requests, the Zionist Organization delved into a number of sensitive areas. It wished the authorities to take all available steps to encourage Jewish participation in the country's administration and to authorize the commission to advise it on the means to attain this goal. It asked for the appointment of a land commission with Zionist representatives on it (although it would not insist on this) that would deal with the full range of land problems: surveys, title verification, land classification, law, and the modernization of law. It also asked for permission to send to Palestine a group of experts to survey the country's resources and study ways to develop them, and in the meantime for authority for the Zionist Commission to proceed with various public works.

Clayton's reply, submitted on 20 November and accepted as a basis of policy, gave small comfort to the Zionist Organization's efforts to increase the scope of its authority in Palestine. He had no objection to the continuation of the commission so long as it was understood that it had no executive function in Palestine's administration. The commission could continue to organize the Jewish population so long as this did not imply anything more than what was already being done. There was no objection to Hebrew, but the only official language was English; there was no objection to work on the site of the Hebrew university and none to settling Jewish soldiers, if the Jewish regiment were disbanded; and there was no objection to a Zionist link with Faysal, but Clayton suggested that Faysal be consulted while he was in Europe.

On the more sensitive issues, Clayton's answers were equally definite. The Zionist Commission could not participate in the present administration. Jewish personnel was being used and such connection would continue to receive sympathetic consideration, but the question of employment must rest with the military authorities. The work of a land commission must wait until a civil government was set up; a cadastral survey was at present too expensive; and the Zionist Commission could under no circumstances participate in a land commission or contribute to its expenses. As for the surveying and developing of Palestine's resources, experts were free to come out if attached to the Zionist Commission and officially authorized, but their investigations would have to remain within the limits imposed by the military authorities. The carrying out of public works must be confined to the Jewish colonies. Finally Clayton expressed the general observation that the time was particularly unsuitable for Zionist activity owing to the increased openness of Palestinian antipathy to Zionism ever since the publication of the Anglo-French declaration. He advised delay until the status of the country and the form of its administration had been finally decided upon.[28] In effect, the Zionist initiative had resulted in virtually no progress toward the furtherance of its aims.

On the occasion of the first anniversary of the Balfour Declaration, the Zionist Commission had organized a large public celebration in Jerusalem that had ended with a minor scuffle due in large measure to a party of Zionists overstepping the bounds of public display recommended by the military governor.[29] The incident had produced complaints from Zionists, Muslims and Christians. Clayton forwarded a report on the celebration and its aftermath to Balfour, adding in a brief letter that the display of hostility caused by the "overzealous" celebration might have served a useful purpose in that it gave rise to an expression of feeling which otherwise might not have been fully appreciated. It made clear the considerable apprehension which non-Jews in Palestine felt about the scope of the Balfour Declaration, which, he added confidently, had received "on the part of many local Jews a more liberal interpretation than was ever intended." He continued to warn, as he had done ever since Zionism had become a major concern and responsibility of his, that the more impatient elements of Zionism must be restrained and tact and discretion employed, if serious friction were to be avoided.[30]

By mid-November Sykes, in the Middle East for the first time since the issuance of the Balfour Declaration and the occupation of Palestine, added his views on the tension in Palestine. After speaking with both Arabs and Jews in Jerusalem and Jaffa, he had gathered the impression of crackling excitement in the air and thought both parties estimated the time was ripe for starting a riot in order to draw world attention to their competing claims. Zionist complaints were mainly directed at the military authorities, who were being charged with bias toward Arabs and not giving sufficient prominence to Zionist wishes. The Arabs, on the other hand, complained that the Zionists were "aggressive, demonstrative, and provocative, and threaten them with a Jewish Government," and that the British government in London was working toward subjecting Palestinian Arabs to Jewish rule. As usual, Sykes was for swift action. He strongly recommended that Dr. Sokolow, the Polish Zionist political leader, writer, and philosopher, be dispatched to Palestine to take charge of Zionist affairs and allay Arab fears. The Palestinian Jews and the Zionists as a whole, Sykes had decided, lacked "sober, tactful, and authoritative leadership." In their recent emergence from political silence and obscurity, they were at present "dazzled with the light, and lack balance and political reticence." There was a considerable one-sidedness in their views, he said, and they were "apt to take offence on very small provocation, and I think occasionally invite trouble by injudicious acts and speech."

On the other hand, Sykes thought the Arabs no better. The Muslims feared Jewish intelligence and enterprise and were affected by "Arab nationalist effervescence" and a "tincture of race hatred." The Christians disliked the Jews for religious, racial, and political reasons. The Muslims and Christians were bound together strongly by mutual antipathy to Zionists and both were being stirred up by "Turkish agents, Arab hotheads, and the idle intriguers with whom the country abounds."[31]

Sykes continued his analysis of the situation two days later in a cable to Ormsby-Gore in London. He appeared surprised that the Jews in Palestine were drifting toward hostility but he still was firmly convinced that the problem stemmed from misunderstanding rather than from a permanent incompatibility of view. He faulted the Jewish tendency to believe that forcing the pace was the only way to achieve the realization of their ideals. He pointed out that tension had recently been increased by two articles in the Zionist periodical *Palestine*.[32] The 19 October and 2 November issues had both spoken of an independent Jewish state. One article had insisted that all of the arable land east of the Jordan should be included, while the other had advocated extending Palestine northward to Beirut.[33] These examples of Jewish ambition, while no doubt honestly given, were not calculated to foster a reputation for moderation nor were they politically realistic. They served to point up the lack of unified Jewish leadership as well as to expose the maximum aims of Zionism.

Upon being shown Sykes's cable, Weizmann grew alarmed and suggested to the Foreign Office that he make a flying trip to Palestine in order to give the Jewish population a "correct political orientation."[34] Ormsby-Gore suggested that Clayton be sounded out about Weizmann's proposal, which Allenby eventually rejected, and about whether he and Allenby thought a further declaration of the government's Zionist policy might be beneficial.[35]

This question of a further official statement had been growing for some time. The Zionists were in the process of preparing a statement which they hoped would meet with government approval, and Sykes in Palestine was in close contact with Zionist leaders who wished to enlarge their sphere of security. Sykes's analysis of the situation in Palestine had thus pinpointed two key questions that were constantly being asked there, and he thought a new declaration might help answer both. The Jews were anxiously concerned with the question of Palestinian boundaries and the Arabs with the question of the ultimate objective of Zionism. Was Palestine to be an independent Jewish state, or would it be under British tutelage until both parties jointly demanded independence? Accordingly, the Political Intelligence Department (PID) of the Foreign Office was given Sykes's cable for analysis. A.J. Toynbee, then a member of the PID, thought both questions lent themselves to easy solutions. He saw no reason why Palestine's northern boundary should not extend to the mouth of the Litani River and the eastern boundary to the Jordan River, possibly even including the valley of the Jordan east of the river. He would also include the Wadi Arabah south of the Dead Sea to the

Gulf of Aqaba. The Zionists, he said, have "as much right to this no-man's land as the Arabs, or more."[36]

On the issue of the ultimate destiny of Palestine under the British, Toynbee's views make very interesting reading and deserve full quotation.

> As regards *B*. (Sykes' second question) surely our foundation shall be a *Palestinian* state with *Palestinian citizenship* for all inhabitants, whether Jewish or non-Jewish. This alone seems consistent with Mr. Balfour's letter.
>
> Hebrew might be made an official language, but the Jewish element should not be allowed to form a state within the state, enjoying greater privileges than the rest of the population.[37]

The solution envisaged by Toynbee was, of course, not likely to be endorsed by the Zionists, especially since the Zionist leadership was still trying to cement an alliance with the Syrian and Hijazi Arabs in return for exclusive rights in Palestine. It does, however, make clear what the PID of the Foreign Office understood concerning British plans at that time for the future of the country. The national home policy was still vague, but was thought by an informed observer to go no further than providing facilities for immigrating and colonizing.

In the meantime, Sykes continued to work hard at finding a formula that would resolve nationalist differences in Palestine. On 19 November he met at length with the members of the Zionist Commission in Tel Aviv. They agreed that in the immediate future two declarations should be issued concerning Palestine. The first, which Sykes thought should emanate from the Zionists, would state that the tutelage of Palestine "should be permanent until both Jewish and non-Jewish elements by decisive respective majorities elected otherwise." The second would deal with the administrative functions of the tutelary government and would cover policy on immigration, language, maintenance of civic equality, and control of land transactions "with a view to giving full scope to the Zionist movement while safeguarding economic and political interests of [the] non-Jewish population."[38] He had concluded that it was most important that the Balfour Declaration be amplified so people would know where they stood. As it was, he said, the Jews were vacillating between fear that the declaration would be abandoned and the "most extravagant ideas stimulated by various resolutions and unauthorized statements of Zionist policy of Jewish republic, etc."

Allenby's initial reaction was swift and crushing. He doubted that Sykes's suggested declarations would be expedient or that any amplification or modification of the Balfour Declaration would produce a good effect in Palestine. In any case, he said, neither the Zionists nor the Arabs were proper parties to issue declarations.[39]

Clayton apparently managed to modify Allenby's decision, however, by talking to the Zionist Commission again and getting it to agree to a more precise wording of the proposed declaration. The new wording provided that the tutelage of Palestine would continue until both Jews and Arabs in Palestine "agree mutually that it should cease. Agreement would necessitate a majority of both Jews and Arabs respectively in favor of complete autonomy and tutelage would continue if either party refused to agree." In addition, Allenby stipulated that any such declaration would have to come from the Entente powers, and should be deferred until Palestine's future was definitely settled.[40]

Despite this ready acquiescence on the part of the Zionists to a formula designed to safeguard the Arab population of Palestine, Zionist leaders in London continued to work to enlarge the scope of the Balfour Declaration. A special committee of Jewish leaders in London led by Herbert Samuel and including Weizmann and Sokolow as well as members of the non-Zionist League of British Jews, submitted to the British government of 20 November a group of proposals, which defined the ultimate goal of the Balfour Declaration as a Jewish commonwealth.[41] The only section of these proposals to survive Foreign Office review was the one in which the Zionists let it be known that they wanted Great Britain to have the trusteeship of Palestine. The sections regarding the development of a national home into a Jewish commonwealth and the one on borders that stretched from north of Litani River to the Hijaz Railway to Aqaba were deleted summarily by Sir Eyre Crowe, the assistant undersecretary of state.

At this time, Clayton presented to the Foreign Office a full explanation of his views on the reconstruction of the Middle East.[42] His arguments were very well received in London, especially by Lord Curzon, who noted in a subsequent memorandum that they were practically identical to resolutions taken by the Eastern Committee.[43] Clayton suggested that France be made trustee over Lebanon, and otherwise compensated with a trusteeship over Armenia, including the port of Alexandretta. Great Britain was to advise an independent Arab state which would include the sanjak of Tripoli and the port of Latakia as well as the land east of the Jordan. He noted that such an arrangement would greatly facilitate the settlement of the Zionist question by leading to the development of the arable country east of the Jordan, which would in turn allow for considerable Arab emigration from Palestine, "thereby making room for Jewish expansion." In view of all the assurances coming from London that the Sykes-Picot Agreement was defunct and in view of the way the Arab and Zionist movements seemed to be meshing at the top, he was certainly justified in being optimistic about his plan. He once again advised the Foreign Office to impress on the Zionists that "undue haste in pushing their programme will only react against their own interest."

Weizmann, however, was not in a position to be patient. He had an unruly, expectant people behind him, and was constantly receiving encouraging private assurances from members of the British government. He realized that the British had developed a Zionist policy for reasons of state. To maintain their position as benefactors of Zionism, the British had to keep Weizmann, the most ardently pro-British among the Zionists, at the head of a successful Zionist movement. It was a careful policy but one that imposed upon Weizmann the necessity of constantly taking the initiative. The policy seldom rewarded Zionist proposals with the adoption of concrete measures and offered no real security that the British might find the Zionist future in Palestine too burdensome to support any further. In essence, the British were inviting Weizmann to advance proposals which they had no intention of underwriting.

Weizmann knew Zionism's assets lay in Europe and its liabilities in the Middle East. Thus, in an interview with Balfour on 4 December, he stressed the critical nature of the Jewish position in Europe.[44] It was events in Poland, Lithuania, and Rumania that accounted for the great tension and anxiety being felt by the Jewish communities all over the world in regard to the fate of Palestine, Weizmann told the foreign secretary. The Jews were being driven to despair and might turn to revolution, and the "only possible antidote lies in Zionism." A strong Jewish community of four to five million with a sound economic base from which the Jews could radiate out into the Near East would solve the Jewish problem. And until it was solved, Weizmann asserted, the world would have no real peace. The solution, however, could not be one of mere appearance. There must be "free and unfettered development of the Jewish National Home in Palestine." The extension of facilities for immigration was insufficient; there must also be opportunities for carrying out "colonising activities, public works, etc. on a large scale so that we should be able to settle in Palestine about four to five million Jews within a generation, and so make Palestine a Jewish country." Weizmann's exposition of Zionist aims was certainly as clear as it was different from that he had expressed to the Arabs of Palestine in the spring of 1918. At one stroke Britain could ease the pressure toward revolution in Eastern Europe, while gaining a loyal client state in the Middle East. As an added bonus for a sorely tried British empire, Weizmann offered the comforting picture of a stable Jewish community spreading out into the Middle East undoubtedly to pour oil on troubled Arab waters.

To Balfour's query about the place of the Arabs in such a scheme, Weizmann referred to the analogy of England, whose institutions were English in their preponderant influence even though not all citizens carrying on normal lives were of English extraction. "There is room in Palestine," he said, "for a great Jewish community without encroaching upon the rights of the Arabs." Balfour agreed that in this sense the Arab problem "could not be regarded as a serious hindrance," but he added with understatement that it would really be very helpful if the Zionists and Faysal could reach an agreement on possible points of conflict.

Weizmann had hoped to publish this very encouraging interview. Upon advising the Foreign Office of his intention, however, he received a polite letter from Balfour, noting that their discussion had not been meant for any such use, but for Weizmann's personal guidance.[45] Weizmann was being encouraged, but the government was also remaining careful to commit itself publicly no farther than it already was committed. Gently and with some humor, Balfour added that a new statement of government policy was not desirable, and even if it were, he said, it should not "be embodied in the report of a conversation of which I fully recognize that all the most interesting and important portions were contributed by yourself. Such a procedure is almost certain to lead to misunderstanding and controversy."

On 28 November, as Weizmann was setting his initiative in train, he had cabled Eder in Palestine informing him of the proposals, including the Zionist definition of the meaning of the national home, which had been submitted to the Foreign Office on the 20th.[46] He asked that Eder explain to the authorities that world Jewry was disappointed with the "moderation and timidity of our demands." In his view, the Arab national ambitions were fully satisfied in the new Syrian state and hence Palestine must be afforded the opportunity for ultimate development into a Jewish commonwealth. Threats and appeals to violence would not intimidate the Jews, who were "determined to press their just demands."[47]

Weizmann, with his eyes on the coming peace conference and his dream of a Jewish state, was deliberately blind to the situation in Palestine. He failed to see what Clayton saw so clearly: that if Zionism continued on an aggressively threatening course, the Arabs might resort to violence "in order to show opposition to Zionism which they cannot express by other means."[48]

Clayton, agitated by Weizmann's opinions, cabled the Foreign Office on 5 December that the Zionists in Palestine were causing distrust and apprehension by making their demands known in public speeches and press articles. If the Jews were erring, he said, it was not on the side of moderation and timidity. If they continued with their "indiscreet declarations of policy and exaggerated demands," Clayton noted presciently, they will only "militate against their success by arousing permanent hostility and laying themselves open to the charge of securing their aims by force." The Zionists must be patient and show sympathy for the majority of the population of Palestine, he added. "If they force the pace now their whole structure will be based on insecure foundations."[49]

The next day Clayton followed up his warning by dispatching to Balfour a recent report by the chief administrator of OETA(S), General A.W. Money. Money was convinced that giving the Jews a preferential share of the government of Palestine would be disastrous in regard to peaceful settlement and the country's regeneration. It would, he said, have an unfortunate effect among all the Arabs in the Middle East, and eventually on all Muslims in the British Empire. Clayton also attached a letter from the military governor of Jaffa, who was being besieged by Palestinians fearful of dispossession either of their lands or of their hoped-for sovereignty.[50] With their proposals thus emasculated by the Foreign Office and sharply criticized by Clayton and other British officials in Palestine, the Zionists abandoned all thought of immediate publication.[51]

While Clayton was in Palestine following through on the plans developed during the summer for a Zionist-Sharifian alliance, important meetings were being held in London. Shortly before Faysal and Weizmann met for the second time, the Eastern Committee gathered in Lord Curzon's room at the Privy Council Office to thrash out the whole question of British commitments and the Syrian and Palestinian issues.[52]

Twice that day the methodical Lord Curzon reviewed at length the historical facts, the current situation, and the possible lines of policy to follow in preparing for the peace conference. Twice he began by spelling out his understanding that McMahon had promised Husayn that Palestine would be Arab and independent. Simply acknowledging this promise, he passed on to the commitments embodied in the Sykes-Picot Agreement and the Balfour Declaration. The situation had become difficult of late, he said, owing to the fact that the Zionists had taken full advantage, and were disposed to take even fuller advantage, of opportunities offered them. In fact, he added, their program was expanding daily. "They now talk about a Jewish State. The

Arab portion of the population is well-nigh forgotten and is to be ignored." The growing communal friction, caused by Zionist energy, foreshadowed a difficult situation arising in Palestine itself, Curzon said, compounded by the bombshell of the November Anglo-French declaration which was encouraging both parties to exploit the situation in their own interests.

The "ridiculous and unfortunate boundaries" of the Sykes-Picot Agreement should be modified, according to Curzon, so that Palestine would have its old boundaries from Dan to Beersheba. After specifying that the northern boundary must extend to the Litani River, whether Palestine be "Hebrew, Arab, or both," Curzon contented himself with merely discussing considerations to be kept in mind in regard to the other frontiers.

As for the country's future administration, Curzon dismissed an international arrangement as being "singularly unsuited to the conditions of Palestine." France's presence there would be "intolerable to ourselves" as well as to the inhabitants, and Lord Robert Cecil agreed that the French were "entirely out of the question." It came down then to a question of the United States or Great Britain. Cecil thought Palestine was no "great catch" because if the British became trustees, they would "simply keep the peace between the Arabs and the Jews."

Curzon viewed Palestine in relation to the British Empire. It was not sufficient merely to keep it free from invasion as a buffer zone against powers situated in the north. Palestine must prosper and flourish commercially in connection with surrounding areas, especially Egypt. He pointed out that, strategically speaking, Palestine was the buffer of Egypt and any further defense of the Suez Canal would have to be made in Palestine. Palestine's commercial and strategic relations with British or British-influenced territory in the Middle East, while not ruling out the Americans as trustees, might not always be a help to the British.

Curzon's final point was that both Arabs and Jews wanted the British in Palestine and thus Britain could play the policy of self-determination for all it was worth and be the gainer by it. His recommendations, therefore, were to drop the idea of international management, plump for the best possible boundaries, and then if it became a question of the United States or Great Britain, encourage both parties to speak for themselves under the principle of self-determination.

Cecil was willing to go along with Curzon in general, although he thought the strategic argument of no real merit. There was some slight chance of the Americans taking Constantinople or Palestine, he said, "because of the great swagger of it." But in any case, he added, "Whoever goes there will have a poor time." General Macdonough also agreed with Curzon, but could not resist adding that a Zionist had warned him that if the Jews did not get what they wanted, the whole of Jewry would turn Bolshevik and support Bolshevism worldwide. To which Cecil replied, "Yes, I can conceive the Rothschilds leading a Bolshevist mob!"

A few days later, on 9 December, the War Office issued a memorandum which scathingly denounced the 1916 agreement from a strategic point of view and gave considerable support to the Foreign Office's political thinking.[53] It concluded that the British should aim at a politically isolated Syria under British influence and at the retention of Islamic goodwill. As for Palestine, the creation of a "buffer Jewish State" was strategically desirable for Great Britain, provided its creation did not disturb Islamic sentiment and it was not controlled by a potentially hostile power. In other words, the memorandum found no place for France in Arab lands, except for Lebanon.

One week later, the Eastern Committee adopted a series of seven resolutions stemming from Curzon's earlier review.[54] The fourth one read: "While we would not object to the selection of the United States of America, as trustees, yet if the offer were made to Great Britain, we ought not to decline." The fifth one stated that the choice of a trustee should be made, so far as possible, in accordance with the expressed desires of both the Arabs and the Zionist community in Palestine.

This was still a very flexible policy. The country had to be under the tutelage of one of the victorious belligerents, for it was impossible to restore the Turks to any shadow of sovereignty over their Arab territories. The Allies had taken up the cause of self-determination, and while that might mean little or much in specific circumstances, it certainly eliminated the Turks from consideration. The French, despite their lingering, affectionate regard for the Holy Land, were automatically excluded because of their potential for hostility and because their part in the military victory had been minimal. The British could still view the presence of Americans in Palestine with relative equanimity. They might bungle the job, but they were a friendly power and it might be wise to associate them with British imperial responsibilities in the Middle East. In the meantime, the British were supporting Faysal in Syria and pushing the Zionists to come to terms with him.

Weizmann met Faysal for the second time at the Carlton Hotel in London on 11 December, the day after Faysal had arrived from a two-week stay in France. According to Weizmann's record, after listening to Faysal outline the weakness of his position in Syria, Weizmann expressed sympathy with his problems and in turn disclosed the Zionist program for the peace conference.[55] Faysal was to recognize the historical and national rights of the Jews to Palestine; Britain was to be trustee; the Jews were to have a share in the government and to develop the country so it could accommodate four to five million Jews without encroaching on Arab rights. In return the Zionists would give Faysal aid and advice.

Weizmann thought his interview most successful. Faysal had agreed completely with the Zionist proposals, he cabled Eder in Palestine, and had promised to spare no effort in supporting Jewish demands at the peace conference.[56] By 17 December, Weizmann had prepared a set of nine proposals for Faysal's signature. They were indeed ambitious. The whole administration was to be formed to make Palestine a Jewish commonwealth under British trusteeship. Jews were to participate in the administration, Hebrew to be an official language, the Jewish population to be allowed the "widest practicable measure of local self-government," and the Jews to have extensive rights in regard "to the taking over of land including the right of expropriating the effendis." Jews were to have the right to pre-empt public works. In Jerusalem a Jewish congress would be set up which would function largely as a Palestinian government. In addition, the Jewish population was to be educationally and culturally autonomous and the sabbath and Jewish holidays to be legal holidays.[57]

Weizmann's far-reaching proposals, however, met with a substantial official chill from Allenby and Clayton.[58] Even if Faysal could accede to such a list of demands, their institution in Palestine would be highly injudicious. Certainly, the expropriation of the larger landholding Muslims would lead to "serious trouble." The Englishmen suggested strongly the adoption of a gradual approach which would take into account Muslim and Christian "proportionate claims to attention." As for the unclear expression regarding public works, they had no doubt but that "a discreet Government would avail itself of Jewish efficiency in the execution of necessary public work." Other pressure in addition to that applied by Allenby and Clayton must have been used on Weizmann, for the agreement he produced on 3 January 1919 was far different from the one he disclosed to Eder. Lawrence had been doing the interpreting during the 11 December meeting, and in his desire to bring the two sides together, he may have given Weizmann an optimistically misleading idea of Faysal's position. In any case, Faysal was not now eager to sign an agreement; what he wanted and needed was recognition from the powers at the peace conference along with aid, financial and otherwise.

According to Antonius, Faysal would rather have delayed signing an agreement until the peace conference had begun, but he was being pressured by the Foreign Office and by friends who used similar arguments. In addition, Lawrence was "showing uncommon zeal in persuading him that there was no harm in his concluding the proposed Agreement with the Zionists subject to the Arab claims to independence being fully recognized."[59] On 3 January 1919, when they met to sign the agreement, Faysal balked at the phrases "Jewish state" and "Jewish government", which Weizmann had included in the draft. After altering them to read "Palestine" and "Palestine government" he signed, adding in a postscript in Arabic the reservation that if any of his demands for Arab independence before the peace conference were modified in the slightest, then the agreement would be considered void.[60] In view of the sweep of this proviso, it is doubtful that Faysal was ever fully committed to an alliance with the Zionists. He signed to satisfy the Zionist and British passion for legality and organization, but was fully content to wait and see how pledges were carried out when they counted: at the peace conference.

The Faysal-Weizmann agreement appealed in the preamble to the "racial kinship and ancient bonds" between Arabs and Jews and noted that their close collaboration was the "surest means of working out the consummation of their national aspirations." The agreement provided for the mutual accreditation of representative agents of the Arab state and Palestine; a boundary commission; the inclusion of the Balfour Declaration in the constitution and administration of Palestine; the encouragement and stimulation of Jewish immigration into Palestine, while Arab rights were to be safeguarded; the free exercise of religion; protection of Muslim holy places; "complete accord and harmony" on these matters when dealing with the peace conference; and reference to the British government of any matter of dispute. Article 7 declared that the Zionist Organization would send a commission of experts to survey and report on the country's economic potential. The article also contained the only reference to Zionist aid to Faysal, promising that the aforementioned commission would be placed at the disposal of the Arab state for similar purposes. The Zionist Organization also pledged to use its "best efforts to assist the Arab State in providing the means for developing the natural resources and economic possibilities thereof."

Faysal had gone far toward satisfying Zionist objectives. He had recognized their special position in Palestine in exchange for possible future aid. However, he had not, nor would he ever, imply his acquiescence in any future Jewish sovereignty over the land. Without doubt he had been shown the formula, worked out by Sykes and

Clayton with the Zionist Commission, which safeguarded the Arab population by assuring them that the British would not leave if the Arabs or the Jews wanted them to stay. He also had the assurances of Hogarth, given the previous January, that no people was to be subject to another, and the word of Weizmann in June that the Zionists did not seek to establish a Jewish government. On the other hand, his attachment to Palestine was far from firm. Perhaps if events had developed differently, if he had been given the time to strengthen his hold on Syria, and if the French had not chosen to crush him, he would then have been willing to abandon Palestine totally to the Zionists. But this line of thought will always remain highly speculative, because Faysal did not have the time he needed, nor were the Zionists willing to back him against the French.[61]

While the Foreign Office was working toward the Faysal-Weizmann agreement and building a case for revising the Sykes-Picot Agreement with a view to obtaining better terms from the French over Syria, the prime minister in an independent move had gotten the French premier, Clemenceau, to agree verbally that Mosul would be attached to a British-dominated Iraq, and that Palestine, from Dan to Beersheba, would go to the British.[62] Despite this agreement, which went unrecorded at the time and seemed to imply that the French were still assured of their position in Syria under the 1916 agreement, the Foreign Office continued to try to secure an Arab state with a capital at Damascus which would be under British control or influence. On 19 December, the Foreign Office memorandum by Curzon had pointed out that Damascus was the key, not only to the area assigned to the French in 1916, but to the area assigned to the British.[63] Curzon argued that if the French were to take Damascus, they would "make their influence felt over a great part of the Arabian peninsula." It was no exaggeration, he continued, to say that the "presence of the French here would be at least as detrimental to British interests as the presence of the Russians was in the zone of Persia which they held before the war."

It was the Lloyd George-Clemenceau agreement, however, that eventually formed the basis for a reconstruction of the Middle East. Although Lloyd George did not mention in his memoirs what the French hoped to gain from Clemenceau's concessions, it became clear in time that Lloyd George had assured France a share in the oil of Mosul and the control of Syria, including Damascus and Aleppo.[64] Thus, while the Foreign Office was working toward its grand design of a British-controlled Middle East, with both Zionists and Arabs satisfied and the French restricted to mandates in Lebanon and possibly

Armenia, the prime minister had neatly cut the ground from under it by making his independent deal with Clemenceau. By doing so, he rendered the Faysal-Weizmann agreement a dead letter even before its signing.

As the peace conference opened in mid-January, Curzon, now acting foreign secretary, wrote to Balfour in Paris about Zionist ambitions. He said that General Sir Arthur Money, the chief administrator of Palestine, had come to talk to him about the risk they were running of jeopardizing the entire British position in the Middle East unless they moved toward a "Zionist state" with extreme caution. A Jewish government in any form, Money had maintained (and Allenby agreed), would lead to an uprising in which "the nine-tenths of the population who are not Jews would make short shrift with the Hebrews." Curzon acknowledged that he, too, shared these views and had "for long felt that the pretensions of Weizmann & Company are extravagant and ought to be restricted."[65]

Balfour replied calmly, and not altogether truthfully, on 20 January that so far as he knew, Weizmann had never "put forward a claim for the Jewish Government of Palestine." He added that such a claim would in his opinion be "certainly inadmissible and personally I do not think we should go further than the original declaration which I made to Lord Rothschild."[66]

Thus, in the interval between the Armistice and the beginning of the peace conference, the Zionists had initiated several attempts at getting the British to define more fully what the Balfour Declaration meant. Their proposals for publication of declarations, definitions, and interviews had all been refused or severely limited. In the Middle East, Clayton, Allenby, Money, and Sykes had all taken their turns at criticizing Zionist forwardness. In Europe, Balfour thought the British had gone far enough with his original declaration and was still of the opinion that an American protectorate over Palestine might be desirable.[67] Curzon had consistently pointed out the practical difficulties of British Zionist policy and was now advocating a check to Weizmann's "pretensions."

On the other hand, Lloyd George, a former lay preacher, was fascinated by the idea of returning God's chosen people to the land of their ancient frontiers from Dan to Beersheba. In addition, Weizmann now had a signed document proving that the Arabs, represented by the head of an Arab government situated at Damascus, welcomed the Jews to Palestine. The paper might have proved worthless as an agreement, a fact neither Weizmann or Faysal understood at the time, but it was priceless as documentary and political proof that not all Arabs looked upon Zionists as interlopers, and indeed that the Arabs and Zionists had signed an alliance as equals.

During this interval, even the most tactful of the Zionist leaders were coming closer to an open statement of their goals in Palestine. After a year's experience of working with the Balfour Declaration, Weizmann thought the Zionist movement strong enough that he was prepared to tell Balfour of the Zionist intention to settle four to five million Jews in Palestine, from whence they expected to radiate out into the Arab countries. He was even prepared to discuss the expropriation of Arab landowners in Palestine. As these leaders pushed harder, the pressure was felt in Palestine. Palestinian Arabs became increasingly restless and the authorities on the scene relayed their concern to London in the hope that some curb could be placed on the Zionists before actual violence broke out. As a period of preparation for the last crisis of the Eastern Question, this time was a failure.

8

PALESTINE IN THE PEACE

On 18 January the peace conference formally opened in Paris. Compared with the major issues the conference delegates confronted, the question of Palestine's fate was a matter of extremely small moment. Germany's future was the main problem. Other major uncertainties included Russia, the fear of revolution, the reconstruction of Europe, and the role of Wilson and the United States. Statesmen worn out by war and victory, who had had no opportunity to study Eastern issues properly, set out to resolve the Eastern Question at the odd moments when other and bigger questions ceased to press them. Ignorant of the Question's problem potential, they treated the territories of the Middle East as if they were insignificant pieces in a European chess match, to be used in gambits for imperial advantage.

By developing the mandate system, the conference was able to reconcile European and American views about the rest of the world. Article 22 of the Covenant of the League of Nations, approved on 28 April 1919, provided a rationale whereby the various nations with colonial interests could exercise their rights under the legal supervision of a supranational body. Territories formerly belonging to the Ottoman Empire were thus to be assigned to tutelary powers, since they had developed to the point where their provisional independence could be recognized, "subject to the rendering of administrative advice and assistance by a Mandatory until such time as they are able to stand alone."[1] Under this covering legalism, Britain and France continued their time-honored struggle for supremacy in the Middle East, abiding by much the same rules that had governed previous practice. Not until years later would they realize that more than mere form had changed. Thus casually laid in Paris, the foundation of the modern Middle East carried within it the flaw that gradually expanded into the New Eastern Question.

In a memorandum dated 1 January 1919 and later amplified before the Supreme Council of the Paris Peace Conference, the Amir Faysal, head of the Arab government in Syria since 5 October 1918,[2] appealed to the representatives of the powers to "lay aside the thought of individual profits, and of their old jealousies," and to recognize the independence of the whole of Arab Asia from "a line Alexandretta-Persia southward to the Indian Ocean."[3] He attributed the blame for Arab differences of opinion to the hundreds of years of Turkish efforts at absorption and asserted that the Arab nationalist movement aimed to unite the Arabs into one nation. He recognized, however, that the differences of the Arab provinces made it impossible for the moment to unite them under one government, and so he divided them into Syria, Iraq, Jazirah, Hijaz, Najd, and Yemen, the last two of which he passed over lightly since they "look after themselves." For Syria, which "we have just won for ourselves by force of arms," he stressed its ability to direct its own internal affairs with "foreign technical advice and help." Iraq and Jazirah were threatened by exploitation and therefore, Faysal believed, should be "buttressed by the men and material resources of a great foreign Power" even though the government should be "Arab, in principle and spirit." The Hijaz, as a tribal area, should retain its past pattern of sovereignty, which the Arabs understood much better than the Europeans.

Palestine, which stood within the area claimed for Arab unity, he treated as a special matter. In open display of amity with the Zionists, he moved toward fulfilling the spirit of the Zionist-Sharifian alliance.

> In Palestine the enormous majority of the people are Arabs. The Jews are very close to the Arabs in blood, and there is no conflict of character between the two races. In principles we are absolutely at one. Nevertheless, the Arabs cannot risk assuming the responsibility of holding level the scales in the clash of races and religions that have, in this one province, so often involved the world in difficulties. They would wish for the effective super-position of a great trustee, so long as a representative local administration commended itself by actively promoting the material prosperity of the country.

On 6 February, presenting his case before the conference, Faysal did not ask that this Arab confederation be placed under a single mandatory, although that was clearly the intent behind his argument for Arab unity. Even when pressed by President Wilson after his address, Faysal would only go so far as to express his personal fear of the results of partition, leaving the conference to draw its own conclusions about his relations with France.[4] After basing his whole case squarely on the principle of self-determination, he suggested that if the conference were in doubt as to Arab wishes for complete independence or in regard to the power they would prefer as a mandatory, then some sort of international inquiry commission could be sent to the area to determine the desire of its inhabitants.

There was little chance of Faysal's views being accepted by the conference. France had refused to acknowledge his authority to speak for all the Arab areas, as he had done, and was in fact reluctant to allow the Hijaz full representation.[5] According to Lawrence, Balfour had even forgotten to include the Hijaz delegation in the conference's opening ceremonies, an omission quickly corrected despite French objections.[6] Balfour's forgetfulness was undoubtedly of the diplomatic variety, since he did not want to begin the conference by ruffling French feathers with too strong support for a client who was openly anti-French.[7] This was in fact a reliable foreshadowing of Britain's unwillingness to back a pro-Arab policy at the cost of incurring French hostility.

In the meantime the Zionists were also having trouble backstage. Weizmann had come to the Foreign Office complaining that the Jews in Palestine were not being given due consideration. In a talk with George Kidston, he instanced the minor but symbolic facts that Hebrew was not an official language while Arabic was and that Arabic and Turkish inscriptions appeared on postage stamps. In general Weizmann thought the administration, apart from Generals Allenby and Clayton, was showing signs of impatience with the Jews. He accused Storrs of having a faulty attitude and referred to him as a "Levantine." Kidston told Weizmann he would be better off bringing up his grievances with the experts in Paris, adding pointedly that accusations of impatience "could much more justly be levelled against the Jews in Palestine than against our administrative Officers." The officers, Kidston continued, were finding it difficult to reconcile so many conflicting claims and the Jews were only making their task more difficult by their "importunity" and by their presumption that the national home "must be handed over to them ready-made at a moment's notice." Graham supported Kidston's rebuke of Weizmann and noted in reply to a query from Curzon that the Zionist leader had never "publicly" demanded anything more than a Jewish national home, but that the idea of a Jewish commonwealth was "always looming in the background." In a minute to Kidston's memorandum, Curzon took up the term "commonwealth," which he had previously noted in Weizmann's cable to Eder on 17 December. It was simply a less direct way of saying "state" or "republic." "What then," he asked, "is the good of shutting our eyes to the fact that this is what the Zionists are after, and that the British Trusteeship is a mere screen behind which to work for this end?" The straightforward and testy Lord Curzon thought the subterfuge rendered the situation worse, "if Weizmann says this sort of thing to his friend but sings to a different tune in public."[8]

The day after Weizmann's interview in the Foreign Office, Curzon wrote to Balfour in Paris about his conviction that Weizmann was out to get a Jewish government, "if not at the moment, then in the near future." In his opinion Weizmann was discussing one thing with British officials, while actually aiming at something very different: a Jewish state or nation with a subordinated population of Arabs being ruled by Jews who would possess the land and direct the administration. Curzon concluded that he would not envy those who wielded the trusteeship of Palestine "when they realize the pressure to which they are certain to be exposed."[9] Never having believed in the viability of Jewish nationalism in a Muslim country of doubtful fertility, Curzon had now gone a step further. He saw that an aggressive Zionism was alienating British officials in Palestine and disturbing the native population, effects that were certain to spread beyond the borders of Palestine into other Arab areas and equally certain to affect British administration in these other areas.

On 3 February, the Zionist Organization had submitted its case to the conference in the form of resolutions, explanations, and proposals. It asked for recognition of the "historic title of the Jewish people to Palestine and the right of the Jews to reconstitute in Palestine their National Home." It asked for Great Britain to be the mandatory power, which would then so order Palestine politically, administratively, and economically as to "secure the establishment there of the Jewish National Home and ultimately render possible the creation of an autonomous Commonwealth." Other special tasks to be performed by the mandatory power included promoting Jewish immigration and "close settlment on the land," with equitable safeguards for the existing non-Jewish population; accepting the cooperation of a council of world and Palestinian Jewry which would develop the national home and oversee the organization of Jewish education; offering the council priority in any concession for public works or for the development of natural resources; and encouraging the widest possible measure of local self-government.[10]

The boundaries of Palestine were to extend from the Mediterranean near Sidon in the north eastward to a point not far south of

Damascus, and from there to Aqaba following a line close to and west of the Hijaz Railway. The boundary with Egypt would be determined later. A special boundary commission with Jewish representation would settle any details of boundary adjustment.

In an attached statement, the Organization stressed that its claim lay on the historic Jewish connection with Palestine, the congested Jewish population of Eastern Europe which lacked the opportunity for healthy development, and the need to redeem the "desolate" land of Palestine. Two things were needed to revitalize Palestine: an energetic, intelligent and devoted citizenry backed by large financial resources; and a stable and enlightened government. Only the Jews, said the Zionists, could supply such a population. With these conditions met, and boundaries drawn to include the bulk of the water resources of the Levant, Palestine could eventually contain a large and thriving population.

The Zionist Organization proposed to set up a Jewish council (later agency) which would function as a government under the mandatory government. It would represent the Jewish people in all matters affecting them, particularly in the development of immigration, settlement, credit facilities, public works, services, and enterprises. It would have the right to acquire and hold real estate, gain and exercise concessions for public works and develop natural resources, to levy taxes for purposes of Jewish education and welfare, and to issue bonds, debentures, or other obligations, whose proceeds would then be expended for the benefit of the Jewish people or for the development of Palestine. The Zionists also made provision for the mandatory power to appoint a land commission with representatives from the Jewish council. The land commission's wide powers were to include surveying and making proposals concerning the whole range of land questions.

On 27 February, Sokolow made the formal presentation of the memorandum to the Supreme Council and read an extract from it. Weizmann also spoke to the council, but his answer to a question asked by Secretary of State Lansing proved more interesting than his speech. Lansing asked Weizmann to clear up the confusion about the meaning of *national home*. "Did that mean an autonomous Jewish government?"

Dr. Weizmann replied in the negative. The Zionist Organization did not want an autonomous Jewish Government, but merely to establish in Palestine, under a Mandatory Power, an administration, not necessarily Jewish, which would render it possible to send into Palestine 70,000 to 80,000 Jews annually. The Organization would require to have permission at the same time to build Jewish schools, where Hebrew would be taught, and to develop institutions of every kind. Thus it would build up gradually a nationality, and so make Palestine as Jewish as America is American or England is English. Later on, when the Jews formed the large majority, they would be ripe to establish such a government as would answer to the state of the development of the country and to their ideals.[11]

Weizmann could scarcely have been clearer or more candid about ultimate Zionist goals.

In submitting its maximum claims, the Zionist Organization had thus established a strong negotiating position in a forum where it was not under the exclusive control of the British. American Zionists—Justice Brandeis, Felix Frankfurter, and Rabbi Stephen S. Wise—had all exercised their influence on the American delegation. In later years, Weizmann, paid generous tribute to Frankfurter in particular for helping him understand the ideas and practices of American politicians.[12] Armed with the knowledge that these men were strong Zionists and supported a British mandate,[13] Weizmann and other Zionist leaders felt themselves strong enough to resist the efforts of Ormsby-Gore to produce a more moderate Zionist Program. The preliminary draft—prepared by an advisory committee made up of John Maynard Keynes, Lionel Abrahams, and James de Rothschild, with Herbert Samuel as chairman—thus survived this British official's "unpalatable advice" and subsequently provided the substance of the formal memorandum.[14] Weizmann's answer to Lansing, which stopped just short of spelling out the Zionist intention of establishing a Jewish state in Palestine, was also based on recognition of the strength of the American Zionists, which had given him a measure of independence from the British. In fact, as Brandeis's biographer put it, the "Zionists were now so confident of statehood that in March 1919 Israel Zangwill, a former opponent of Zionism, proposed that Brandeis be elected the first President of Palestine."[15]

It is worth noting that in the midst of this bold presentation by the Zionist Organization, one discordant note was struck. Professor Sylvain Levi, the unofficial French representative of the original Zionist Commission to Palestine and a member of the faculty at the College de France in Paris, spoke to the Supreme Council from his personal vantage point as a French Jew on the Zionist movement, which he favored, despite his profound doubts about the virtues of nationalism. It seemed shocking to him that the Jews, who were on the verge of obtaining equal rights all around the world, would seek to obtain exceptional privileges in Palestine. "Privileges so obtained," he said, "as a rule did not profit either the giver or the receiver."[16]

In addition to questioning the morality of the movement, he pointed out a number of difficulties in the realization of Zionist goals. In the first place, there were too many Jews for Palestine to hold them all, and in the second, the standard of living in Palestine was too low even for the oppressed Jews of Eastern Europe. In the third place, the type of person who would be drawn to Palestine from Europe, where there was persecution, would carry into Palestine "highly explosive passions, conducive to very serious trouble in a country which might be likened to a concentration camp of Jewish refugees." Finally there were the problems of dual citizenship and the fusing together of Jews from so many different national backgrounds.

Weizmann, horrified by this display of academic objectivity and logic and worried by its possible political impact, never forgave Levi. Both he and Sokolow refused to shake hands with him after the meeting was over, referring to his speech as the work of a traitor.[17] This was only an incident, however, and seemed to have no deleterious effect on Zionist progress.

Meanwhile, Mark Sykes had returned from the Middle East where he had been working sixteen hours a day. As his biographer remarked, "Eastern questions come and go in phases, and the momentary phase was an unlucky one for Mark."[18] And not just for him. Even those most sympathetic to him realized that his policies had resulted in a great tangle.

> From being the evangelist of Zionism during the war, he had returned to Paris with feelings shocked by the intense bitterness which had been provoked in the Holy Land. Matters had reached a stage beyond his conception of what Zionism would be. His last journey to Palestine had raised many doubts, which were not set at rest by a visit to Rome. To Cardinal Gasquet, he admitted the change of his views on Zionism, and that he was determined to qualify, guide and, if possible, save the dangerous situation which was rapidly arising.[19]

On 16 February, Sykes, stricken with influenza, died in Paris at the age of thirty-nine. It may be that Clayton, Sykes's alter ego in the Middle East, was right to say later: "It is permissible to believe that had he lived the situation in the Near East would not be what it is today."[20] Indeed it is hard to believe that Sykes would not have had an impact on the peace conference. His death removed the most articulate and acceptable of Arab advocates just as his ideas of Zionism were changing and, as events were to show, it removed his protection from the man he had installed as CPO. Sykes could scarcely have died at a worse time.

When the Arabs and Zionists had been presenting their cases to the peace conference, the British and French had been moving toward collision over Syria. The British had been weakened by the tendency of the prime minister to intrude into Foreign Office matters, by the inability of that office to control Middle East policy while the India Office ran Mesopotamia and part of Arabia and while the War Office was still deeply involved in Syria and Palestine, and by the division of the Foreign Office into a Paris branch under Balfour and a London branch under Curzon. They had thus been unable to come to a quick agreement with the French over Syria. Early in February the signs had been good. Lloyd George and Clemenceau had had friendly talks over Syria and Morocco.[21] On 6 February the French handed the British a new "liberal-looking" draft offer. The British, however, became suspicious of the offer and analyzed it as a French attempt to extend influence into the Arabian Peninsula, an area reserved for the British. As a result of this uncertainty over French intentions regarding the Arabs, Lloyd George decided that the British would stay in occupation of Syria until their pledge to Husayn could be fulfilled.[22] In so doing Lloyd George seemed to have forgotten his talk with Clemenceau in December in which he had given up claims to Syria. At any rate he had justified his maneuvering to gain further concessions from the French by appealing to his honorable commitments to Husayn.

On 8 February, the British proposed that the Syria outlined in the 1916 agreement be cut down by about a third by extending the British-influenced Arab area so that a line from Haifa to Mosul would be wholly within the British area. This would have achieved the British objective of cutting off the French from the heart of the Arab interior.[23] It would also have secured the strategic Hauran for Britain and served to meet admiralty wishes for a Mosul-Mediterranean corridor for the movement of petroleum. Although immediately rejected by the French, the line desired by the British coincided with the one the Zionists were campaigning for, at least in some of its more important aspects.[24] Thus the Arab question, by coming between Britain and France, postponed a quick solution to the problem of Palestine. The Arabs, caught in the rift between the two imperialist powers, had little or no room for maneuver. The Sharifian party could only depend on the hope that Britain would continue to see its interests served by retaining its intimacy with Husayn and the Hijazis. The contrast with the independence the Zionists had gained by using the similarity of views of the American and British delegations could not have been greater.

Faysal's speech before the Supreme Council on 6 February, in which he argued for an Arab confederation under a single mandatory, had the effect of hardening the French attitude toward him.[25] To counter his arguments, the French on 13 February brought forward a Syrian, Shukri Ghanim, who had lived the previous thirty years in France. As chief representative of the Central Syrian Committee, Ghanim rejected the thesis of Faysal that the Arabs were a unit only artificially divided by the Turks. There was no affinity between the Hijazi and the Syrian, between the bedouin and the farmer, he proclaimed, aside from their having one language, and that resemblance was more apparent than real. Historically, he said, Syria had never been ruled by Arabia for more than the few years between its conquest in 635 A.D. and the proclamation of Mu'awiya as caliph, and Syria would not accept such rule now. In conclusion, he asked for a Syria separate from Arabia and under a French mandate.[26]

While the Arabs were thus split, at least seemingly, and the British and French were irritating each other with counter-claims, Lloyd George had temporarily become disillusioned with the Zionists. Probably upset by the ambitious designs revealed in their conference memorandum, he seized upon a letter from Cardinal Bourne in Palestine complaining about Zionist claims that they were to dominate the Holy Land. He wrote to Kerr from London on 15 February to say that Balfour should be informed of the situation, adding that if the cardinal's report was accurate, "then they are certainly putting their claims too high." He had heard from other sources, he said, that the Arabs were disturbed by Zionist claims and by the threat that they would be expropriated in order to make room for the Jews. He continued: "We certainly must not have a combination of Catholics and Mohammedans against us. It would be a bad start to our Government in Palestine. The letter itself is revelation to me of the reason why the Catholics hate the Jews so badly."[27] The prime minister's letter was not an indication of a change in policy. He had consistently supported the formula of the Balfour Declaration,[28] but it was plain that the growing assertiveness of the Zionists did not meet with full British approval.

In a letter drafted by Ormsby-Gore for Balfour's use, it was apparent that the Foreign Office was still depending on the Faysal-Weizmann agreement and that British officials were aware that if Arab aspirations in Damascus and eastern Syria were not satisfied, then a general anti-European reaction might arise throughout the Arab world, causing the British "serious embarrassment in Palestine as elsewhere."[29] An accompanying memorandum, drawn up by the staff in Paris, emphasized that there was no question of immediate Jewish domination. It was expected that Jewish influence would grow as Jewish numbers increased, but no discrimination for or against Jews was anticipated "in the selection of persons fitted to take their share in the administration of the country."

Balfour refused to take refuge in this roundabout way of saying that the Jews were to have preference in Palestine, even though there would be no official discrimination. Forthrightly, he pointed out that the weak point of the British position on Palestine was that "we deliberately and rightly decline to accept the principle of self-determination." He could not have been clearer. Continuing, he said he suspected that most anxiety over Palestine was motivated by "hatred of the Jews."

> Our justification for our policy is that we regard Palestine as being absolutely exceptional: that we consider the question of the Jews outside Palestine as one of world importance, and that we conceive the Jews to have an historic claim to a home in their ancient land; provided that home can be given them without either dispossessing or oppressing the present inhabitants.

In any case, Balfour wanted to avoid public statements about Palestine until the whole Middle Eastern situation had cooled down and they could deal with the critical problems which were "hanging fire."[30] On the other hand, he saw the danger in letting these problems ride unchecked too long and agreed that an official statement might be the lesser of two evils. At this stage of the conference, a public quarrel with the Zionist Organization was the last thing the British wanted. After all, if a decision on Palestine's mandatory could be reached in the near future, there would still be time to rein in the extremists before they went too far in the Middle East.

During the month of February, the Zionists gained a valuable ally in the person of Colonel Richard Meinertzhagen, wholly English despite his name, an Army intelligence officer who had served with Allenby in Palestine and who would succeed Clayton as CPO to the EEF in the Middle East. He had met Weizmann in London and later had a long talk with him in Paris, where he became convinced that Zionism was a constructive form of Bolshevism, as opposed to the destructive form found in Russia.[31] A confessed anti-Semite who wished that Zionism could be separated from Jewish nationality,[32] he came to be a fanatical pro-Zionist who believed Zionism "to be a world force which will outlive its lawless cousin—Bolshevism—and . . . will become a model for all communities on which to build a healthy prosperous state, immune from wars and civil strife."[33] This intemperate idealist began in February to carry on his own underground campaign for Zionism within the British delegation at Paris.

Meinertzhagen was dissatisfied with the Balfour Declaration, which he said Weizmann regarded as a "great document, a charter of freedom," but which was "in fact a paradox, meaning nothing at all, like so many other things emanating from A.J.B."[34] Acting on his own, he told Weizmann that now was the time to go all out for Jewish sovereignty in Palestine, pledging his personal support for such a move. He wrote in his diary that he thought Lloyd George and Wilson would support him and that he had consulted Smuts, who eventually agreed to back Meinertzhagen's efforts. He talked with the Greek premier, Venizelos, the British chief of staff, General Sir Henry Wilson, and even with the Japanese delegation, and got Lawrence to agree that the time was ripe.[35] It is indeed ironic that such an energetic intruder into policy should later have been so bitter about other officials' disregard for settled policy.

By the beginning of March, Faysal had begun to be disturbed by the trend of events. In an interview given to the French newspaper *Le Matin* on 1 March, he said:

> The unhappy Jews will find an asylum in Palestine. But they must behave there like good citizens. Our humane heart will only be happy about this. But it is necessary that the rule over them be in the hands of a Christian or Moslem government, appointed by the League of Nations. And if they will want to set up a state and to demand the right to rule in this country, I must express serious doubts. It is to be feared that there will be clashes between them and the other races.[36]

According to the Israeli historian Aharon Cohen, it was about this time that Faysal met with a group of Palestinian Jews, giving them a warm welcome and speaking to them "as to brothers." Cohen went on to point out that Faysal also referred unfavorably to a proposal by Zangwill that the Arabs in Palestine be transported by camel to Iraq and Arabia.[37] Clearly Faysal was not finding his alliance with the Zionists a profitable one. The status of Syria was far from being settled and there was little the Zionists could do to help him, while, on the other hand, the Zionists appeared to be achieving success, much of which was due to his understanding with Weizmann.

The Zionists, upset in turn by what Weizmann called this "frankly hostile" interview,[38] protested to Faysal. The latter's secretary disavowed the statements attributed to him, explaining that Faysal had actually said: "If the Zionists wished to found a Jewish state at the present moment, they would meet with difficulties from the local population."[39] After being visited by several American Zionists[40] and meeting with Lawrence,[41] Faysal on 3 March sent his famous letter to Felix Frankfurter, in which he described the Zionist proposals currently before the conference as "moderate and proper" and promised that his party would do its best "to help them through."

Despite this attempt to paper over the rift, Faysal said nothing that would lead the reader to believe that he had acceded to the idea of Jewish sovereignty in Palestine. His letter struck a very cordial tone throughout, especially as he noted his appreciation of Weizmann, but the fact remained that Faysal was not budging on the ultimate fate of Palestine, at least until he had in hand something more tangible than a precarious semi-desert kingdom. He noted that neither the Arabs nor the Zionist movement was imperialist; they were both national, and as such, he said, "there is room in Syria for us both."[42]

Meanwhile in Palestine, agitation had been stepped up. On 28 January 1919, Arab notables rallied in Jerusalem. Their slogans included: "Palestine is part of Syria, and the Arabs of Palestine are part of the Arab nation!" "Complete independence for the Arab countries!" "No Jewish immigration to Palestine!" On 4 February they issued a manifesto called "The First Warning," addressed to the world, in which they declared that they would fight for their land before they would be driven from it. In the same month, the Palestinian Arabs formed the Muslim-Christian Association and at its first national meeting in Jaffa passed various resolutions of opposition to the Balfour Declaration and to Zionist activities and set up branch offices all over Palestine. According to Cohen, Arab terrorist groups began operating in Palestine, trying to drive out both British and Jews.[43]

In the midst of these strong currents running in the Arab East, Clayton decided that it was time to inform officials in London that their incompatible promises had produced liabilities that were not all dischargeable. Syria and Palestine were interdependent problems in his view, and he strongly recommended that the British weigh the various alternatives and choose either a whole loaf or no bread.[44] With a fine clarity of analysis, he set out to explain, step by step, Britain's alternative means of achieving its objectives in the area. His recent months of experience as CPO in the eastern Mediterranean had led him to the conviction that the promises to France, Husayn, and the Jews were impossible to reconcile.

In 1916, he said, Britain had renounced any claim to predominant influence in Syria, while to Husayn Britain had promised support for an Arab state or confederation "from which we cannot exclude the purely Arab portions of Syria and Palestine." Finally, Britain was

committed to a "large measure of support of Zionism," even though
the initial Zionist program had been "greatly exceeded by the proposals now laid before the Peace Conference."

Unfortunately, the French were totally unwanted in Syria, except
by the Maronites of Lebanon, and dual control of a homogeneous
Arab state would be impracticable owing to the radically different
methods of administration used by France and England. Furthermore, Zionism was "increasingly unpopular" in the Middle East,
where the "somewhat exaggerated programme put forward recently
by the Zionist leaders has seriously alarmed all sections of the non-
Jewish majority." The British situation in Palestine would be rendered even more difficult if Syria were handed over to France,
thereby undermining Arab confidence in Great Britain. The British
therefore were forced, Clayton said, "to break, or modify, at least one
of our agreements."

Clayton then presented three alternatives. Under the first, the current arrangement with France would be maintained. The French
would have to assume full responsibility for the bedouin tribes who
depended on Damascus, Aleppo, and the Hauran, because any dual-
ity of control over the Syrian hinterland would lead to continual friction between Britain and France. He predicted that the French would
meet with "great obstruction and possible armed resistance" from
Syrian Arabs, who would be supported by the Arabs of the Hijaz.
Great Britain, the controlling power in Palestine charged with carrying out a Zionist policy, would in turn be pressed by France to
enforce the neutrality of the tribesmen in the Palestinian hinterland
and to close the lines of communication between Arabia and Syria.
The results would be calamitous. Britain's influence with the Arabs
would be greatly impaired, first by the sellout in Syria and second by
the support of an unpopular Zionist program.

Meeting French demands, then, would probably require the use of
force, which would necessitate the maintenance of a large army of
occupation in Palestine and would react harmfully on "British interests and influence in Arabia, and even in Mesopotamia, by definitely
alienating Arab sentiment." This solution could only lead, Clayton
thought, to a serious menace to vital British interests.

A second alternative was to reason that if France must have Syria,
then an American mandate for Palestine would be preferable to a
British one. Britain would thus escape the odium of having to impose
a Zionist policy on Palestine. The loss of prestige in the Arab world,
however, would still be great. This solution was really not much of
an improvement over the first, and Clayton passed over it quickly.

The third alternative was to offer France an inducement to re-
nounce Syria and to give the United States or Great Britain the mandate for both Syria and Palestine. Only in this way, he asserted, could
a compromise be reached "between Arab aspirations for a united and
autonomous Syria and Zionist demands for a Jewish Commonwealth
in Palestine." A U.S. mandate would place the Levant under the
control of a power which was meeting with increasing favor among
the Syrians and which had few interests liable to conflict with those
of Britain. It would also, Clayton noted, "relieve Great Britain of her
conflicting pledges to France, to the Arabs and to the Zionists." The
disadvantages were the uncertainty about U.S. acceptance of such a
mandate and the "inevitable and serious loss of British prestige which
stands high in the East as a result of British victories in this area."
Clayton continued:

> A mandate to Great Britain would entail grave responsibilities and would
> mean undertaking a difficult and possibly thankless task. On the other
> hand it would put the seal on British predominance throughout the Arab
> countries; would render Great Britain paramount in Islam; and would
> safeguard the Eastern Mediterranean and the routes to Mesopotamia
> and India by securing control of the Aleppo-Mosul line.

After his survey of alternatives, Clayton presented a suggested
course of action, which would modify earlier strategic designs. France
might be satisfied with control of Constantinople and the task of
reorganizing and reconstructing the "future Turkish State, in view
of her large interests in the Ottoman Public Debt and in the Anatolian
Railway system." This would also entail the control of the southern
Black Sea and the Caucasian states. The United States co·'ld undertake the construction of Armenia as an autonomous state acting as a
buffer between French and British interests. And Great Britain would
take the mandate for the "eventual establishment of autonomous
Government in Syria and Palestine with due regard for Arab aspirations and Zionist aims." There were only two courses open to
Great Britain: either it would press for control up to the Aleppo-
Mosul line or it must withdraw to the Egyptian frontier, which would
then be extended to include southern Palestine up to Beersheba and
the southern end of the Dead Sea, and south to Aqaba.

Clayton's plan for meeting British requirements in the area was
well thought out and logically and forcefully presented. Clearly it was
a projection of his strategic ideas of the previous summer. The
French presence in Syria did indeed considerably weaken the British
position in the Middle East in the interwar period and the Second

World War. Syria and Damascus were the very heart of Arabism, and the Syrians became exceedingly bitter over the French policies of direct rule, hostility to nationalism, and "divide and rule." This bitterness was not confined to Syria nor was it directed only at France. It spread to the entire Arab world and was aimed at the West in general. Britain could hardly hope to escape this emotional reaction, since Britain, more than France, was the standard-bearer of Western civilization in the Middle East. The error in Clayton's thinking lay in his hope that concern for the security of the British Empire would force the British to back the Arabs at the expense of the French, rather than the other way around. Lord Robert Cecil had expressed nothing less than the truth when he said in December 1918 that the French would not give up the "whole of Syria without the most tremendous convulsion. They would rather give up anything in the world than give up that claim to Syria; they are mad about it, and Cambon himself is quite insane if you suggest it."[45]

Clayton was not an isolated figure arguing for an unrealistic solution. Lord Milner, who was "totally opposed to the idea of trying to diddle the French out of Syria," recognized that he had "almost every other Government authority, military and diplomatic, against him." As colonial secretary, his solution was to get the French to agree to a "liberal interpretation" of British mandates in Mosul and Palestine, and to have Britain play the honest broker in promoting a rapprochement between Faysal and France.[46] Milner, however, was desperately tired, according to Lloyd George, and never able to "settle down to business" and concentrate on arriving at the urgently-needed decisions.[47] Whether Milner was to blame for the French failure to come to terms with Faysal, as Clemenceau charged, or the fault was Curzon's, as the French also suspected, the "Syrian tangle" continued to defy efforts to unknot it.[48]

On 20 March, the Council of Four came together in the prime minister's Paris flat on the Rue Nitot for an important meeting. The French foreign minister, Pichon, and Lloyd George eventually reached a critical point, with the former claiming that under the mandate system, the whole of Syria should go to France, while Lloyd George insisted that the French were bound as tightly as the English to the promises embodied in the McMahon letter to Husayn.[49] When Pichon maintained that the promise was made by England alone and it became obvious that the two sides had reached an impasse, President Wilson intervened. The 1916 agreement, he said, was out of date now that Russia had "disappeared," and besides, he continued, dismissing the agreement entirely, the United States adhered consistently to the principle of the consent of the governed. Turning to General Allenby, Wilson asked him what would happen if the French were give permission to occupy Syria. Allenby replied that he had no doubt that war would result. If Faysal were directing it, he continued, "there might be a huge war covering the whole area, and the Arabs of the Hedjaz would join." He also thought Palestine and possibly Egypt would become involved, in which case "the consequences would be incalculable."

Wilson then suggested that an inter-Allied commission be formed to inquire into the state of opinion in Syria. Clemenceau, who had let his foreign minister do all the verbal sparring with Lloyd George, agreed to the principle of the inquiry, adding that the commission must not be confined to Syria.[50] Its scope must be enlarged to take in Palestine, Mesopotamia, Armenia, and any other parts of the Ottoman Empire which would be under the mandate system. Lloyd George had no objection, although Balfour, with good reason, protested that the sending of the commission would delay a peace settlement. Wilson brushed aside Balfour's protest and at Lloyd George's request undertook to draw up the terms of reference for the commission.

Curzon welcomed the commission, later known as the King-Crane Commission, as providing the opportunity for extricating the British from their position in Palestine. He had been increasingly dismayed, he wrote Balfour on 25 March, at the thought of the responsibilities Britain would have to undertake in Palestine and at the boundless ambitions of the Zionists.[51] The Zionists had just held a conference in Britain, he said, at which they had gone on record committing themselves to the following propositions:

1. absolute control of immigration;
2. all Jewish Holidays to be observed officially;
3. immediate control of water rights, carrying with it control of the land;
4. Jewish nationalization of all public land and of the surplus land of all private estates exceeding a certain size;
5. complete control of all public works;
6. Jewish supervision of all educational institutions; and
7. use of Hebrew as a main language in all schools.

Curzon, who was worried about the "manifest symptoms of Allied weakness or disunion" in the entire East,[52] confessed to Balfour that he shuddered at the "prospect of our country having to adjust ambitions of this description with the interests of the native population or the legitimate duties of a mandatory Power."[53] Although the Turks knew that they could not regain their lost Arab provinces, he wrote in a memorandum on the same day he wrote to Balfour, they "cannot fail to see with a chuckle of deep satisfaction that there is a serious and widespread revolt against the British in Egypt, and that the Turkish flag has actually been raised again in the valley of the Nile." He warned of "fresh trouble . . . brewing in the East, which may disarrange some of our best laid plans."[54]

With this deep trouble looming in the background, it seemed folly to Curzon to persist in a policy certain to bring the British to grief. To Balfour, he wrote:

> I look back with a sort of gloomy satisfaction upon the warnings that I ventured to utter a year and a half ago in the Cabinet as to the consequences of inviting the Hebrews to return to Palestine. It is now clear that to these difficulties will be added great troubles with the Vatican; and altogether the position in Jerusalem will be such that I should rejoice at nothing more than that the Commission should advise that a mandate be conferred upon anyone else rather than Great Britain.[55]

While Curzon was fulminating powerlessly in London, the prime minister was being influenced in another direction by the private efforts of Meinertzhagen. On 24 March, Lloyd George, Philip Kerr, and Meinertzhagen lunched together in Paris, talking of Zionism during the whole meal. Although Meinertzhagen failed to pin Lloyd George down on what he thought of an ultimate Jewish sovereignty, he did succeed in interesting him in a scheme for annexing the Sinai.[56] In a memorandum on the subject requested by Lloyd George, Meinertzhagen set out the future course of events with uncanny precision. "This Peace Conference has laid two eggs," he said, "Jewish Nationalism and Arab Nationalism; these are going to grow up into two troublesome chickens." He predicted that if Zionism succeeded, it would have to expand, which would lead to bloodshed. Since there was going to be a clash, Britain should choose sides well in advance with the likely winners, the Jews, in order to gain their lasting gratitude. The Egyptians, on whom the British position in the Middle East depended, Meinertzhagen marked out as Palestine's "potential enemy." While all this was well in the future, it was not too soon to establish the Sinai as a strategic base with access to both the Mediterranean and Red Seas. The Sinai would serve as a buffer between Palestine and Egypt and no problem of nationalism would arise, since the land was nearly uninhabited.[57]

According to Meinertzhagen, Lloyd George was sufficiently impressed with the memorandum to approach President Wilson on the subject of British sovereignty in the Sinai. Wilson, however, was shocked by the idea of inflicting a permanent grievance on Egypt, and Lloyd George dropped the subject.[58] Though the idea of a Gibraltar in the eastern Mediterranean was never officially revived, despite Meinertzhagen's repeated efforts through Eyre Crowe and Vansittart, its main influence may have been to resolve Lloyd George's personal doubts about Zionism and to convince him of the utility of a Jewish client state in the Middle East. Certainly something took place around this time which set the highly-placed British officials in Paris on a collision course with Britain's highest political advisers in the Middle East.

The mystery of this abrupt change in Britain's Middle East policy is explicable only in terms of the general situation in Europe. Bela Kun's Communist revolution in Hungary, the Spartacist revolts in Germany, and the Bolshevik occupation of Odessa, in addition to labor unrest in Britain and the erosion of coalition support in two British by-elections, all led Lloyd George to make a weekend review of England's basic political and diplomatic strategy. On 25 March he produced his famous Fontainebleau Memorandum, "Some Considerations for Peace Conference before They Finally Draft Their Terms." According to him, Europe's greatest danger in the coming years would be Bolshevism. "Already it had gripped most of Russia and was spreading to neighboring countries from the Baltic to the Black Sea and Mediterranean. These countries were too weak to resist and too divided to combine."[59] Hence Germany had to be built up to resist revolution, rather than, as France demanded, demilitarized and dismembered in both the east and west. A conference crisis ensued, continuing into mid-April and ending only when France accepted a number of safeguards: demilitarization of the Rhineland, Allied occupation of the Left Bank for fifteen years, and an American-British-French security treaty (which was later rejected by the U.S. Senate). While Lloyd George and Wilson were pressing France to be generous to Germany for fear of revolution, it was clearly no time to extract further concessions on Syria. Furthermore, intensified fear of revolution would have an impact on Palestine policy. A Zionist Palestine would be the "only possible antidote" to revolution by East European Jews.[60] Once again, as they had from the beginning, European considerations were outweighing Middle Eastern realities.

On 26 March, Clayton informed the Foreign Office that Palestinian Arabs, fearing that the peacetime conference might confer political and economic advantages on the Jews, were reacting with high feeling and increased anti-Zionist propaganda. Emotion was being heightened by the "rash actions and words of the Jews themselves and by pronouncements which appear by leading Zionists in the press in

England, America and elsewhere."[61] Clayton alerted London to the possibility of anti-Jewish outbreaks of violence, especially if there were any announcement of special privileges going to the Jews. Curzon commented laconically that the Zionists would have only themselves to thank if they lost the prize.[62] A few days later, writing to Wavell, Clayton welcomed the sending of a commission of inquiry, saying it would have a quieting effect in the East while all parties got busy "propagating and collecting signatures to monster petitions." He was taking steps to see that all reasonable precautions were taken to prevent anti-Jewish outbreaks, and he thought that the Jews, too, must be kept quiet.[63]

From Paris, where a much different view of Zionism prevailed, Hogarth wrote Clayton that Weizmann and Frankfurter were putting up an "exceeding moderate programme" and agitating for some certainty about the status of Palestine. He had dined recently with both of them, he said, and found them "singing very low, and talking of thirty, forty, fifty years' delay of a political Jew state." Weizmann was talking of half a million Jews in Poland "with loins girt and staff in their hand" even though probably no more than ten thousand a year could be introduced in practice. Though Hogarth was backing what he thought was a moderate version of Zionist policy in Palestine, he evinced a cynically sympathetic regard for the methods being used. Weizmann, he said,

> tried to frighten Wilson with Bolshevism, but I gather without much success; and he is to try it on A. J. B. tomorrow. I am personally backing him wholeheartedly so long as he is moderate, but I fear things have gone too far in Palestine for us to take over, with that Jew Council in evidence, without trouble. Still,—there stands H. M. G.'s Declaration about the National Home! It must mean something, and this is about the least it could mean!

On 31 March Balfour, who did prove highly sensitive to arguments about Jews being pushed into revolutionary postures in Eastern Europe,[64] wrote to Samuel that, according to information received from reliable sources, the Zionists in Palestine were "alienating the sympathies of all the other elements of the population" and their behavior was having bad repercussions in Paris.[65] He requested Samuel to "warn the Zionist leaders both here and in Palestine that they would do well to avoid any appearance of unauthorized interference in the administration of the country." On 3 April he wrote much the same to Weizmann, adding that he should take the necessary measures to alleviate the dangers.[66] Samuel agreed to try to calm the situation, but he insisted that there was a second side to the story. He relayed to Balfour the sense of grievance felt by the Jewish population of Palestine against the military authorities who were believed to be unsympathetic. Nevertheless, he said, he hoped it would be possible to impress upon the Jewish population the need for restraint.[67]

Weizmann, too, agreed to take steps to curb the pent-up exuberance of the Zionists, assuring Balfour that everything possible was being done to avoid misunderstanding. However, he blamed the real trouble on agitators in Damascus, talk in the French press of a Jewish state, and the British officials administering Palestine. The Britons at the top were all right, he said, but the proper spirit was lost in transmission to the lower echelons. What he wanted in view of the gravity of the situation were "men of fresh outlook and full understanding and sympathy for the purposes which lie before the Balfour Declaration, the acceptance of which, we are confident, will be made part of the peace of the world."[68]

In mid-April Curzon sounded the alarm again. The policy being pursued in Paris, he said, was totally at variance with the "absolute concurrence of opinion from every authority whom I have seen, consulted, or read." The position of the British in the Middle East was dangerous and the policy favored in Paris seemed likely "to produce disturbance, if not disaster." Curzon had had the Eastern Department of the Foreign Office prepare a summary of the existing situation, which, he said, revealed

a position of divided councils and conflicting ambitions among the Great Powers, of profound and increasing unrest in the regions affected, of military insecurity, and of impending bloodshed and chaos, that may rob us of many of the fruits of victory and create a standing menace in the Middle East, both to the peace of Europe and to the security of India.

In Palestine, he said specifically, a dispute which had appeared capable of reconciliation at the end of the war had, through the "exaggerated demands of the Zionists in Palestine, produced a new situation of unrest and tension which was likely to become more acute."[69] The Eastern Department's summary added that anti-Zionist feeling in Palestine had reached "fever heat," that Zionist claims had become "more and more exorbitant," and that France and the Vatican were in varying degrees opposed to Zionism.[70]

By the beginning of May, the Syrian question had become yet more complicated. Soon after the Council of Four decided to send a commission to the Middle East, Henry Wickham Steed, editor of the London Times, brought together a number of British and French Middle Eastern experts. In the course of a six-hour meeting, they reached substantial agreement that they must try to prevent the commission from arriving in Syria because it would have an unsettling effect there and would undermine the prestige of the peace conference.[71]

Unaware of this backstage maneuver, President Wilson went ahead and appointed two American commissioners, Dr. Henry C. King, president of Oberlin College, and Charles R. Crane, a Chicago businessman who was well known in the Democratic party. Although much has been made of their unfamiliarity with the area they were to poll, they had the support of an experienced and talented staff. According to the historian of the commission, they were both "men of experience and sound judgment."[72]

While the Americans prepared for the commission's inquiry and the British appointed Hogarth and McMahon to the commission, with Toynbee as an expert adviser,[73] Faysal and Clemenceau met at the Hotel de Matignon on 13 April to try to come to an agreement on the future of Syria. These talks were supposed to be formalized by an exchange of letters, but Faysal's 17 April reply to Clemenceau's draft was rejected by Robert de Caix, acting for the premier. Faysal sent another letter on the 20 April, just before he left Paris for Syria, containing vague and amiable assurances of his willingness to work "to increase the friendly bonds between the French and the Arabs."[74] Apparently Faysal, acting on the advice of Lawrence, had no intention of coming to terms with the French and was trying instead to play for time to build up strength at home and hoping for American intervention and a report from the inter-Allied commission that would be sympathetic to Syrian opinion.[75] This was very dubious strategy and it was no wonder that Lawrence immediately left France for an ill-starred flying trip to Egypt that took three months to accomplish.[76]

On 2 May Clayton took an important and probably decisive step. Like Curzon, he was disturbed by the deterioration of the British position in the Middle East and by the prospect of having to administer a Palestine saddled with a pro-Zionist policy while the Arabs were being abandoned to the French. The coming of an inter-Allied commission, however, presented one last opportunity to achieve a settlement along the lines of his March memorandum, or, failing that, a settlement with a greatly moderated Zionist program. With that in mind, he forwarded to the Foreign Office a report by General Money, the chief administrator of Palestine, in which the general asserted that, since the Palestinian Arabs identified Great Britain with the Zionist program, they would prefer either a French or a U.S. mandate to a British one.[77] The Palestinians, he said, would resist Jewish immigration, however gradual, by "every means in their power including active hostilities." Money thought the Arabs would continue to oppose a British mandate so long as they continued to fear Zionism. He said:

> If a clear and unbiased expression of wishes is required and if a mandate for Great Britain is desired by His Majesty's Government, it will be necessary to make an authoritative announcement that the Zionist programme will not be enforced in opposition to the wishes of the majority. In conclusion, the idea that Great Britain is the main upholder of the Zionist programme will preclude any local request for a British mandate and no mandatory Power can carry through a Zionist programme except by force and in expressing opposition to the wishes of the large majority of the people of Palestine.

Clayton underlined Money's evaluation by telling the Foreign Office in the same dispatch that he considered the above an accurate reflection of the true situation. "Fear and distrust of Zionist aims grow daily," he said, "and no amount of persuasion or propaganda will dispel it." His definite conclusion, in short, was that a "British mandate for Palestine on the lines of the Zionist programme will mean the indefinite retention in the country of a military force considerably greater than that now in Palestine."

On the same day Clayton's cable arrived, Lloyd George suggested in Paris that the Allies temporarily redistribute their responsibilities for various parts of Turkish territory with the United States getting Constantinople and Armenia and France getting Syria, on the assumption that Britain would get Mesopotamia and Palestine. Wilson, however, did not know where he would find the necessary troops, and besides, he added, it was impossible for him to know whether or not the United States could take a mandate.[78] Lloyd George did not press the matter and the subject was dropped for the time being. However, the suggestion of moving toward a quick settlement of the Turkish situation, coming as it did on the same day as Clayton's cable, must have been more than a coincidence.

On 8 May, an even stronger reaction took place. The Zionists had been very unhappy from the first with the idea of an inter-Allied commission, since they were well aware of the anti-Zionist agitation in Palestine. But it was not until 8 May that Felix Frankfurter, a member of the American Zionist delegation in Paris, wrote an urgent letter to President Wilson from the headquarters of the Zionist Organization in Paris, informing him of Jewry's "deepest disquietude" over the commission's appointment and the consequent postponement of a peace settlement. Such a delay, Frankfurter wrote, was bound to intensify unrest and stimulate religious animosities. As it was, the English authorities were eager to have Weizmann and him go to Palestine to assure the population there of Jewish restraint, but he dared not leave Paris before a settlement was reached, preferably while Wilson was still in Paris to participate in the decision. He concluded by stressing the president's responsibility for the "peace of the world," which, Frankfurter wrote, depended on the "disposal before you return to America of the destiny of the people released from Turkish rule."[79]

Wilson addressed a reply to Frankfurter on 13 May, making a perfunctory acknowledgment of the letter and assuring Frankfurter of his profound appreciation of the whole matter. Frankfurter immediately wrote back in anguish, saying that Wilson's brief note had "occasioned almost despair to the Jewish representatives now assembled in Paris, who speak not only for the Jews of Europe but also for the American Jewish Congress, the democratic voice of three million American Jews." Having thus reminded Wilson of the magnitude of the American Jewish vote, Frankfurter wrote about the "uncertainty, indefinite delay, and seeming change of policy" which were producing a feeling of helplessness among the Jews. The Zionists were "bending every energy," he wrote, "to prevent the slow attrition of the spirit of such a people." This time he left no doubt in the president's mind about the Zionists' requirements!

> Therefore, you will forgive me for submitting to you the wisdom and justice of a reassuring word, written or spoken, even though it be repetitive—that you are purposing to have the Balfour Declaration written into the Treaty of Peace, and that you are aiming to see that declaration translated into action before you leave Paris.

Wilson's reply came with a faint air of surprise. He wrote that he had "never dreamed" he would have to give "renewed assurance of my adhesion to the Balfour Declaration," adding that he had yet to find anyone who seriously opposed its purpose. He mildly rebuked Frankfurter for reading discouragement into his letter, concluding that he saw no reason to be discouraged but rather "every reason to hope that satisfactory guarantees can be secured."[80]

On 19 May, three days after Wilson wrote to Frankfurter, Balfour replied to the two-week-old dispatch from Clayton which had stressed the need for "an authoritative announcement that the Zionist programme will not be enforced in opposition to the wishes of the majority." Balfour's message,[81] addressed to Curzon, was a decisive rejection of this advice to drop or restrict the Balfour Declaration. He said there could "of course be no question of making any such announcement as that suggested in . . . General Clayton's telegram," and he instructed Curzon to remind Clayton that the governments of the United States,[82] France, and Italy had all approved the Balfour Declaration. He continued, "General Clayton will doubtless have opportunities of emphasising the general unity of opinion among the Allies on this matter in responsible quarters in Palestine." In fact, he wrote, he had been advised by the director of military intelligence, General Thwaites, that it might be best to send to Palestine "a further adviser on Zionist matters to assist General Clayton . . . preferably some representative who has been in Paris during the last few months and understands the different currents of opinion here." Balfour was clearly telling Curzon that the latter did not understand the strength of pro-Zionist influence in Paris, if not among all the Allied powers, then at least among the U.S. and British delegations. His words may also be read as a veiled reference to his inside knowledge of Wilson's stance on Zionism, even though he was not officially presented with the Frankfurter-Wilson correspondence until 21 May. Frankfurter did not receive Wilson's official permission to use the correspondence until that day and Balfour had had to wait until then to inform Curzon of the exchange, but it was obvious that the correspondence had been initiated for Balfour's use and that Balfour was intimately acquainted with its purport and results even before official clearance was received.[83] Balfour then said that General Thwaites had proposed Colonel Meinertzhagen as the most suitable person to perform the duties of adviser on Zionist affairs. In view of Meinertzhagen's uninhibited lobbying for Zionism, this suggestion amounted to an announcement of loss of confidence in Clayton.

Balfour's cable signaled a significant change of policy, a new determination to back Zionism despite informed advice from the Middle East and from the rump Foreign Office in London. On 7 May, Balfour had cabled Curzon, for relay to Cairo, a dispatch enjoining the military authorities in Palestine to use caution in regard to political and economic favors to the Jews. At that time, it was still not certain that Britain would take the mandate or adopt the Zionist program, and therefore, it was

> essential . . . that as long as His Majesty's Government are in military occupation of the country, no policy should be adopted or step taken which would enable commercial interests, however reputable, and whether British or foreign, to establish themselves in Palestine or obtain

control over the land or the principal industries until the decision of the Conference enables His Majesty's Government to work out the full implication of their acceptance of a mandate for Palestine and of the policy of the national home for the Jews.

Then Balfour did a complete turnabout. On 5 July, after Wilson's letter to Frankfurter, Balfour told Curzon that the land registers, which OETA had closed in November, could be opened on a limited scale, "provided that, as far as possible, preferential consideration is given to Zionist interests."[84]

As for the explosive situation in Palestine itself, Balfour wanted Ormsby-Gore and Samuel to study Clayton's cable "with a view to ascertaining whether they have any further proposals to offer as to how the present hostility to Zionism in Palestine can best be allayed by the administrative authorities on the spot." In other words, not only were those administrative authorities out of favor, but Balfour was handing leadership and initiative over to the Zionists. No longer were the Zionists merely putting up proposals for review by a cautious Foreign Office; now their views as to policy, program, and execution were actually being solicited.

With policy on Palestine thus changing, it seemed clear that British enthusiasm for the inter-Allied commission, never great, would reach a new low. Lloyd George and Clemenceau had agreed in mid-May that Sir Henry Wilson and Andre Tardieu would draw up a map of occupation zones for Syria.[85] The British War Office was short of troops at the time, owing both to demobilization and to emergencies in Egypt and northwest India, and would have been happy to relinquish responsibility for part of Syria. The French, on the other hand, feared the findings of the inter-Allied commission's inquiry if they could not control Syria with French troops. When the map was brought in to the Council of Four meeting on 21 May, however, the British northern boundary had been drawn by Henry Wilson to include the Mosul-Haifa line and much of southern Lebanon, so that it passed only forty miles south of Damascus.[86] Clemenceau angrily accused the British of a breach of faith.[87]

After further discussion of possible breaches of faith, Clemenceau, who had never appointed French commissioners in the first place, said that his representatives were ready to go as soon "as the British troops in Syria had been replaced by French."[88] On 22 May, after Lloyd George had stoutly defended the line which would have given the British the Hauran and Tadmor (Palmyra), Clemenceau said that if Lloyd George insisted on leaving his troops there, then France would no longer cooperate with Britain in the Middle East. Lloyd

George saw that Clemenceau had been provoked far enough and assured him that if the French would send no commissioners, then he would not send his.[89] The American commissioners, who were on the point of departure,[90] would have to go alone, thus fatally weakening in advance any findings of theirs in the Middle East.

It may be going too far to suggest that the clash between Lloyd George and Clemenceau on 21–22 May was engineered by Lloyd George for the primary purpose of scuttling the inter-Allied commission. Lloyd George was well aware that the French did not view the commission as furthering their interests and hence would be very happy if they could find an excuse for stopping it. The British held a similar view of the commission, as witness the meeting of the British and French experts initiated by Wickham Steed in March, but wished to avoid the odium of breaking with the Americans over Wilson's pet idea. In addition, Lloyd George knew the French would refuse to accept the Hermon-Tadmor line,[91] and would strongly object to taking the pulse of the country while it was beating to a British occupation tune.

It is true that the British were anxious about the strong possibility of an Arab uprising should the French land troops in Syria. However, they knew they would have to give up Syria, at least most of it, to the French at some time in the near future, and whenever they did, the possibility of Arab-French hostilities would probably still exist. The fact is that after this clash in the council, events were left to drift during the summer until the British agreed in September to withdraw their troops and let the French replace them. Nevakivi has said that the prime minister in May had "obviously not made up his mind as to the best policy to be pursued over Syria."[92] It is, however, possible that Lloyd George, fearing the results of an Allied inquiry into the Middle East, deliberately manufactured the incident with Clemenceau or even stage-managed it with him in order to stop or discredit the commission. He could then wait a decent length of time before coming to an agreement with the French, hoping that the situation in the Middle East would in the meantime sort itself out. The idea that British policy, as determined by Lloyd George, was already set by the time of the 21 May debate in the Council of Four is supported by a letter from Hogarth to Clayton on 19 May.[93] Hogarth wrote that he was thinking of resigning and going back to Oxford, "sick at heart at all this fiasco and the melancholy consummation of four years' work." "To think," he said, "that we are to hand over Feisal and Syria to Senegalese troops, and take Palestine with our hands and feet tied!" He added that he would not "blame the Arabs of either land if they get out their rifles again." Curzon had come over to Paris to argue against the drift of British policy, but it was clear that he was losing. He and Curzon were doing what they could, Hogarth added, but no one could do "much in the teeth of ignorance, inertia and natural greed at the top. Curzon, who does know what he is talking about in this matter, has come over to fulminate, but he spoils his case by playing Jove too long and too loud."

For his part, Curzon played the incident down, claiming that it must have been based on a misunderstanding or misreport of what had acutally happened and that its only significance was to indicate the "passionate intensity with which France . . . means to adhere to her Syrian pretensions."[94] At any rate the Foreign Office did not see Clemenceau's outburst as affecting British policy; it was only an inexplicable display of Gallic temper.

On 31 May Lloyd George made a final attempt to get the whole commission going. He read to the Council of Four a cable from General Allenby, who described the situation as "extremely grave." If he could not tell Faysal that the commission was coming out to determine the future of the country, then the British could look for a rising of the bedouin east of the Jordan and in the Sinai which would endanger Palestine and Allenby's long lines of communication. Allenby also predicted serious trouble in Egypt and the Sudan, which he would be unable to handle with the troops at his disposal.[95] Clemenceau held firm. He would not send commissioners until French troops replaced the British in Syria.[96] Balfour immediately sent Allenby a telegram explaining the situation and authorizing him to tell the Americans, who were already en route, that the "British Government will give the fullest weight to the advice which the Council of the Principal Allied and Associated Powers will receive from the American Commissioners."[97] It was not long, however, before the British quietly eliminated the American commissioners from consideration entirely.

Further evidence that British policy on Syria may have been set in May behind President Wilson's back is contained in a cable sent by Clayton to Curzon from Cairo on 1 June. Picot, who was then head of the civil administration of OETA (West), had told Clayton that he knew from official French sources that Syria was being "divided without reference to Feisal and that the American Commission is only coming out to keep Faisal in the dark while partition of Syria is being arranged."[98] As Clayton warned, this was a "dangerous game to play," but if it was a game, it was one the British played successfully, at least for the moment.

Certainly if British policy was settled and if it entailed the disappointment of Faysal, then the question of whether Faysal and the Zionists would ever come to terms was immaterial. In this connection, it is interesting to note that Aharon Cohen, working mainly from documents in the Central Zionist Archives in Jerusalem and the Zionist Archives in London, has concluded that by mid-1919 the British had abandoned their interest in a Faysal-Zionist understanding.[99] Cohen goes on to blame British obstruction, as well as Zionist shortsightedness, for the Zionists' failure to reconcile their differences with the Arabs.[100] In view of later developments in British policy, Cohen is probably correct in his assessment of responsibility for this failure. But however much blame accrues to the British on this point, it is still true that the Zionists made remarkably few efforts to overcome British obstructionism. For instance, Cohen has also noted that the Central Zionist Archives contain no document that could enlighten us as to any direct political efforts by Jewish bodies toward cooperation with the Palestinian Arabs.[101]

On 7 June Clayton pressed both the War and Foreign Offices for permission to announce that "the Peace Conference and not only His Majesty's Government will attach fullest weight" to the advice of the King-Crane Commission. Unless they could assure the Arabs of this, he said, he considered it inadvisable to make any announcement at all.[102] Balfour replied on 16 June that since the French "presumably" would not go along with any such announcement, the most the British could do would be to inform the Allied powers that the British intended to "give fullest weight" to the report of the American commissioners.[103]

On 8 June Clayton reported that feeling in Syria and Palestine was running high. He warned that if the idea were to get abroad that the commission was not authoritative or was merely a matter of form, then there was "little doubt that a grave situation will arise."[104] Four days later he greeted the arriving American commissioners in Palestine and told them he was sorry they had not been given the "full powers" of the original commission.[105]

On 19 June Clayton acknowledged his receipt of Balfour's momentous dispatch of 19 May in which Balfour had announced a loss of confidence in his political officer. Clayton said he was glad to receive copies of correspondence with the French, Italian, and American governments on the subject of the Balfour Declaration which had "not hitherto been communicated to me." He said he had been aware that the governments concerned had some "general unity of opinion" on this matter, but that he was not sure the local French and Italian representatives had "always acted entirely in accordance with the spirit of the declarations made by their respective Governments." In fact, he continued:

> Unity of opinion among the Allied Governments on the subject of Palestine, however, is not a factor which tends to alleviate the dislike of non-Jewish Palestinians to the Zionist Policy. Indeed, it rather leads to further anxiety on their part to express clearly to the world their own point of view, in the fear that a decision will be forced upon them by the Peace Conference before they have had an opportunity of expressing their aspirations.[106]

Embarrassed by having been caught on the wrong side when policy was breaking, Clayton nevertheless stood by his analysis. But British policy on the Middle East had been more decisively influenced by events and views in Europe and the United States than it was by events in the now powerless Middle East itself.

On the same day, 19 June, Curzon sent Balfour the suggestions the government had asked from Samuel on the means the military administration in Palestine could use to allay hostility to Zionism.[107] After consulting Weizmann and Sokolow, Samuel had written condemning the military administration in Palestine for not having an attitude "fully in harmony with that of H.M. Government." He said that as a consequence of the authorities' lax conduct toward the Arabs, the Arabs had gotten the idea that the Balfour Declaration was not a settled line of British policy. He suggested that the government send definite instructions to the administration informing it that policy contemplated "the cession to Great Britain of the Mandate for Palestine" and that the mandate would carry the Balfour Declaration as well as adequate assurances for the Arabs. The local authorities were to impress upon Arab leaders the case closed, "chose jugée," of the British commitment and inform them that "continued agitation could only be to the detriment of the country and would certainly be without result." He also suggested that an officer personally in sympathy with Zionism be sent to Palestine to convey the government's views to the administration and to the Arabs more fully than could be done by correspondence.[108] On 1 July Balfour acknowledged receipt of Samuel's letter and suggested that the matter be discussed with Clayton at the first opportunity, since he was then on his way to England for leave.[109]

A week earlier, on 24 June, an important meeting had been held in Balfour's Paris apartment, bringing together Balfour, Lord Eustace Percy, and the American Zionists Brandeis and Frankfurter.[110]

Balfour emphasized the complexity of the Jewish question that was confronting the statesmen of Europe. Palestine was only a fragment, although an essential one, of the whole problem, which had been made more difficult by the "pressure on Jews in Eastern Europe" and by the "extraordinary phenomenon that Jews now are actually, to a large degree, leaders in such movements." In fact, Balfour said, he had heard from a reliable source that Lenin was a Jew. Clearly, Balfour's concerns regarding Zionism were Europe-centered. Eastern and Central Europe were generally disturbed, Bela Kun in power in Hungary, and the Bolsheviks presenting a powerful challenge to the counterrevolutionary statesmen meeting in Paris. In this context, Balfour once again perceived the actual facts of the case in Palestine as a secondary consideration.

Brandeis interrupted to correct Balfour: Lenin was an upper-class Russian on both sides. Brandeis then proceeded to give his own views on Zionism. He said he believed that "every Jew is potentially an intellectual and an idealist" and that the problem was "one of direction of those qualities." He had come upon Zionism by chance, he said, but had had the opportunity to observe that immigrant Russian Jews in the United States were able to find "constructive channels for expression and make positive contributions to civilization," and had no doubt that revolutionary Jews, through Zionism, could find the same channels and make the same contributions. Balfour agreed enthusiastically, adding significantly: "Of course, these are the reasons that make you and me such ardent Zionists."

Brandeis then outlined three essential conditions for the realization of the Zionist program. First, it must be agreed that Palestine was to be "the Jewish homeland and not merely that there be a Jewish homeland in Palestine." The Balfour Declaration represented a commitment to this, he said (without strict accuracy), and would be confirmed by the Peace Conference. Secondly, a Jewish Palestine must have "economic elbow room" to allow for a self-sufficient and healthy social life. He realized that the question of the northern boundary lay with Britain and France, but he "assumed that Great Britain was urging the northern boundary necessary for the control of the waters." Third, he urged that control of the land and resources go to the state and not to private hands in order to assure the future of a Jewish Palestine.

Balfour agreed with the conditions, but he wished to point out British difficulties in meeting them. After relating these at some length, he asked Brandeis how President Wilson reconciled the principle of self-determination with his support for Zionism. Brandeis replied that the "whole conception of Zionism as a Jewish homeland, was a definite building up for the future as a means of dealing with a world problem and not merely with the disposition of an existing community." Balfour was content with the answer and adjourned the meeting after making sure that Brandeis understood the problems faced by Britain in relation to Palestine.

Shortly after this meeting, in which Brandeis and Balfour seemed to agree so well, Samuel followed up his letter of 5 June by appearing at the Foreign Office on 2 July to complain further to Sir Ronald Graham about the military authorities in Palestine, who, he declared, were taking "every opportunity of injuring Zionist interests." Alluding to "forthcoming changes" in the personnel of the administration, he expressed the hope that the new men would possess a better understanding of the government's intentions. Weizmann also called upon Graham that afternoon to voice his "violent" objections to the British officers, who, he claimed, were "showing a marked hostility to the Jews and lost no opportunity of not only injuring their interests but of humiliating them." The Jews were in a worse position now than they had been under the Turks, Weizmann said, adding that Allenby was too busy and Clayton "showed no strength in handling the situation." Weizmann warned that when the Jews heard about the "true facts of the situation in Palestine," there would be a "violent outburst of feeling in Jewish circles and Jewish gratitude and friendship towards His Majesty's Government would be turned into bitterness and hostility." Knowing that the British were sensitive to American opinion, Weizmann said that Justice Brandeis, then on his way to Palestine, could not fail to discover the deplorable situation in Palestine and as a result Jewish-American opinion, then inclined toward Great Britain, would be drastically affected.[111] Weizmann's passionate feelings were sincerely, though single-mindedly, expressed both in this interview and later in his memoirs. As the Israeli writer and journalist, Amos Elon, has explained:

> The Zionists were fervently, and at great human sacrifice, pursuing a national and social renaissance in their ancient homeland. They were blind to the possibility that the Arabs of Palestine might entertain similar hopes for themselves.[112]

The British, on the other hand, could not afford to have a similar blind spot, since they were ministering to the needs of a non-Jewish majority whose rights they were duty-bound to protect and who feared the aggressive Zionists. It was simply beyond Weizmann to appreciate that he could be wrong. He later would ask why it was "an almost universal rule that such administrators as came out to Palestine favorably inclined turned against us in a few months?"[113] His only recourse was to fall back on European stereotypes and attribute these universal shifts in attitude either to anti-Semitism or to some other basic fault common to gentiles. [114] It never occurred to him to suspect that the Zionists were "reaping the harvest which they themselves sowed," as Curzon commented on Weizmann's complaints to the Foreign Office.[115]

When Clayton arrived in London on leave from his duties in the Middle East, he was quickly called in to meet with the Zionists to discuss the complaints that had been piling up for months. On 9 July a full-scale meeting was held in the offices of the Zionist Organization in London.[116] Weizmann, as chairman, outlined the various problems that had accumulated, such as immigration, land, concessions, loans, and official languages. In conclusion, he disclosed his knowledge that government policy was at the point of changing by saying that he expected that "some trouble might come after the policy of the British Government was declared, but he was sure it would not go to any considerable extent."

Clayton thanked Weizmann for his statement of Zionist difficulties, adding that, to be fair, he should point out that the authorities in Palestine were chosen not to carry out any particular policy but to maintain the country's security. Furthermore, he said, "in the absence of definite instructions from the Home Government, the Administration was, in his opinion, not justified in doing anything which could be construed as in some way forestalling the mandate." He conceded that some individuals might have appeared "to show lack of good will," which could be attributed to the fact that the best men were not available. The solution to the problem was to get a quick settlement of the disposition of former Turkish territories, and he was in agreement with prevailing Zionist opinion when he said he thought "that a clear statement of policy and the declaration of the fait accompli would probably be accepted peaceably by at least 75 per cent of the Arab population." In this way, he said, they could remove any grounds for the Palestinians thinking that policy could be reversed by means of violence. He had changed his mind since coming to Europe. Formerly he had believed that nothing should be done that could lose Palestine for Britain,

> but he thought now that if the decision had really been reached in principle and if a delay of four or five months must elapse before it was announced, definite instructions should be given, and certain lines of action should be indicated to the Administration in Palestine, along which they could proceed in preparing to carry the decision into effect.

Weizmann, after dealing with a few specific problems, courteously acknowledged that almost all the complaints had arisen from the administration's not having received clear instructions. But he also implied in a closing remark that the administration had known that it was running "counter to the policy of the Home Government."

This meeting could hardly have been in stronger contrast to the first meeting of Weizmann and Clayton in EEF headquarters in Palestine. Then Weizmann had been the suppliant, seeking to enlarge the meaning of the Balfour Declaration and lay the foundation for a Jewish national home. Clayton, at Allenby's side, had been the man in power, deciding what the Zionist Commission could and could not do. Now, not yet a year and a half later, Clayton had gone to Zionist headquarters in London, which was almost alien ground to him after so many years in the East, to try to explain to a group of critical Zionist leaders how their loss of faith in the British officials in Palestine had come about.

Clearly, Clayton did not relish the role he was having to play, although no document has come to light informing us of his private thoughts at the time. By 23 July both he and General Money had tendered their resignations from their political and administrative posts and the Zionists were pressing for those posts to be filled with "men who are in complete sympathy with" the Balfour Declaration.[117] Although Weizmann professed regret at the resignations, one Foreign Office official wrote that the Zionists were "triumphant about this, and Mr. Landmann could not conceal his satisfaction at General Clayton's departure."[118]

On 23 July Weizmann wrote to Balfour strongly endorsing the appointment of Colonel Meinertzhagen as Clayton's successor, since he had the "full confidence of the Zionist Organization and of the Jews in Palestine." He added his hope that when the top administrative posts had been filled, opportunity would be taken to change the men in subordinate positions also. "Changes in these offices are, I feel, almost as essential as the filling of the higher appointments with the right type of men.[119] Weizmann's presumption did not go unnoticed at the Foreign Office, where one official noted that the Jews were having things "too much their own way" and that it was "intolerable that Dr. Weizmann should be allowed to criticize the 'type of men' employed by" the government. [120]

Meanwhile the Zionists had been preparing the texts of proposals to be included in the draft mandate for Palestine. On 15 July they presented these to the British delegation in Paris,[121] and on 24 July Noel Baker, British secretary to the Commission on Mandates constituted by the peace conference, noted that in a "startling new development" Weizmann and Lord Robert Cecil had decided that the commission should draw up a draft and publish it at once.[122] This development took Balfour by surprise,[123] but he authorized discussions with the Zionist Organization so long as publication was not decided upon until Balfour had seen the draft.[124]

On 4 August, after the American commission had safely left Syria, the official stamp was affixed to the change of government policy which had led to the embarrassment and resignations of Generals Clayton and Money. The Foreign Office cabled Colonel French, the acting CPO, that British policy contemplated that Great Britain would receive the Palestine mandate and that its terms would follow the Balfour Declaration. Following closely the language of Samuel's letter of 5 June, the Foreign Office's instructions assured the Arabs that they would "not be despoiled of their land nor required to leave the country," nor would they be subjected to the rule of a minority, as this would not meet the Zionist program. The heads of administration and their local representatives were urged to impress upon Arab leaders that policy was firmly fixed and that "continued agitation would be useless and detrimental." Since it was assumed that the Palestinians' chief worry was economic and not political, they were to be told that Palestine's development "under the new regime may be expected to involve [a] large influx of money and all classes and races will benefit by its expenditure."[125] When Weizmann applied to the Foreign Office on 13 August for permission to publish the telegram, however, Balfour refused on the grounds that its publication would appear to "prejudge the question of the mandate" and would raise antagonism in the country.[126]

Although British policy on Zionism seemed settled, some officials still indulged in wishful thinking. On 6 August Robert Vansittart, at the time a member of the political section of the British peace delegation, asked if it was certain that Britain would accept the mandate if it was offered. He wrote that considerations were "beginning to emerge which might conceivably make it wiser for us, while supporting Zionism to the extent of our power, not to be the mandated power." Sir Eyre Crowe agreed and Balfour wrote that he too would agree with Vansittart "if only our own convenience is to be consulted." Personally he wanted "some one else to take the mandate," although he doubted that anyone would. These are very peculiar statements indeed. Balfour, although an "ardent Zionist," was not unaware of the problem of backing a pro-Zionist policy in a predominantly Arab country. Ruthless politician though he might be, he shrank from full acceptance of the consequences of Britain's imperial needs. Yet he was apparently able to comfort himself with the warmth of two considerations: one, that this was a burden of empire which must be borne in order to turn the Jews from revolution in Europe; and, two, that the powerful Americans, though not prepared to take the responsibility, had expressed themselves strongly in favor of Zionism. As casually tough a politician as was ever bred, Balfour would never have advocated a policy emanating from mere sentiment. He did not do so in 1919.[127]

On 30 July Balfour had explained to Meinertzhagen that the government was committed to Zionism but that he personally did not favor a British mandate which would be in charge of making it succeed. All development and industrial plans and financial assistance were to be "based on the principle that Zionists are the Most-favoured Nation in Palestine," he told him, adding that the preparatory work leading to the final settlement of the future of Palestine was to be based on the same principle. British policy had become muddled over Syria, Balfour said, admitting that he "perhaps was personally responsible for it." The British had not been honest with either French or Arabs, but now it was preferable to quarrel with the Arabs, if quarrel there must be. At the end of their interview, Balfour said that Meinertzhagen "had a very difficult task to perform in establishing Zionism in Palestine and in bringing about a workable state of affairs in Syria," and he promised him the confidence and support of the government.[128]

On 11 August Balfour developed some of the ideas he had discussed with Meinertzhagen in a remarkably frank memorandum.[129] After reviewing the history of British commitments in the Middle East, paying particular attention to the French point of view, he concluded that as it was impossible to fulfill all of them, the British would have to do the next best thing and come as close as possible to "the essential spirit of the various international pronouncements."

Palestine was a case in point. The contradictions there were "flagrant" because "we do not propose even to go through the form of consulting the wishes of the present inhabitants of the country." The U.S. commissioners were touring the area only as a matter of form; the powers were committed to Zionism.

> And Zionism, be it right or wrong, good or bad, is rooted in age-long traditions, in present needs, in future hopes, of far profounder import than the desires and prejudices of the 700,000 Arabs who now inhabit that ancient land.

In my opinion that is right. What I have never been able to understand is how it can be harmonised with the declaration, the Covenant, or the instructions to the Commission of Enquiry.

I do not think that Zionism will hurt the Arabs; but they will never say they want it. Whatever be the future of Palestine it is not now an 'independent nation', nor is it yet on the way to become one. Whatever deference should be paid to the views of those who live there, the Powers in their selection of a mandatory do not propose, as I understand the matter, to consult them. In short, so far as Palestine is concerned, the Powers have made no statement of fact which is not admittedly wrong, and no declaration of policy which, at least in the letter, they have not always intended to violate.

His solution was to accept the "fundamental conception underlying the Sykes-Picot Agreement": that the British should have a sphere centering in Mesopotamia, the French one in Syria, and the Jews a "home" in Palestine.

Balfour's memorandum was a landmark in the desultory summer of 1919, when no one seemed really to be in charge of British policy. Tiredness had become a major factor in policy-making. No new regime had come to power after the war was over. The "coupon" election of 1919 had simply confirmed that Britain's weary war leaders would lead the fight for peace. In August Curzon complained to his wife that Balfour was in Paris pursuing one policy while he was in London pursuing another. Balfour, he said, "wants to take a holiday and me to take his place. I have declined. No one knows what ought to be done, and meanwhile, of course, nothing is done, and we go on getting deeper and deeper into the mire. Oh! how I long to get away and have a rest."[130] One cause of Curzon's weariness was his despair over the government's Palestine policy. On 12 August he told C.P. Scott that the "worst of our recent commitments was Palestine." In the course of their conversation that afternoon, he showed, according to Scott, that he was "dead against the whole Zionist arrangement," saying that the Zionists "were very grasping and arrogant and even claimed to expropriate the Arabs though in numbers they were only as one to four."[131]

While Britain's Zionist policy was being confirmed and strengthened in Paris, Middle Eastern stability continued to deteriorate. Early in August Allenby reported to Churchill, then at the War Office, on Justice Brandeis's visit to Palestine. Brandeis, skeptical at first, had become convinced that the military administration was doing its best and that its difficulties had indeed been more numerous and serious than anticipated.[132] Brandeis had not only agreed that the British policy should be "one of great patience and moderation," but he had personally "administered rebuke" to Zionists in Palestine "who had caused trouble by immoderate conduct and self-advertisement." The Zionist Commission in 1919 had been a weak and tactless body. Helen Bentwich, the wife of the Jewish attorney general of the military administration, noted in January that Arab-Jewish antagonism was going very deep and that the "Jews are not as tactful as they might be in trying to make things easier." She longed to see "some really strong Jew here in charge of Zionist affairs." Her husband, a courageous and well-placed Zionist who served in Palestine until 1931, agreed with her analysis, adding that if a British officer tried to resist Jewish pressure, "he was regarded as an anti-Semite, or at least an enemy of Zionism."[133] This situation had certainly not improved by August when Allenby, again writing to Churchill, blamed the Zionist Commission for weakening its own authority by its inability to govern the "unruly spirits of the community" and by making promises of concessions they were powerless to implement. As for the widespread charges of anti-Semitism, he had investigated them and both he and Brandeis had concluded that the charges were unfounded. There had been misunderstandings, Allenby conceded, but the Zionist Commission had often referred its complaints directly to its headquarters in Europe rather than submitting them to the chief administrator. In such a case, Allenby said, relations were bound to be difficult.[134] In late August Colonel French, acting CPO, also observed to the Foreign Office that there was a tendency among leading Zionists to "complain of what the administration had not done for them and to ignore both what has been done and the practical difficulties of the present and the future."[135]

Thus during 1919, while the ablest Zionist leaders were in Europe securing recognition of their program, antagonism built up between the Jews and the administration on the one hand and the Jews and the Arabs on the other. In August Major J.N. Camp, assistant political officer in Jerusalem, turned in a long secret report on the various organizations being formed by Palestinian Arabs to obstruct the carrying out of a Zionist policy. He concluded that nearly all important Muslims and Christians were bitterly anti-Zionist. The Faysal-Weizmann agreement was "not worth the paper it is written on or the energy wasted in the conversation to make it," he said. Faysal was not a Palestinian representative and could not be relied on to make any sort of binding agreement. Only force would see a Zionist policy through. Major Camp's report is interesting, not only because it gives an accurate picture of the situation in Palestine, but also because it reveals an underlying attitude of sympathy for the Arabs who, through no fault of their own, were being done a gross injustice.[136]

On 16 August, General Money's successor as chief administrator of Palestine, General Sir Harry D. Watson, wrote a secret report to the CPO and the chief of the General Staff in which he clearly indicated that merely changing one chief administrator for another was not going to alter the facts obtaining in the country.[137] Watson said he had taken over his position with an open mind regarding Zionism and that he was still in sympathy with its aim for a national home "as long as it is not carried out at the expense of the rightful inhabitants and owners of the land." The situation he found there, he maintained, was serious. The Palestinian Arabs had developed an antagonism motivated by nationalism, not by religion, a deeply rooted feeling that was "fast leading to hatred of the British." If the Zionist program were "forced upon them," the result would be "an outbreak of a very serious character necessitating the employment of a much larger number of troops than [are] at present located in the territory." He concurred with Major Camp's report and urged for "the sake of Zionism" that Zionist "activity be greatly curtailed, and that the work of the establishment of the Jews in Palestine be done very very slowly and carefully." The role of the administration would have to be one of protecting the Palestinians "against the alien coming to their country," and he advocated that the government announce that it would protect all class and religious interests most carefully. He declared emphatically that if a moderate program were exceeded, Britain would not only have to keep a large force in Palestine, but would "lose the lives of many of her sons in a war which will be fought, against the principles of the League of Nations, in forcing upon a small country a population of aliens."

General Watson's courageous and thoughtful report failed to have any effect on the Foreign Office. However, it probably did have something to do with helping to send him the way of his predecessor. In November Watson was replaced by General Sir Louis J. Bols, Allenby's chief of staff, the last of the four generals who headed the military administration of Palestine. Many Zionists, including the fanatical Meinertzhagen, have charged these four men and their subordinates with the responsibility for poisoning the relations of the Arab and Jewish communities in Palestine. Some of them were indeed biased against the Zionists, but the allegation was greatly exaggerated. Christopher Sykes, one of the most evenhanded historians of the British mandatory period, has candidly pointed out that it could be said "with a good degree of certitude that the principal aim of this regime, which it usually carried out to the best of its ability, was impartiality. If it had an ideal, it was strict fairness on the British model."[138]

In September the British, after much discussion and debate, finally produced an aide-memoire, much along the lines of Balfour's 11 August memorandum, to be handled to Clemenceau.[139] Churchill, at the War Office, was being pressed hard to meet a demobilization schedule and also fill requirements for troops. The huge occupation expenses could no longer be tolerated. Therefore, the British announced that they were withdrawing their troops from Syria and Cilicia and turning control over to the French west of the Sykes-Picot line and to the Arabs east of the line of Damascas, Homs, Hama, and Aleppo. In appearance the British had discharged their responsibilities to the Arabs but in reality they had left the young Syrian goverment at the mercy of the French. The British were withdrawing to Palestine, "defined in accordance with its ancient boundaries to Dan to Beersheba," and Mesopotamia. If the French agreed, as they did, there would remain only the question of boundaries.

Meanwhile the American section of the inter-Allied commission had dropped from view. Its final report, which recommend a single mandate for a united Syria and a greatly reduced Zionist program, was handed in to the White House already a dead letter on 27 September 1919.[140] The Americans quietly forgot it and it remained unpublished until December 1922. By arguing for the right of the Arabs to self-determination and their ability to handle it and by urging that the Zionist program be considerably modified, King and Crane had presented a report that was long on courage, sincerity, and historical accuracy, but short on political realism.[141] As the historian of the commission has justly pointed out:

> Developments within Palestine since 1919 would seem, in part at least, to justify the recommendations of the Commission, since Palestine became a battleground among the forces of Zionism and Arab nationalism and British imperialism, centering around the control of the Suez Canal and the eastern Mediterranean sea.[142]

Unfortunately, well-informed and predictably dependable reports have never been prized in regard to Palestine. The non-Jewish people of Palestine were ignored in 1919, and they continued to be ignored for the next fifty years.

1919 was in many ways decisive. Syria was turned over to the French, Lawrence discredited, and Faysal set on the road to disaster in Syria. The Americans, who had arrived with abundant power and hopeful plans, departed with tarnished ideals and a discredited president. Plans for an American mandate over Armenia, Constantinople, or Palestine were swiftly forgotten as it became clear that the American people did not wish to tie their hands with overseas responsibilities. The American commission of inquiry, which had caused so much turmoil in Paris and raised so many hopes in the Middle East, had been shunted aside even before it gave its report. The Zionists were transformed from a body almost totally under British protection to an agressively independent movement with broad international recognition and strong American support. Their leadership no longer went cap in hand to British politicians, but waited in its own headquarters to communicate grievances and formulate policy. The British, at the height of their power a year earlier, had been rolled back from the foothills of the Taurus by economic necessity, political unrest within the empire, and the ambition of their ally and ancient enemy. Saddled with the execution of a policy in Palestine that no one aside from fanatics was enthusiastic about, the British would continue to look for a way out but fail to find it until 1947 when the Americans finally made it impossible for them to stay.

The difference between British policy in Palestine in January and in September was vast. The division of the British Foreign Office and Lloyd George's deplorable habit of acting independently meant that the fatigued decision-makers in Paris did not always have access to the best-informed advice available, even if they had been inclined to take it. During this time the Paris branch of the Foreign Office seemed to be unduly influenced by revolutionary events taking place in Eastern and Central Europe, rather than reflecting on the interests of Britain and the empire. Mark Sykes's death was inopportune. He was the one British official who had followed Middle East policy at the highest levels throughout the war. His counterpart in the Middle East, General Gilbert Clayton, who had been the highest and most knowledgeable British official there throughout the war, was soon afterward embarrassed and unseated. The replacement of Sykes as adviser to the British peace delegation in Paris, by Meinertzhagen, who had just been converted to Zionism, was more than unfortunate for the Palestinian Arabs.

Throughout the peace conference the Zionists made steady progress. When the conference opened, they had the Faysal-Weizmann agreement. Both in the agreement and at the conference Faysal recognized the legitimacy of their aspirations. The American Zionists gave the Zionist Organization a badly needed sense of independence which it did not fail to exploit. Wilson's proposal for an inter-Allied commission, although feared by the Zionists, proved to be the catalyst precipitating a reaction in the Middle East that spread to Paris and eventually forced the British to change their Palestinian policy. Later, as the Americans faded from the Middle East picture, Britain was left with a policy which was not in its own interest[143] but to which it was committed and from which it could not back away without a strong reason.

Far from being settled on its merits or for reasons rooted in the Middle East, the Eastern Question was being settled in accordance with European and American political interests that lay outside the area. The map of the dying Ottoman Empire was redrawn in London, Paris, and Washington with only slight reference to events taking place in the East. The same arrogance of power that was to instruct the Germans that they had the choice only of accepting or rejecting a treaty was to divide the Ottoman Empire in cynical violation of the West's own professed ideals. National interest was sometimes forgotten in the pursuit of sentiment. Lloyd George, an anti-Turk Liberal who was fascinated by the Greek prime minister, Venizelos, unleashed the Greeks in an invasion of Turkey, a move he may have regretted in September and October 1922.[144] And Balfour allowed his growing enthusiasm for Zionism and the prospect of what it could do for millions of potential European revolutionaries, to sway him toward believing that European Jewish aspirations were worth more than "the desires and prejudices of the 700,000 Arabs" who inhabited Palestine. Through inattention, fatigue, sentiment, and fear of revolution, the Western powers had not solved the Eastern Question. They had only altered it.

9

PALESTINE AFTER VERSAILLES

From 1919 to 1925, the British government continued to support, more or less strongly, the policy set forth by Balfour in May 1919 and by the Foreign Office instructions of that August. By 1925, largely owing to the moderating efforts of Herbert Samuel, who was knighted preparatory to his being appointed high commissioner of Palestine, the policy had succeeded so well that a non-Jew could take over from Samuel without arousing Jewish protest and he could write in his *Memoirs* that the second half of his term had been "a time of steady progress and comparative calm." But even Samuel recognized that the quiet was merely on the surface and that the "underlying political issue was unsolved."[1] This was a period of incubation, during which the final convulsive acts of the Ottoman Empire and the conflicting desires of Western imperialists delayed the legal snuffing-out of both empire and Eastern Question. In this period the "national home" settled itself down to a season of hardy growth and consolidation that would earn it a full share of the Question's dubious inheritance.

When Meinertzhagen arrived in Palestine in September 1919 as the symbol of the new policy, he found the situation there much as it had been described by his predecessor. By mid-September he had wired to London for Weizmann to come out to Palestine as head of the Zionist Commission.[2] He hoped Weizmann could put a stop to the "unfortuante conduct" among Palestinian Jewry that was "gradually discrediting Zionism." He was also reporting to Curzon that the people of Palestine were not yet ready to be told about the Allied policy of establishing Zionism in their country, but that if growth were "slow and methodical," then success was assured.[3]

151

In December Lord Allenby, still commander-in-chief of the EEF and high commissioner of Egypt since March 1919, invited Samuel to visit Palestine and advise him on future policy in regard to finance and administration.[4] With the Foreign Office's concurrence, Samuel arrived in Palestine at the end of January 1920, by which time the situation there had calmed considerably. Meinertzhagen reported that Weizmann had been in touch with Arab notables as well as with Jewish extremists and had also established a cordial relationship with the administration.[5]

Although both Allenby and Bols appreciated the assistance Weizmann gave them, the Palestinians still were massively rejecting Zionism. In Damascus in February, the Palestine Congress, a group of self-appointed representatives, passed a series of resolutions proclaiming Palestine's inseparable unity with Syria and opposition to Zionist immigration.[6]

After an extensive and intensive tour of Palestine, Samuel left the Middle East on 31 March and soon reported fully to Curzon, who had become foreign secretary in Balfour's place in October 1919. Samuel played down the Zionist agitation, attributing it to exaggerated fears on the part of the Arabs and some officials. He felt that the administrators, who were loyal to government policy though many lacked conviction as to its wisdom, were unduly apprehensive about anti-Zionist manifestations.[7]

Not long after Samuel's departure, however, on Easter Sunday in April 1920, rioting broke out for the first time between Arabs and Jews in Jerusalem. A number on both sides were killed and several hundred were wounded. The military commission of inquiry called forth by Bols blamed Arab disappointment over the non-fulfillment of wartime promises, Arab fears of being denied the right of self-determination, and the "aggravation of these sentiments" by propaganda from Syria and the Zionists.[8] Meinertzhagen, on the other hand, accused Colonel Waters-Taylor, Bols's chief staff officer, and the recently promoted General Storrs of deliberately fomenting the riot "to impress on the administration the unpopularity of the Zionist policy."[9] The inquiry and its findings were kept secret, but Meinertzhagen made his indictment known to the government, and the military administration became "hopelessly compromised"[10] and therefore expendable in the eyes of its London chiefs.

Shortly thereafter, on 25 April 1920, the Supreme Council, then sitting at San Remo, despaired of ending the Eastern Question with a Turkish treaty. It formally, and some said illegally, gave Britain the mandate for Palestine.[11] Although Lloyd George had probably de-

:ided already to end the military administration, since he had invited
Samuel to San Remo to present the Zionist case,[12] Meinertzhagen's
accusations and a proposal by Bols to abolish the Zionist Commission[13] undoubtedly strengthened his hand. On 26 April Samuel wrote
:o Lloyd George accepting the proffered office of high Commissioner.[14] And on 29 April London announced that a civil administra-
:ion would soon take over in Palestine from the military.[15]

In May Curzon asked Samuel to reconsider because Allenby
thought Samuel's appointment might be the signal for an outbreak
of serious disorders, but Samuel held firm. He wrote to Curzon on
14 May that he had strong Jewish support as well as the support of
two influential British officials in Egypt who were intimately acquainted with Palestinian affairs, namely Generals Deedes and Clayton, and that he was willing to take the risk, which he considered
small. Lloyd George agreed that Samuel should go out, and 1 July
was set as the date for the civil administration to begin.[16]

The acceptance of the mandate and the initiation of civil government were truly decisive moves. Curzon reminded Lloyd George in
October 1920 that the inclusion of the Balfour Declaration in the
Treaty of San Remo was "the Magna Charta of the Zionists."[17] And
Barbara Tuchman years later, in a book which strained to establish
the earliest possible connections between Britain and Palestine, wrote
that it had indeed been the mandate and not the Balfour Declaration
which had given "a footing in public law to the restoration of Israel
in Palestine." She correctly noted that the declaration had been
"simply a statement of policy that any subsequent government could
have ignored, allowed to lapse, or even repudiated."[18]

On 30 June, as Samuel was arriving in Palestine, a revolt was under
way in Iraq which seriously weakened Britain's claim to a mandate
which supposedly rested on the consent of the governed. The stern
measures needed to put down the rebellion not only embarrassed the
British but encouraged the French to move against Faysal's government, which on 7 March had declared the independence and integrity
of Syria under Faysal.[19] On 24 July, after a clash between French and
Arab troops, the Syrian government was forced to evacuate Damascus. Storrs and Samuel went to meet Faysal with an honor guard as
he passed through Palestine en route to Alexandria. The dejected
Faysal was, however, not recognized by the Egyptian sultanate. There
was no honor guard at the Egyptian border "and at Qantara station
he awaited his train sitting on his luggage."[20]

While on his way through Palestine, Faysal met with Dr. Eder, then
chairman of the Zionist Commission. Faysal asked for help from the

Zionists to regain Syria, but Eder accused him of having been anti-Zionist in Damascus and explained that the Jews had to deal with the realities of politics, which in this case included Faysal's clash with France. Under the circumstances, Eder said, the Zionists could not counter the French for his sake. Eder asked Faysal, however, to recognize the Zionists in Palestine, accept the loss of Palestine and Syria, and use his influence to restrain anti-Zionist propaganda among Palestinian Arabs. This unrealistic attempt at bargaining was the last of the Zionist leadership's contacts with Faysal. Indeed, as Cohen has written, it was the end of the Zionist "political initiative towards a Jewish-Arab settlement."[21]

In contrast to Faysal's humiliation and temporary exile, Samuel took over the administration of Palestine with Wyndham Deedes, a strong pro-Zionist, as his civil secretary (later chief secretary). Zionists such as Norman Bentwich and Albert Hyamson held the important and sensitive posts of legal secretary (later attorney general) and head of immigration. On 7 July Samuel spoke to assemblies of notables of Jerusalem and Haifa, promising "absolute impartiality" of administration and assuring them that the "gradual establishment in Palestine of a National Home for the Jewish people" would in no way affect their "civil or religious rights or diminish the prosperity of the general population of Palestine."[22] He also announced that he would soon appoint an advisory council which would have a majority of government officials but would also have ten unofficial members representing Palestine's population. By September Palestine appeared to be quite tranquil and in October Samuel convened the first meeting of his advisory council, calling it a "first step in the development of self-governing institutions."[23]

Events in Transjordan, however, were at this time drawing increasing attention from the Palestine government. An imprecisely demarcated zone of movement between Syria and the Arabian Peninsula, Transjordan worried the Foreign Office because unrest there could cause the French to try to expand from the Hauran southward toward the Hijaz.[24] Since the government refused to occupy the area with British troops despite an oblique appeal by Samuel to the king, a political settlement would have to be found.[25] Late in the year the Amir Abdullah, a more astute brother of Faysal, made no secret of his preparations to advance into Transjordan from the northern Hijaz in order to restore Faysal to his Syrian kingdom. Apart from using Faysal, who was in London at the time, to restrain his brother, the government, in Sir Alec Kirkbride's words, "pursued a policy of masterful inaction.[26]

Meanwhile another version of the same policy was being followed in Palestine. Although the Palestinian Arabs were coming to appreciate Sir Herbert Samuel's exceptional personal integrity, they still had grievances. On 18 December, at the conclusion of the third Palestinian Arab Congress meeting at Haifa, Musa Kazim al-Husayni, president of the congress, presented to Samuel a memorandum appealing "to Great Britain for the justice of immediately proceeding to form a native Government to be responsible towards a Legislative Assembly representative of, and elected by, the Arab-speaking population living in Palestine up to the beginning of the war." On 21 December Wyndham Deedes arrogantly dismissed the memorandum, denying that the congress had been representative of the population.[27]

Early in 1921, in view of widespread trouble in the British Middle East, Churchill moved from the War Office to the Colonial Office, where a Middle East Department was being put together. Sir John Shuckburgh, a longtime India Office official, headed the department, which included T.E. Lawrence as Arab adviser, Hubert Young as second-in-command, and Meinertzhagen as military adviser. In March Churchill convened in Cairo a conference of high British officials involved in Middle Eastern politics. With the Arab territories at last unified under the Colonial Office and for once utilizing the experience of officials in the Middle East, a veritable "galaxy of talent," the conference was able to lay foundations of policy for the following twenty years.[28] By using the ideas of Sir Hugh Trenchard, chief of the Air Staff, and T.E. Lawrence on the use of air power to control the Middle East, and by arranging to put Faysal on the Iraqi throne, the British government managed to reduce its military expenditure and, in Lawrence's opinion, wipe out its wartime obligations to the Arabs.[29] Part of the settlement involved recognizing the establishment of Abdullah as the ruler of Transjordan in return for his promise to let the French alone and keep the bedouin from raiding Palestine. Not until the following year, however, did the government initiate negotiations to formalize Abdullah's fait accompli.[30]

While in Jerusalem in April to deal with Abdullah, Churchill rejected the demands of a deputation of the executive committee of the Haifa congress. Specifically, he refused to repudiate the Balfour Declaration or restrict immigration, adding that Arab fears were unfounded and that Zionist success would make everyone in Palestine prosperous.[31]

Churchill's hard-line approach disappointed and frustrated the Arabs and strengthened Jewish inflexibility toward them. In May, shortly after Samuel had intervened to secure the appointment of Amin al-Husayni as mufti of Jerusalem to replace Kamal al-Husayni, who had died in March,[32] a Jewish labor dispute between Bolsheviks and socialists escalated into a Jewish-Arab riot which lasted for days. It was a bloody affair and was put down only with difficulty. For the first time Samuel was shaken. He directed a commission of inquiry led by the chief justice, Sir Thomas Haycraft, to report on the causes of the disturbance.

In the meantime, Captain C.D. Brunton of General Staff Intelligence investigated and on 13 May reported on the origins of the fighting. He blamed the British government's Zionist policy since 1917 for building Arab resentment and Churchill's treatment of Arab demands, "like those of a negligible opposition to be put off by a few political phrases and treated like bad children," for setting the political scene for violence. He denied that the Arab attack had been premeditated and pointed out that the Arabs were armed mainly with sticks, while the Jews had had revolvers. The Zionists, he said, "above all would like to prove that the attack was not the outcome of the bitter antagonism which by their own methods they have excited in the hearts of the Arabs."[33]

Samuel, an honest, dedicated, and well-meaning man (and by his own estimate) "the last man to take a hand in any policy of oppression,"[34] then thoroughly alienated Zionist leaders by a statement given on 3 June in which he promised that Great Britain would never impose upon the people of Palestine "a policy which that people had reason to think was contrary to their religious, political, and their economic interests." The Zionists were stunned when he redefined the Balfour Declaration as meaning

> that the Jews, a people who are scattered throughout the world, but whose hearts are always turned to Palestine, should be enabled to found here their home, and that some among them, within the limits which are fixed by the numbers and interests of the present population, should come to Palestine in order to help by their resources and efforts to develop the country to the advantage of all its inhabitants.[35]

Weizmann in particular was infuriated by Samuel's "negation of the Balfour Declaration."[36] He and other Zionist leaders decided, however, not to attack Samuel publicly but to circumvent his position by dealing with government leaders in London.[37]

On 14 June, speaking to the House of Commons, Churchill dismissed Arab grievances again as owing to the excitable nerves of a people who really had nothing to be frightened about. In the ensuing debate, it became apparent that all parties were committed to the Balfour Declaration. Christopher Sykes has maintained that this consensus presented the government with an opportunity, which was "not to come again," to issue another official declaration which would clarify all the ambiguities of the original one. That the opportunity was not taken, he thought, was due to "that arrogant British mood of carelessness, that over-confident conviction," epitomized by Balfour in his old age, that "Britain and her Empire had nothing much to be alarmed about in a problem involving small populations in a small area."[38] It is more likely that the party in power would consider such an obvious consensus as an invitation to continue with its present policy, in order to keep the Middle East from becoming a matter for party or parliamentary debate, rather than viewing the consensus as an opportunity for a more precise definition of that policy. In any case, the opportunity, if there was one, was not taken.

On 22 July Lloyd George and Balfour met somewhat lightheartedly with Weizmann and Churchill to discuss measures to be taken in view of the imminent arrival of the Palestinian Arab delegation which had left Palestine for London on 19 July. The three officials agreed, when pressed by Weizmann, that they had conferred representative government on Mesopotamia and Transjordan only because they had had to, and Lloyd George told Churchill that he must not give this type of government to Palestine. Weizmann was still dissatisfied. He said he regarded the "Arabs as political blackmailers and could only talk with them when he knew the position of the British Government." Lloyd George then said, "Frankly speaking, you want to know whether we are going to keep our pledges?" Weizmann answered affirmatively and Balfour nodded. "You must do a lot of propaganda," Lloyd George said. "Samuel is rather weak."

Not content with undermining one of his own officials, the prime minister later suggested that the Zionists set aside some of the money they were spending in Palestine "for the purpose of bribing the Arabs." Weizmann, to his credit, rejected the idea as being neither moral nor rational. He added that it was the British presence in Palestine that made "it difficult to enter into intimate relations with the Arabs," implying that the British should shoulder the responsibility for correcting the situation.[39]

On 11 August Churchill presented to the Cabinet a memorandum calling for the adoption of a series of measures designed to secure the success of the government's Zionist policy. At the same time he advocated as a sop to the Arabs the conversion of the advisory council into an elective body which should be so constructed that it could not obstruct government policy, while otherwise remaining free "to express . . . legitimate views on all proposals for the economic development of the country."[40]

But Churchill was not willing to act energetically. He wanted the Zionists to come to a friendly understanding with the Arabs, but the Palestinian delegation's intransigence and Weizmann's ill-concealed contempt for the Arabs made that impossible. Meinertzhagen was disgusted with Churchill. "Winston does not care two pins," he said, "and he does not want to be bothered about it. He is reconciled to a policy of drift. He is too wrapped up in Home Politics."[41]

In October, the Haycraft Commission submitted its report on the May riot in Palestine. It enumerated the principal Arab grievances and concluded that the fundamental cause of the May disturbances was "a feeling among the Arabs of discontent with, and hostility to, the Jews, due to political and economic causes, and connected with Jewish immigration, and with their conception of Zionist policy as derived from Jewish exponents."[42] The commission reported, for instance, that Dr. Eder had said that only the Jews should be allowed to bear arms and that "there can be only one National Home in Palestine, and that a Jewish one, and no equality in the partnership between Jews and Arabs, but a Jewish preponderance as soon as the numbers of the race are sufficiently increased."[43]

The Russian Zionist Asher Ginsberg, a prominent thinker and writer better known as Achad Ha-Am (one of the people), was also highly critical of this type of statement. In June 1920 he blamed Zionist exaggeration for arousing "friction and bitterness on both sides." He maintained that the Jews had learned nothing from experience. Shortly after San Remo, he said, "we began once more to blow the Messianic trumpet, to announce the 'redemption' and so forth." Philip Graves, an English author and journalist who had worked with Clayton during the war, commented with approval on Ginsberg's remarks, saying that it was "this unreflecting 'Messianism' revealing itself in wild and sometimes provocative words that has been the principal cause of Arab anti-Zionism."[44]

In August the Palestinian Arab delegation, appointed by the Fourth Palestine Arab Congress on 29 May 1921, arrived in London. Little came of its meetings with Churchill and Balfour despite Samuel's warnings of the consequences of a failure to reach accommodation.[45] In February 1922, Churchill proposed to both Jews and Arabs an elective legislative council that would consist of nine Muslim Arabs, three Christian Arabs, and three Jewish and eleven official representatives (who would be appointed).[46] Since it was obvious that the government was not offering any real legislative power and that its policy had not appreciably changed, the Arabs turned the proposal down. It might have been cleverer of them to accept this halfway measure and later try to modify it to their benefit, as was accepted Zionist procedure. But they were politically naive (Weizmann called them "fifth-rate people")[47] and possibly the recipients of bad advice from an anti-Zionist group within the Conservative party.[48]

At any rate, Samuel came to London in May to press upon the government what he regarded "as an imperative need—that their intentions should be clarified." Churchill and the Cabinet agreed, Samuel said, and in June 1922 the government issued a white paper, usually called the Churchill White Paper, in which an attempt was made for the first time to explain publicly and definitively the government's policy on Palestine.

Churchill tried to calm the fears of both sides. He assured the Jews that the policy of the Balfour Declaration had been affirmed more than once and was "not susceptible of change." On the other hand, Arab apprehensions, based on certain unauthorized statements "to the effect that the purpose in view is to create a wholly Jewish Palestine," had no foundation in government policy. Churchill continued:

> When it is asked what is meant by the development of the Jewish National Home in Palestine, it may be answered that it is not the imposition of a Jewish nationality upon the inhabitants of Palestine as a whole, but the further development of the existing Jewish community, with the assistance of Jews in other parts of the world, in order that it may become a centre in which the Jewish people as a whole may take, on grounds of religion and race, an interest and a pride. But in order that this community should have the best prospect of free development and provide a full opportunity for the Jewish people to display its capacities, it is essential that it should know that it is in Palestine as of right and not on sufferance. That is the reason why it is necessary that the existence of a Jewish National Home in Palestine should be internationally guaranteed, and that it should be formally recognized to rest upon ancient historic connection.[49]

As for the important question of immigration, the principle was invented that immigration would be limited by the economic capacity of the land to absorb new immigrants. Finally, Churchill carried on at some length about the proposed legislative council, which would bring about self-government by "gradual stages." According to Sykes, the above redefinition of the Balfour Declaration had been drafted by Samuel and there were many Zionists who later regarded him as a "renegade for having done so, for having conceded so much to Arab nationalism, to the enemy whom they could not acknowledge as one."[50]

Weizmann and other Zionist leaders were disappointed by what they considered this "serious whittling down of the Balfour Declaration."[51] In their view, it was futile to try to placate the opponents of Zionism, since, in Weizmann's words, "their objection to the Jews is that the Jews exist, and in this particular case, that they desire to exist in Palestine." It was true that the maximum demands of the Zionists were diminished by the white paper, but it is entirely untrue that the new declaration of government policy in any way reduced governmental commitment to Zionism. Rather, Churchill's pronouncement, by defining more surely the government's intentions, tied the government more closely to the task of assuring Zionist success.

For the first time, then, the government had had to deal with a delegation representing Palestinian interests, and for the first time Palestinian considerations had made an impact on the formulation of British policy. The result was a compromise, carrying the two clauses of the Balfour Declaration forward a step. The ambiguity of the original statement and the subsequent British reluctance to elaborate on that promise had encouraged the Zionists in the hope that their demands would be met, but each step taken since 1917—the administrative instructions of August 1919, the San Remo Conference and adoption of the mandate in 1920, and the white paper of 1922—had confirmed in increasingly definite terms the essential commitment of the British government to Zionism. The development of policy from the vague political promise of 1917 to the legal commitments of the mandate and the white paper meant a hardening, an institutionalizing of the government's will to carry Zionism through to success, though not necessarily to success as defined by the wishes of the more extreme Zionists.

Since the British government was making it clear that confirmation of the mandate was conditional upon Zionist acceptance of the terms on the white paper, Zionist leaders had little choice but to announce their agreement with the government. Most of them did so with qualms, but Vladimir Jabotinsky, the fierce Zionist extremist, nervously approached by Weizmann, merely remarked that it "would still afford us a framework for building up a Jewish majority in Palestine, and for the eventual emergence of a Jewish State."[52]

On 21 June, following the publication of the white paper, a motion in the House of Lords to repeal the Balfour Declaration passed by a large majority. However, in the House of Commons on 4 July, in a vote on the Palestine mandate which Churchill had made a vote of confidence, the government won by the overwhelming majority of 292 to 35, thus reversing the "few foolish lords."[53] Churchill immediately informed Samuel of the vote, adding that the policy would "therefore be pursued vigorously, as it is clear that the country supports his Majesty's Government in their Palestine policy."[54]

With this apparent settling of the government's policy, the stage was set for the League of Nations Council to vote on the mandate. After a last flurry of propaganda by the Zionists, directed especially toward Spain and Brazil, the League's approval was gained on 24 July 1922, thus finally formalizing Britain's rule in Palestine.[55]

Earlier in the year, Deedes had let Samuel know that he wished to resign as chief secretary to the government of Palestine in order to return to England and take up social work in East London. Samuel persuaded him to stay another year while he looked for a successor.[56] In May Samuel had written to Clayton, "much the best man in view,"[57] inviting him to take up Deedes's post, but Clayton, who had been knighted in 1919, replied on 5 June 1922 with a polite rejection. However, immediately after the publication of the Churchill White Paper, Clayton wrote to Samuel again, saying that in light of this fresh statement of policy, "the situation as regards myself has altered considerably, as I must confess that the former vagueness in regard to the policy of H.M.G. greatly influenced me in framing my reply to your suggestion." He explained that he had been "apprehensive of possible personal embarrassment in view of my intimate political connection with Palestine and with the Arabs during the war and during the earlier phases of the Military Administration," but that now with the enunciation of a definite policy, he felt he could accept a renewed offer gratefully.[58]

Churchill was delighted that Clayton had changed his mind and Hubert Young minuted that it was excellent news. "Nothing could be better for the prospect of success in Palestine," Young wrote," than that Sir Gilbert Clayton should accept the post of Chief Secretary. He is universally beloved of the Arabs and his appointment will do more than anything to reassure them."[59]

Much had happened to Clayton in the years he had been away from Palestine. Back in 1919, Allenby had selected him for the position of adviser to the Egyptian Ministry of the Interior, where his mission had been to establish peace in Egypt and to restore confidence and good relations between Egypt and Great Britain. His views had changed considerably from those he had expressed in June of

1917, when he had argued for the annexation of Egypt at whatever cost to that country. According to Gertrude Bell, who talked with him in Cairo in September 1919, he agreed in the main with the arguments of the Egyptian nationalists. British objectives could be met, he said, by guarding "imperial necessities in Egypt . . . and international interests for which we had made ourselves responsible." All the rest could go. He would maintain control of the Suez Canal, the Nile, the army, and the police. The Egyptian ministers would probably make mistakes, but they had a right to a fair trial. These concessions, Clayton felt, would win most of the country to the British side. On the other hand, he said, "If however we refuse to take very bold liberal measures we shall create in Egypt an Oriental Ireland."[60]

As his editor has said, this was a courageous and "most unpopular policy" from the British government's point of view.[61] Wingate's advocacy of just such a policy in March 1919 had brought his career to an abrupt and ignominious end. In 1921 Clayton officially recommended that the protectorate be abolished, and in February 1922 he and Maurice Amos, the British adviser to the Justice Ministry, accompanied Allenby to London to persuade the government of that policy's feasibility.[62] The government reluctantly accepted Allenby's ultimatum and on 28 February 1922 the protectorate was abolished.[63] Once again Clayton had talked himself out of a job, but this time he left with the full confidence of his superiors and the knowledge that his patience and understanding had helped the empire survive a serious crisis.

The change in Sir Gilbert's thinking and the new policy in regard to Egypt, however, were not based entirely on his Egyptian experience. As Clayton revealed in a note cited by the Colonial Office's Middle East Department in February 1923, it was "hardly conceivable that the present policy . . . would have been either recommended or accepted had it not appeared certain that the British control in Palestine would be maintained for at least a considerable period of years." In his view the key to British communications through the Middle East had shifted from Egypt to Palestine, whose retention now became "essential from the standard of Imperial strategy." Control of the canal was still vital, but with

> Palestine under British control, with the British position maintained in the Sudan and on the western littoral of the Red Sea, and, above all, with adequate British naval power in the Eastern Mediterranean, Egypt becomes of minor importance, provided always that foreign intervention in her affairs is not permitted.[64]

This, then, was the clue to Sir Gilbert's conversion to a liberal policy in Egypt. Just as Britain's key position in the East had once been Constantinople, only to shift after the 1880s to Egypt, so the march of events since the war was to lead to a similar shift from Egypt to Palestine, where the British were already deeply committed to an illiberal policy backed for the foreseeable future by the strength of British arms.

While Clayton was waiting to take over his new position, he carried on negotiations with Abdullah that eventually led to the independence of Transjordan, which was announced on 25 May 1923.[65] Clayton was later to follow up this type of careful negotiation, and secure an unbroken line of communications across the Middle East, in his talks with Ibn Saud and the Iman of Yemen.[66]

In August 1922 the British government passed a Palestine Order in Council providing for elections to a Palestinian legislative council. The Palestinian Arabs were not inclined to accept the legislative council in any event, but before the elections could be held two events occurred to strengthen their attitude of non-cooperation. The first was Mustafa Kemal's victory over the Greeks and successful confrontation of the British at Chanak, and the second was the change of governments in Britain brought about by the breakup of the Lloyd George coalition. As Samuel pointed out in a report to the Colonial Office in December 1922, Palestinians paid extraordinarily close attention to the course of British politics. The policy of the new government of Bonar Law, with the duke of Devonshire installed in the Colonial Office, was not known with certainty. Palestinian Arabs hoped for further changes. Samuel urged an immediate reaffirmation of previous policy in order to encourage the moderates and discourage the proponents of a policy of non-cooperation.[67]

While the new government in London was still in the process of deciding what its policy would be, the Palestinians in February successfully boycotted the legislative council elections. Samuel then suspended his attempts to form an elective council and revived a plan for a new advisory council. By August this plan too had met defeat as a result of Arab non-cooperation.[68]

On 17 February 1923 Devonshire presented the Cabinet with a substantial review of the previous government's Palestine policy. The review, conducted by the Colonial Office's Middle East Department, concluded that the British government was "in fact, committed to the Zionist policy before the whole world in the clearest and most unequivocal fashion."[69] The charge that the McMahon pledges had been violated was rejected, as was the allegation that an injustice was being forced upon the majority of the people of Palestine. According to the memorandum, the idea of a Jewish state in Palestine had "been definitely ruled out, and the Zionists have implicitly acquiesced in its culmination." Therefore, the fears of the Palestinian people, while originating, the department felt, in genuine feeling, were "largely coloured by a misunderstanding of the real aims and intentions of the Government."

Accordingly, there were four possible courses open to the government, the first three of which involved repudiating the Balfour Declaration and hence giving up the mandate. This would involve an "act of perfidy," the memorandum continued, "from which it is hardly too much to say that our good name would never recover." It would also involve establishing another power in Palestine, or, failing that, the return of the Turks, either alternative being intolerable to Great Britain. Clearly, then, the fourth possibility, as formulated by the Colonial Office, was the only honorable choice:

> They might take the same ground as the late Government, viz., that looking at the pledge as a whole, they find that there is nothing in what was said to the Arabs to preclude the due fulfillment of the Balfour Declaration; that they regard the policy of the White Paper as adequately safeguarding both parts of that Declaration and see no reason for making any departure from it.

This moderate and rational memorandum, which seemed entirely consistent with the Hogarth assurances to King Husayn in January 1918,[70] was, however, difficult to apply in Palestine. Time had entrenched attitudes of hostility. The long silences of the British government in the face of extreme Zionist claims and the long trail of unfortunate events since the Mudros armistice in 1918 had ended in the discrediting of verbal assurances from the British government.

Deedes, back in London after resigning his post in Palestine, showed a great deal of insight into this problem in an address before the Royal Central Asian Society on 17 May 1923. The Zionism being opposed in Palestine, he said, was not the Zionism adhered to by the government, "but it is the Zionism preached by the extremists to-day and the professed Zionist leaders some three or four years ago, and never contradicted until the other day by His Majesty's Government." Deedes then outlined briefly what the Palestinian Arabs feared: a flood of Jewish immigrants, the loss of their lands, and the diminution of their trade and business because of competition with a more intelligent people. "If this were indeed our Zionist policy," he continued, "my sympathies would be entirely with them; that they still believe it to be so is not altogether inexcusable." The problem was plainly one of credibility and the "years of exaggeration and misrepresentation as to Zionism take a lot of living down, and the more recent and moderate statements of policy are simply not as yet believed."[71]

This, then, was the position Sir Gilbert found on his arrival in Palestine in April 1923. The government, owing partly to the fall of Lloyd George, had to a large degree recovered its control of Zionist policy while remaining committed to the national home idea. But the Palestinian Arab leaders had lost faith in British policy statements. They waited for the actions to follow, powerless (because divided) to seize the initiative themselves. On 26 June Stanley Baldwin, who had been prime minister since May, appointed a committee to advise the Cabinet on policy in Palestine. It was chaired by the duke of Devonshire and included Curzon (foreign affairs), Derby (war), Peel (India), Hoare (air), Amery (admiralty), and Joynson Hicks (financial secretary, treasury).[72]

Exactly one month after the appointment of the committee, Devonshire circulated its completed report on "The Future of Palestine." On the whole, the report closely followed the Colonial Office memoranda of February and March. Candidly, it admitted that not all members of the committee were happy with the policy of the Balfour Declaration; but whether wise or unwise, that had been an accepted policy of the government for years and figured in several legal commitments. These considerations, the report continued, "possess a cumulative weight from which it is well-nigh impossible for any Government to extricate itself without a substantial sacrifice of consistency and self-respect if not honour." The grounds for retaining the previous government's policy were almost wholly negative. They were summarized as follows in the report:

1. We see no way of reversing the policy without throwing up the Mandate.

2. If we return the Mandate another claimant would very quickly be forthcoming. Whether that claimant were France or Italy, the result would be equally injurious to British and, as we think, to Palestinian, interests.

3. If no applicant were forthcoming and the Palestinian Arabs were left to work out their own destiny, the sequel could hardly fail to be the return at no distant period, of the Turks. This would be an even more disastrous consequence, and would, indeed, involve the final sacrifice of all for which we fought and won the Eastern war.

4. Although the strategical value of Palestine is rated by the Imperial General Staff less highly than it had been placed by some authorities, yet none of us can contemplate with equanimity the installation in Palestine of another Power.[73]

The final sentence in the select committee's summation encapsulated Britain's irreducible desideratum in Palestine and her whole reason for being there. In the committee's pessimistic logic lay the inherited thinking of generations of British diplomats and warriors: no other power must be allowed to threaten the passageways to India.

Going on to blame the "exaggerated pretensions of the Zionist organizations and press" for frightening the Arabs through "mistaken tactics," the committee reasoned that Arab objections were aimed not so much at the Balfour Declaration, the mandate, or the national home, as they were at the "preferential position which has been accorded to the Zionists in the country, and the universal Arab belief that the scales are weighted against the Arabs in the Administration." The committee accordingly proposed the setting-up of an Arab agency along the same lines as the Jewish agency that had been established under the mandate. Its members would, significantly, be "suitable persons" appointed by the high commissioner, and hence would not have the same degree of autonomy as was exercised by the Jewish agency. The Arab agency would advise and cooperate with the administration, and, "subject to the control of the Administration," participate in the country's development. Samuel, the report said, thought the proposal had some chance of acceptance by the Arabs and was on record as predicting a rosy future for Palestine.

The committee, however, was clearly assigning greater weight to the more pessimistic forecasts of Sir Gilbert Clayton. Clayton had written, in a report which Meinertzhagen found to be in bad taste,[74] that there was no need to abandon the Zionist policy or relinquish the mandate; but he asked whether "a way cannot be found, by modifying objectionable Articles in the Mandate, or at least by moving all possible grounds for any charges of partiality or bad faith, to dissipate the present fear and distrust of the Arabs." That, the committee concluded, was the "precise object" of the proposals included in the report.

At the second meeting of the Imperial Conference in October, Devonshire brought up the subject of Palestine in the course of a review of crown colonies and protectorates. Smuts was for holding on to Palestine because of the assumed international importance of the Jews. "There is no more subtle influence in the world," Smuts asserted, "I hope for good, than the influence of that international people (the Jews), full of brains and character, and dominating much bigger nations in many parts of the world through the filtration of their ideas and policies."[75]

Curzon then agreed that Britain could not back out now, since the French would step in and camp on the threshold of Egypt and the Canal. Besides, so long as they were in Palestine, there was a need for development and the rich Jews of America could be relied on to subsidize that development. Still, Curzon cautioned, the Arabs must be treated fairly and firmly: there must be "no invidious preference to the Zionists."[76] Curzon's statement served to underline the July report of the Committee on Palestine. Britain was committed in the eyes of the world to the national home policy, but the only reasons for retaining that commitment were negative: Palestine must not fall to any other power, especially France, and America's Jews would relieve the British taxpayer in the matter of development. All this was too late, however. If there was a cumulative weight of circumstances keeping the British in Palestine, there was also a cumulative weight of time and fear restraining the Palestinians from exploring other avenues of policy than that of non-cooperation.

On 11 October, at Government House in Jerusalem, Samuel communicated the government's proposal of an Arab agency to a representative group of Arab leaders. It was refused, as Samuel by then knew it would be. As Paul Hanna has written, the Arab agency was not "exactly analogous" to the Jewish agency, as was claimed by the Committee on Palestine, but the Arabs "were in no mood for compromise even if the concession offered had been greater than it was."[77] The policy of non-cooperation had been too successful in the recent past for them to recognize that the time to take a positive initiative had arrived. The next day, 12 October, the Colonial Office drafted instructions to Samuel to break off negotiations with the Arabs and proceed to administer the country under its mandatory obligations without assistance from the Arab community.[78] The instructions were sent on 9 November.

The cooperation of the Arabs now seemed to be of little importance. Order was being maintained without their participation. Samuel's next annual report, sent in January 1924 within a few days of Britain's first Labour government's taking office, noted that since May 1921 the political situation in the country had shown remarkable improvement, despite successive failures to come to an accommodation with the Arabs. He attributed the establishment of tranquility to a combination of causes: policy in Palestine had become settled, the white paper had had a moderating effect on both Jews and Arabs, peace had been concluded with Turkey, and the population had become reconciled to the rule of his administration. True, the Jews were disappointed with the slow pace of development toward their ideals, but, he said, they were "full of confidence that their undertaking in Palestine taken as a whole, in spite of all obstacles and difficulties, will succeed."

Samuel reported happily that while the Arabs were subsiding toward "their usual attitude of placid acceptance," the Jews were forging ahead with enormous energy. "Almost all" of the new economic activity in Palestine was Jewish, Samuel said, adding that the process was "capable of almost indefinite expansion." He saw the country as "empty and undeveloped," but with the potential of sustaining a much larger population "with no disturbance or loss to any of the present inhabitants." It was going to require capital, enterprise, and additional labor, Samuel said, and it was "the Jews, and the Jews alone, who are able and willing adequately to supply all three."[79]

On 19 February J.H. Thomas, the new colonial secretary and the general secretary of the National Union of Railwaymen, circulated in the Cabinet a memorandum urging an immediate reaffirmation of the policy of the Balfour Declaration "as interpreted by the late government." He said he was not underrating the difficulties, but he was satisfied that any alternative course of action would lead to even greater trouble.[80] On 21 February, the Cabinet agreed with Thomas, and on 25 February the announcement of the continuity of government policy was made in the House of Commons.[81]

Much of the credit for this continuity of policy of coalition, Conservative, and Labour governments and for the relative calm in Palestine must go to Samuel, who had been closely connected with the development of British policy in Palestine right from the beginning. Sir Geoffrey Furlonge, a former head of the Foreign Office's Eastern Department and ambassador to Jordan, has noted in his biography of the Palestinian Musa Alami that Samuel had indeed been "assiduous in cultivating the influential Arabs, punctilious in his respect for their customs and susceptibilities, tireless in lulling their fears . . . ."[82] Samuel wrote in his memoirs that he had aimed to administer the country for the benefit of all sections of the population.[83] This, no doubt, was true. Samuel's real objectives, however, were never in doubt. He was a convinced Zionist who steadily contemplated the establishment of a Jewish state in Palestine at some future date.[84]

As Musa Alami noted in 1924, when he was not only a large landowner in Palestine but a junior crown counsel under Norman Bentwich in the Legal Department, Samuel was dedicated to the success of the national home and "never envisaged the Arabs as having any significant power, still less political parity with the Jews, in the future State."[85] Samuel's policy was indicated in his January 1924 report to the Colonial Office when he took credit for guaranteeing the country's tranquility by making small concessions to the Arabs in order to make them amenable in matters essential for Zionist success. In fact Samuel was not running Palestine according to the policy laid down by successive governments. Ever since 1922, they had expressly ruled out a Jewish state in Palestine. But Samuel chose to disregard their clear intent. Years later, the uninhibited pro-Zionist Meinertzhagen apologized for his references to Samuel's weakness. "What I took for weakness," he said, "was in reality a determination to be just and impartial." For Meinertzhagen, this accolade could only be bestowed on those who worked hard and consistently for Zionism.[86]

According to Furlonge, Musa Alami in his official work in Samuel's administration noticed the adoption of a series of policy decisions designed to advance Zionist aims even at the expense of the Arabs. It seemed strange to Alami that all the key posts in Samuel's administration had been entrusted to strong Zionists. Men such as Hyamson of the Immigration Department, Harari of Customs, and Bentwich, who was both attorney general and legal adviser to the government, were all Jews. In addition, Abrahamson of the Lands Department was a Christian of Jewish origin. In the Secretariat, Sir Wyndham Deedes was a "passionate Gentile Zionist."[87] Even Sir Gilbert Clayton was being used by Samuel to reassure the Arabs of Britain's good intentions.

There were other instances of favoritism, some of which Musa Alami thought must have originated with Samuel and Bentwich. One was the reclassification of village pasturage or common land as government land, which was then handed over to the Jews. This decision was eventually reversed, but, as Furlonge has written, not until "many thousands of acres had been alienated and many peasants ruined." Other instances were the institution of an urban property tax and the abolition of the Ottoman land bank without any substitute for it being set up, both steps which damaged undercapitalized Arabs and helped the Jews. There may have been excellent reasons for each of these measures, reasons unknown to Musa Alami, but the significant thing is that he perceived them as injuring the Arabs and as having been prepared and administered by men with a pro-Zionist bias. The men were honorable and efficient government servants, but, as Furlonge has written, "they were in a position to interpret policy in numerous ways, and would have been less than human had they not done so in favour of the principles which they espoused."[88] For instance, Bentwich conceived of his duty as discharging a dual obligation. But these obligations were not to the Arabs on the one hand and to the Jews on the other. He thought of the mandatory as administering "the country not simply as guardian of the nation which is there, but with a view to help a people who desire to come there."[89] This widening of an administrative constituency was hardly specifically countenanced by government directives. Clearly Bentwich's "nation" was Jewish, not Palestinian, as were the people who wished to emigrate to Palestine, and hence his guardianship went a good deal beyond fidelity to Churchill's formula of the economic capacity of the land to absorb population.

Clayton was well aware of what was going on in Palestine. He had been convinced in 1922 that British policy was at last on the right track. He knew and respected Samuel and in August 1923, when he was still acting high commissioner, had, in the face of widespread Arab criticism, strongly defended continuing the appointment of Hyamson to the Immigration Department. In his view, the British administration, to be successful, must convince both Arabs and Jews of its absolute impartiality and be free to take whatever measures it deemed best without being deterred by representations and criticisms from either side.[90]

By 1924, however, Clayton had become thoroughly disillusioned with British policy in Palestine. There had been a long and bitter struggle over the position of Ernest Richmond, an architect by training, whom Samuel had appointed as his assistant secretary (political) in 1920.[91] Samuel had found him useful as his adviser on Muslim affairs and as a sympathetic intermediary with the Arabs. In December 1922, when Richmond threatened to resign if his title were changed to second assistant secretary as part of an organizational shakeup, Samuel wrote on his behalf to the Colonial Office that there was no one to take his place if he left. Clayton, too, thought he was worth keeping. In July 1923 he described Richmond as being regarded by the Arabs "as to some extent the counterpart of the Zionist Organization."[92] A friend of his, C.R. Ashbee, then civic adviser in Jerusalem and an anti-Zionist who claimed Jewish ancestry, called Richmond the "sheet anchor of Zionism in Palestine" in 1923 because it was he who gave the Arabs "confidence in an administration that for them would otherwise be wholly Zionist."[93]

In March 1924, however, Richmond stormily resigned. He wrote to Samuel that while he had been part of the administrative machine, he had tried to alter it but had failed. He said he had been led gradually and most reluctantly, but definitively to a conviction that the Zionist Commission, the Middle East Department of the Colonial Office and this Administration are dominated and inspired by a spirit which I can only regard as evil, and that this spirit is, through the agencies I have mentioned, acting in a manner that is not merely unwise and impolitic but evil.[94]

Since he found himself, "unhappily, in complete opposition" to the general drift of events, he was resigning. It was truly a remarkable letter, as Kedourie has noted,[95] and one not likely to win him high praise from political professionals, but Richmond was hardly unique in expressing a lack on confidence in Samuel's administration.

At nearly the same time Richmond was demonstrating one method of displaying disagreement with his superiors and in the process severely damaging his own reputation, Sir Gilbert Clayton was indicating his own deep disenchantment and discouragement. In a letter to Walford Selby, a close friend from his days with the Interior Ministry in Cairo who was then principal private secretary to the foreign secretary, Clayton explained his thoughts and feelings of the moment. First of all, he too disliked the Middle East section of the Colonial Office, "with its mixture of Colonial Office bureaucracy and so-called expert local knowledge. Such an institution," he said, "should never have been allowed to leave the F.O. which alone knows how to use it." As for the situation in the Middle East, he felt he could cope with Egypt, but he was displeased with Palestine "under the present regime and with the present methods" of implementing policy.

> There is an intangible "something" behind everything, an unseen influence—something unhealthy and certainly not British, which has to be felt to be realized. Frankly, unless the place is to be run by Englishmen on British lines, I am off and that within a few months. To you in confidence I will say that this Palestine policy—difficult and contradictory as it is—has only one chance of success, which is that it be implemented by pure-bred Britishers whose justice and impartiality cannot be questioned. If I were to say that this is so openly, I should not unnaturally be accused of wanting the job, but you know that that has nothing to do with it—indeed I should envy no man the task. But the long and the short of it is that you cannot have Jews—however upright and honorable—in control, and hope to convince the Arabs that they are going to get a fair run.

The conclusions he had drawn from his year in Palestine were prophetic.

> In general, a year in Palestine has made me regard this whole adventure with apprehension. We are pushing an alien and detested element into the very core of Islam, and the day may come when we shall be faced with the alternatives of holding it there by the sword or abandoning it to its fate!

The Arabs were underdogs now, he said, but they would bide their time. Perhaps England would have to go for a "white" empire policy and forget all ideas of dominating "brown" peoples.

Although he had spent most of his official life working to safeguard Britain's imperial lifelines, his brief experience with Samuel's administrative policy in Palestine made him wish for freer alternatives.

> Ocean routes, open seas and no commitments in confined spaces like the Mediterranean. That is freedom in war and the ability to take the initiative from the very outset. In peace, the same chance for all everywhere and the most energetic man of business gets the trade and economic power. Think of the freedom if we could say that if war were to come again, we did not care a d—n for Mediterranean or Suez Canal. A strong Home Fleet, Gibraltar blocked and the Red Sea stopped from the East, and the Mediterranean stews in its own juice with Dago pulling Dago's tail to their hearts' content.[96]

Here is a bitterness to match Richmond's. But Clayton knew there was no chance of fighting policy publicly. A public uproar over his leaving would serve no purpose save perhaps to cut short his own career. Little wonder, then, that he was ready to cut and run. Selby, in reply, agreed that in their Zionist policy the British were liable to "reap the whirlwind." He even substantiated the unease felt by both Richmond and Clayton, saying that he had experienced it himself in the spring of 1920 when he had been in Palestine to help deal with the situation brought on by the political tension over the new Syrian state and the San Remo Conference. "I well remember the nervous strain," he said, "under which practically all our officers representing us in Palestine were suffering. There was something intangible and unhealthy about the whole thing, and I can see that this atmosphere persists." Allenby, as Selby reminded Clayton, had in 1920 vigorously expressed his opinion that the Palestine administration would have to be a British one and that while there could have been no better appointment than that of Sir Herbert Samuel, he deprecated it because of the latter's being a Jew.[97]

Clayton's own impartiality during his tour of duty in Palestine was unquestioned, even in the midst of profound personal disillusionment. Brigadier Fred H. Kisch, chairman of the Palestine Zionist Executive (successor to the Zionist Commission) from 1923 to 1931, who had fought for Richmond's removal,[98] wrote in late February 1924 that his impression of Clayton was that he was "a very capable administrator, painstaking and conscientious and thoroughly loyal to the policy which he has been sent here to execute."[99] In fact Kisch, a hard-driving British Zionist who had been handpicked by Weizmann to succeed Eder in 1922,[100] had by midsummer of 1924 lost confidence in Samuel "from the Zionist point of view"[101] and in August confided to his diary his wish to see Clayton installed as high commissioner.[102]

Norman Bentwich wrote in later years that Clayton "had a talent for keeping his own counsel, and a simple integrity and courtesy which disarmed those he must disappoint," adding that over the last two years of Samuel's administration, Clayton had displayed "a fairness which prevailed over all the little frictions, and helped to make the second half of Samuel's term a blessedly peaceful period."[103] In any case, he persisted in his duties, avoiding Richmond's spectacular example, until April 1925, shortly before Samuel gave way to the elderly Lord Plumer.

One of his last tasks in the spring of 1925 was to escort Lord Balfour around Palestine. Balfour was making his first visit to the land with which his name had been so closely linked in order to participate in the imposing ceremonies of the opening of Hebrew University. Balfour had no idea of the risk he was running, Storrs has written, "or of the strain which his presence imposed."[104] The seventy-one year-old statesman was greeted by Jews with enthusiasm and by Arabs with a general strike. His secretary destroyed scores of abusive telegrams without telling him about them. When he and the popular Storrs walked through the narrow lanes of the old city of Jerusalem, Balfour took the friendly salutations from onlookers as being addressed to him, as Storrs had hoped he would.[105]

George Antonius, a Christian Arab of Lebanese origin who held several posts in the Palestine government at various times and accompanied Clayton on his missions to Arabia and Yemen, had been assigned to travel with Balfour. Antonius took the opportunity to explain to Balfour Arab nationalism and the anti-Zionist movement. Balfour listened closely but apparently with his customary academic disinterest, remarking that the consequences of his "experiment" were "extraordinarily interesting."[106] In Damascus, his next stop, matters were not handled so well as they had been in Palestine. Violence broke out and Balfour's life was "in serious jeopardy before he could be spirited away and deposited safely on board a steamer" in Beirut harbor.[107]

Arab feeling was indeed running deeply against the supposed author of their troubles and it was journalist and author H. Charles Wood's opinion that in that critical period

> Sir Gilbert's wisdom and knowledge were important factors in the prevention of an outbreak . . . . I saw him repeatedly at that time; he was constantly pouring oil on troubled waters, and when difficulties were overcome, one realised that this was largely the result of the work of a man who was trusted by Arab and Jew alike.[108]

Clayton retired from the Palestine government well liked by everyone. His editor, Robert O. Collins, has written that even "today he is still remembered as the best of Englishmen by the few who remain in Jerusalem from those quiet days."[109] In November 1925, while visiting Jerusalem, he was recognized at a performance of *Carmen* and given a standing ovation by the Palestinian audience. At that time he had recovered from his jaundiced view of a year and a half earlier and thought that Jerusalem had a "wonderfully home-like and affectionate atmosphere."[110] Of course, by that time he was in the midst of another assignment.

By the time Samuel and Clayton departed from Palestine in 1925, the Balfour Declaration had acquired a political and legal significance and mythology that had given it a life of its own apart from actual British policy. That policy, though defined by Samuel in 1921 and Churchill in 1922, was still a matter for debate. In addition, it had become a political device as difficult to run against as motherhood. More important for the future were the concrete facts of Zionism in Palestine. Zionism and its many organizations had grown and were firmly established in Palestine; in 1925, for the first time, the growth of the Jewish population exceeded, if not by much, the growth of the Arab population.[111] From 1920 to 1925, the Jewish community doubled in size. Jewish agricultural settlements expanded in number from forty-four in 1918 to one-hundred in 1925. Jewish representative bodies had gained recognition from the government of Palestine. And the Hebrew University, symbol of intelligence and stability, opened in 1925.[112]

Although Zionists and government officials alike did not know it at the time, the foundation for a vastly increased Jewish population had been laid, without which the Jewish exodus from Nazi Germany in the 1930s and after 1945 would have had even more tragic consequences than it did. In addition, an Arab moderate party, the Hizb al-Watani (national party), had been formed in November 1923; although the new party owed more to personal than to political rivalries, its existence meant the breaking-up of total Arab hostility toward Britain. The Palestine garrison in 1925 had been reduced to a minimum, as had expenditures.[113] There would be no fresh outbreak of violence until the Wailing Wall riots of 1929.

One thing, however, stands out about the 1917–1925 period in regard to British policy. Far from there being a uniform British enthusiasm for a thorough pro-Zionist policy, there is more evidence of the precise opposite. Important individuals, such as Lloyd George and Balfour, had their reasons for supporting the policy and spoke on occasion of their wish to see a Jewish state in Palestine one day. But government policy consisted of much more than the sentiments of these men, and government policy over the entire period of this study was carefully framed to give the government a minimum commitment to Zionism.

Once the British government had accepted publicly at San Remo the responsibility for establishing the Zionists in Palestine, there was no turning back. But what did a national home policy mean? Various historians have unearthed statements by British leaders confessing that they were for the eventual emergence of a Jewish state, but as policy surfaced in the pages of government documents purporting to set forth official policy, what emerged was something quite different.

> There was no place in these plans for a Jewish national home ... Competent spokesmen of His Majesty's Government made no secret of their emotional and political approach to the problem: While they saluted the idea of the return of the people of the Bible to the land of the Bible, they were not unmindful of the more concrete political benefit to British imperial interests. Such benefit, it was often declared, was bound to accrue when a (not too large) Jewish community became dependent for its survival on British protection, and thereby provided a moral pretext for continuous, perhaps perpetual, British control.[114]

In 1922 the Lloyd George government specifically repudiated Weizmann's celebrated statement that the aim of the Balfour Declaration was to make Palestine "as Jewish as England is English."[115] In 1923 the Colonial Office under the Bonar Law government said that the idea of a Jewish state in Palestine had "been definitely ruled out."[116] In 1924 the Labour government accepted the policy defined by the 1922 white paper, which it understood did "not aim at the conversion of Palestine into a Jewish State."[117] And in 1925 L.S. Amery, colonial secretary in Baldwin's second Cabinet, told Haj Amin al-Husayni, the mufti of Jerusalem:

Now I did make it clear, and I want to make it clear to His Eminence, that there is no idea in this country of subordinating the Arab Nation or the Arab language or culture in any way behind the Jewish. There is no idea of creating a Jewish Political Nation which should have domination over the other inhabitants of Palestine. All that the Mandate makes clear is that the development of the present Jewish Communities in the country shall proceed freely, guaranteed by the League of Nations and not dependent only upon the good will of the particular Government at any moment in this country, and to my mind any development that will proceed in that way to the Jewish Communities by bringing in capital and productive development, must always benefit the rest of the country as well.[118]

What then were the governments' reasons for their continuing interest in a Zionist establishment? As these emerge from government memoranda, they seem to form a continuity with past British policy toward that part of the Middle East. Once committed to the mandate, as the British were at San Remo, they could not repudiate the vague policy of the Balfour Declaration without giving up the mandate, which would endanger the imperial lifeline to India by inviting a foreign power to camp at once on the land route to the head of the Persian Gulf and the outskirts of the Suez Canal. These governments had sufficient time and evidence to see that their commitments to Arab and Jew were irreconcilable, but the alternative would have been intolerable and dangerous. Better to try to satisfy both sides, with peacekeeping between the two communities as the only real British responsibility. Just as the British during the nineteenth century had worked to keep the Ottoman Empire intact and free from the control of any other power, so in 1917–1925 they restructured a policy of keeping the southern portion of the defunct empire intact and free of the influence of other powers, besides making it part of a continuous belt of British-controlled territories. When the United States refused to commit itself to responsibility in the Middle East after World War I, the British were forced to take a Palestine that even Balfour did not want in order to prevent France from realizing its ancient aim of dominating the Holy Land.

The British did not want the territory or the responsibility for their own sakes, but they were obsessed with security. "The empire has reached its maximum and begun the descent," Hogarth wrote in April 1920, just before Britain was awarded its Middle Eastern mandates at San Remo. "There is no more expansion in us . . . and that being so we shall make but a poor Best of the Arab Countries."[119] The theme of *Africa and the Victorians,* still held true for the early interwar years: "Over and over again, [the British] show an obsession with security, a fixation of safeguarding the routes to the East."[120]

Arnold Toynbee, who was a member of the Foreign Office's Political Intelligence Department late in the war and then a member of the British delegation to Versailles, writing in the early 1920s, referred to the strength of Britain's fixation on security against the French. He said:

> One cannot understand—or make allowances for—the postwar relations of the French and British Governments over the 'Eastern Question' unless one realizes this tradition of rivalry and its accumulated inheritance of suspicion and resentment.[121]

Curzon, who had been highly critical of the Balfour Declaration and the ensuing measures to give it effect, did not oppose; he contented himself with a verbal display. He and the other members of the succeeding Cabinets of the early 1920s agreed with Sir Halford Mackinder, the geopolitician, that the war had shown that the Suez Canal carried "the rich traffic between the Indies and Europe to within striking distance of an army based on Palestine . . ."[122]

Hence Britain's "Suez fixation"[123] assured that the partition of the Ottoman Empire, while calling for adjustments and new tactical measures, would only continue the Eastern Question "by other means."

> Mandates replaced pashaliks under the new dispensation, with sovereignty residing in London and Paris instead of Constantinople. These fundamental changes, however, are more apparent than real. During most of the nineteenth century the real authority in eastern affairs resided in London and Paris. One intermediate state—that of Constantinople—has since been removed in the application of that authority. But in those portions of the former Turkish domain essential to the control of the two trunk routes to the East, the territories embraced in the kingdoms of Egypt, Iraq, and the Hedjaz, in Palestine and the Emirate of Transjordania, Great Britain still prefers to apply a sovereign power more or less indirectly.[124]

Thus we can see that British policy in Palestine was dictated by the same elements of security and imperial psychology that had helped to determine the shape of the classical Eastern Question.

Clayton, at various points in his career, adapted himself to the obsessions reigning in London, even though he knew and tried to point out that Britain was borrowing unnecessary trouble by backing the Zionists. While in Egypt, he thought that the British stronghold in the eastern Mediterranean had shifted to Palestine, thus allowing a relaxation of Britain's tight hold on Egypt. The white paper of 1922 had strengthened this idea, and he had gone to Palestine with the hope that there he would again be at the center of Britain's imperial strategy in the Middle East. Instead he found himself installed as a genial figurehead, being used to assure the Arabs of Britain's reliability, while Samuel went ahead and quietly laid the foundations of the national home for the Jews. Having spent his career in Egypt, the Sudan, and Arabia, he did not relish the task of cynically reassuring both sides in Palestine that the government was with them. Palestine was no place for a man with ambition for imperial advancement. Clayton, like a minor Pilate, could do nothing to change the situation. Instead of symbolically washing his hands, he only wished privately to leave the Mediterranean to stew "in its own juice."

Since Britain was mainly concerned with security, it followed that policy in Palestine would be directed at keeping the Arabs quiet so that there would be no danger of disturbances spilling over the borders and at encouraging the Jews to build up an establishment, preferably a small one, which would bring in the outside capital needed for development. The British role would be confined to keeping the peace between the two communities, along the lines of British responsibility for Hindu and Muslim in India, Greek and Turk in Cyprus, and Protestant and Catholic in Ireland.

The Zionists saw what was happening. The chairman of the Palestine Zionist Executive, Fred Kisch, wrote in 1938 that his organization had done its best in the 1920s to reach an accommodation with the Palestinian Arabs and that some Arabs were ready to follow a lead from the mandatory government. While the meaning of this "best" may be open to interpretation, it was nevertheless true that the lead was not given. "On the contrary," Kisch said, "the Government never ceased to maintain the authority and power of the Arab extremist groups, headed by the Mufti of Jerusalem," Haj Amin al-Husayni.[125]

Agreeing with Kisch, the Israeli historian Aharon Cohen has concluded in a lengthy study that the "policy of both Jewish and Arab leaders was largely the effect, rather than the cause, of basic British policy and orientation" and that British policy was "decided in accordance with British imperial needs and contingencies, which were all too frequently founded on the 'divide and rule' method in opposition to the legitimate national interests and aspirations of the peoples concerned."[126] In his view, the two peoples, left alone, would have been able to come to an understanding.

And yet, as we have seen, the pattern for Zionist-Palestine Arab relations was created early by Weizmann and the Zionist Commission. It is evident that they knew their interests ran counter to those of the Arabs. Weizmann's first concern was with consolidating his hold over

Palestinian and world Jewry and his second with trying to come to terms with the Arabs. But the Arabs he dealt with were not Palestinians but bedouin whose interests lay in Syria and the Hijaz. Furthermore, his contempt for Arabs in general and Palestinians in particular was difficult to conceal. Late in life, he wrote:

> The Arab is a very subtle debater and conversationalist—much more so than the average educated European—and until one has acquired the technique one is at a great disadvantage. In particular, the Arab has an immense talent for expressing views diametrically opposed to yours with such exquisite and roundabout politeness that you believe him to be in complete agreement with you, and ready to join hands with you at once. Conversations and negotiations with Arabs are not unlike chasing a mirage in the desert: full of promise and good to look at, but likely to lead you to death by thirst.[127]

Eventually his British-sponsored attempts to obtain Faysal's approval for Zionism foundered on the rocks of imperial expediency and a rising Palestinian Arab nationalism. As an anonymous reviewer on Cohen has written:

> There was a fundamental clash of interests which could not be resolved through talk. The Arab argument was irrefutable, and it is disingenuous to claim that the conflict could have been resolved by some diplomatic legerdemain.[128]

Weizmann's negotiation with Faysal was not, however, the only time a connection was tried. Several times in following years some Zionists attempted to arrive at a political rapprochement with the Arabs outside Palestine. After the British and the Zionist Organization dropped their efforts with Faysal in the spring of 1919, Dr. Chaim Kalvarisky, a Polish Zionist who was then an administrator with the Jewish Colonization Association, accepted an Arab initiative to talk about how the Zionists thought Palestine should be governed. Kalvarisky drafted a statement for the Arab leaders and the Palestinian delegates to the midsummer 1919 Pan-Syrian Congress in Damascus. The Palestinians favored it as a basic Palestinian constitution and asked him to obtain official Jewish approval. The Jewish community, however, would have nothing to do with it. Kalvarisky attributed their disapproval to "contempt for the Arab national movement and the Arab people, which were dismissed as unimportant, and an exaggerated appraisal of our own strength and the help of Europe and America."[129]

Another attempt was made in the spring and summer of 1922, but it did not involve Palestinians and it failed soon after the formal adoption of the mandate.[130] There was still another attempt late in 1922, but talks between Abdullah and Weizmann came to nothing.[131]

Thus British policy from 1917 to 1925 was not, as Paul Hanna wrote in 1942, marked by "reluctance to take a definite decision" nor by a struggle "to harmonize two irreconcilable interests."[132] Rather, it was marked by exceeding boldness and ruthlessness, qualities met by the Zionists with steadfast determination to gain final sovereignty over Palestine, a sovereignty that may have been gained only in 1948 but whose crucial origins lay in an earlier period.

Bibliographical Note

This work is based on several collections of papers, on documents in Great Britain's Public Record Office and on numerous published works. References to the most helpful books will be found in the footnotes. The following collections of papers were used: the papers of Sir Gilbert Falkingham Clayton and the papers of Sir Reginald Wingate in the Library of the School for Oriental Studies at the University of Durham; the letters of D.G. Hogarth, Lord Herbert Samuel, Sir Mark Sykes, and Lord Edmund Allenby at St. Antony's College, Oxford University; the papers of David Lloyd George at the Beaverbrook Library in London; and the letters of Lord Balfour, Lord Curzon, and Sir Mark Sykes in the Public Record Office.

List of Abbreviations

Cab.	Cabinet
CO	Colonial Office
CP	Committee on Palestine
DBFP	Great Britain, Foreign Office, *Documents on British Foreign Policy, 1919–1939,* First Series, vol. 4 (London: Her Majesty's Stationery Office, 1952). Edited by E.L. Woodward and Rohan Butler.
DNME	J.C. Hurewitz, ed., *Diplomacy in the Near and Middle East: A Documentary Record, 1914–1956,* vol. 2 (Princeton: D. Van Nostrand, 1956.
EC	Eastern Committee
FO	Foreign Office
FRUS	United States, State Department, *Foreign Relations of the United States,* the Paris Peace Conference Series and the Lansing Papers (Washington, D.C.: Government Printing Office).

Notes

Chapter 1: Eastern Questions

[1] Halford L. Hoskins, *The Middle East* (New York: Macmillan Co., 1954), p. 10.

[2] (London: Macmillan & Co.; New York: St. Martin's Press, 1966).

[3] For instance, J.C. Hurewitz, writing in 1953, in *Middle East Dilemmas* (New York: Harper & Brothers, 1953), characterized the period after 1923 as proceeding from the "ghost of the old Eastern Question" after improper interment in 1923 to the "'new look' of the old Eastern Question" after 1947. Elie Kedourie, in "Britain, France, and the Last Phase of the Eastern Question," in J.C. Hurewitz, ed., *Soviet-American Rivalry in the Middle East* (New York: Frederick A. Praeger, 1969), pp. 189–97, has described the demise of the classical Eastern Question as taking place in 1955, when the Baghdad Pact marked the transition to a new and more dangerous question. Yet another writer, Jon Kimche, journalist, editor, and author of several books on the Middle East, has recognized that the Eastern Question in its varying national interpretations survives to the present day, although in an altered historical context. Curiously, Kimche has added the Chinese and Egyptians to the Russians and Americans in the great power contest for control of key political and strategic positions in the Middle East. Jon Kimche, *The Second Arab Awakening* (New York: Holt, Rinehart & Winston, 1970), pp. 13–14. Still another recognition of the ongoing nature of the question is contained in G.D. Clayton, *Britain and the Eastern Question* (London: University of London Press, 1971), p. 244: "One Eastern Question was concluded in 1923. There is as yet no answer to the new one." In this connection it is instructive to turn to the older and still valuable standard work of J.A.R. Marriott. His *The Eastern Question*, 4th ed. (Oxford University Press, 1940), was primarily concerned with the nineteenth-century aspect of an age-old problem. For him the "primary and most essential factor in the problem is the presence, embedded in the living flesh of Europe, of an alien substance . . . the Ottoman Turk" (p. 3). But he also viewed the problem in a vastly broadened historical context. "From time immemorial," he wrote, "Europe has been confronted with an 'Eastern Question.' In its essence the problem is unchanging . . . . But although one in essence, the problem has assumed different aspects at different periods" (p. 1).

More specifically, he wrote in a third epilogue in 1939 that the problem's modern phase had "evidently closed with the transference of the Turkish capital from Istanbul to Angora . . ." and he added, "Other factors in that problem . . . still obstinately await solution" (p. 577).

⁴ Antonius, *The Arab Awakening* (1938; reprint ed., New York: Capricorn Books, 1965). Antonius was a Lebanese Christian who served the government of Palestine early in the mandate.

⁵ Sylvia G. Haim, ed., *Arab Nationalism* (Berkeley and Los Angeles: University of California Press, 1964), p. 3.

⁶ Bernard Lewis, *The Middle East and the West* (Bloomington, Ind.: Indiana University Press, 1964), p. 57.

⁷ See ibid., p. 90, and Ben Halpern, *The Idea of the Jewish State*, 2nd ed. (Cambridge, Mass.: Harvard University Press, 1969), p. 4.

⁸ J. C. Hurewitz, *Diplomacy in the Near and Middle East*, vol. 1: *1535–1914* (Princeton, N.J.: D. Van Nostrand Co., 1956), p. 209.

⁹ In July 1963 the papers of Sir Gilbert F. Clayton, covering the years 1898–1929, were presented by Lady Clayton to the Sudan Archive of the School of Oriental Studies at Durham University.

¹⁰ As Sudan agent, Clayton acted as liaison between the Egyptian high commissioner, Lord Kitchener, and the authorities in the Sudan.

¹¹ From the introduction to Gilbert F. Clayton, *An Arabian Diary*, ed. Robert O. Collins (Berkeley and Los Angeles: University of California Press, 1969). p. 54. The diary is Clayton's personal account of his negotiations with Ibn Saud and the Imam Yahya in the Arabian Peninsula in 1926. Professor Collins expresses the opinion that "no history of Britain in the Middle East or the national questions in Egypt, Palestine, Arabia, or Iraq can be adequately studied without reference to the Clayton Papers" (p. viii). I am deeply in his debt for the pioneer work he has done on Clayton's life and character.

Chapter 2: Great Britain and Palestine in the War, 1914–1917

¹ Cited by Elizabeth Monroe, *Britain's Moment in the Middle East, 1914–1956* (Baltimore: Johns Hopkins Press, 1963), p. 36.

² Cab. 42/2, 27/1; see Aaron S. Klieman, "Britain's War Aims in the Middle East in 1915," *Journal of Contemporary History* 3 (July 1968), 237–51.

³ Cab. 27/1.

⁴ Storrs, *Orientations* (London: Ivor Nicholson & Watson, 1937), pp. 142–43, 172–73.

⁵ DNME, p. 14. For the complete Husayn-McMahon correspondence, see Antonius, *Arab Awakening*, pp. 413–27, and Cmd. 5957 (1939).

⁶ Sir Henry McMahon's account of the origin of serious British efforts toward Arab revolt, in Wingate papers, 12 September 1916; Elie Kedourie, "Cairo and Khartoum on the Arab Question, 1915–1918," in *Chatham House Version and Other Middle Eastern Studies* (London: Weidenfeld and Nicholson, 1970), p. 14. According to Isaiah Friedman, McMahon wrote

to Husayn on his own responsibility after listening in early October to the arguments of Muhammad Sharif al-Farugi, an Arab officer who had deserted from the Ottoman army. Al-Farugi had claimed that an Arab secret society, of which he was a prominent member, could produce a large-scale revolt against the Ottomans, but that the Turks and Germans were aware of the society's influence and were themselves trying to come to terms with its leaders. Actually, Friedman writes, there was no such German attempt, and indeed, German records directly contradict al-Farugi's contention regarding his society's influence and the Syrian population's readiness to rise in revolt. McMahon and Clayton, however, chose to believe al-Farugi and in the urgency of the moment wrote the crucial letter to Husayn. "The McMahon-Hussein Correspondence and the Question of Palestine," *Journal of Contemporary History* 5 (1970), 89–93. Albert J. Toynbee has agreed that al-Farugi's arrival in Cairo after deserting at Gallipoli constituted the turning point in the negotiations with Husayn. "The McMahon-Hussein Correspondence: Comments and a Reply," *Journal of Contemporary History* 5 (1970), 186. Certainly al-Farugi was a vital ingredient in the Husayn negotiations, but this fact must be viewed in conjunction with the military disaster at Gallipoli and the apparent need for political steps to be taken to divide Arab from Turk.

⁷ Monroe, *Britain's Moment,* pp. 31–32.

⁸ DNME, p. 15.

⁹ For much the best and most complete account, see Friedman, "McMahon-Hussein Correspondence," pp. 83–122. For other useful general versions, see Monroe, *Britain's Moment,* ch. 1; Antonius, *Arab Awakening,* chs. 7–12; Zeine N. Zeine, *The Struggle for Arab Independence* (Beirut: Khayats, 1960), ch. 1; Paul L. Hanna, *British Policy in Palestine* (Washington, D.C.: American Council on Public Affairs, 1942), ch. 2; and P.M. Holt, *Egypt and the Fertile Crescent, 1516–1922* (London: Longmans, Green and Co., 1966), pp. 266–68.

¹⁰ McMahon's statement (23 July 1937) and Clayton's (12 April 1923) are printed in Herbert Samuel, *Memoirs* (London: Cresset Press, 1945), pp. 172–73. In March 1922, McMahon wrote a letter to the Colonial Office at the request of Sir John Shuckburgh, for use in discussions with a Palestine Arab delegation, in which he expressed himself emphatically. He explained that he had restricted specific mention of towns to places in Syria which the Arabs considered vital and that at the time he could think of no place "of sufficient importance for purposes of definition further South." He had rejected mention of the Jordan, he said, because of the possible desirability of finding "some more suitable frontier line east of the Jordan and between that river and the Hejaz Railway." He added that he had "no recollection of ever hearing anything from the Sherif of Mecca, by letter or message, to make me suppose that he did not also understand Palestine to be excluded from independent Arabia." It seems peculiar, despite the fact that the letter was apparently not meant for publication, that McMahon rests his claims on the British reservation regarding areas which "cannot be said to be purely Arab," in the words of his original letter, instead of using the stronger historical argument of French interest in Palestine. Since by 1922 it was obvious that the French had given up their interests in Palestine, it may be that McMahon felt compelled to rely on a strained

interpretation of his original letter. McMahon's letter is printed in Aaron S. Klieman, *Foundations of British Policy in the Arab World* (Baltimore: Johns Hopkins Press, 1970), pp. 228–29n.

[11] Leonard Stein, *The Balfour Declaration* (London: Vallentine, Mitchell & Co., 1961), pp. 218–32.

[12] "Report of the Committee on Asiatic Turkey," June 1915. p. 26; Cab. 42/3.

[13] Clayton to Sykes, 4 April 1918. FO 371/3391/76678.

[14] Samuel, *Memoirs*, p. 173. See Kedourie, "Cairo and Khartoum," pp. 21–25, for further evidence and discussion of British policy in 1915 and 1916.

[15] Elizabeth Monroe complained, "It is galling to think how easily McMahon could have devised some form of words intimating to the Sharif that several faiths held that land in reverence, and that there must be multilateral agreement about it." *Britain's Moment*, p. 34.

[16] Even after the war, Palestinians were deliberately not informed that the Anglo-French Declaration of November 1918 did not apply to them. See chapter 7. The Arab world was well aware of the general terms of Britain's pledges, even though they remained unpublished officially until 1939 (Great Britain, *Parliamentary Papers*, 1939, Misc., no. 3, Cmd. 5957). Antonius, *Arab Awakening*, p. 180.

[17] 5 December 1918. Cab. 27/24. Foreign Secretary A.J. Balfour, also not in the government in 1915, was one of those present.

[18] Antonius, *Arab Awakening*, p. 179.

[19] The best account of the making of the agreement is in Jukka Nevakivi, *Britain, France and the Arab Middle East, 1914–1920* (London: University of London, Athlone Press, 1969), ch. 2. For a brilliant defense of the arrangement as a "workman-like device of reconciliation," see Elie Kedourie, *England and the Middle East* (London: Bowes & Bowes, 1956), p. 42.

[20] "Memo on Asia Minor Agreement (S-P)," 14 August 1917. FO 371/3059, 159558/159558. Although these words were written in 1917, they fairly represent Sykes's thoughts of a year earlier.

[21] The text of the Anglo-French Agreement of 1916 is reproduced in DBFP, pp. 245–47.

[22] These citations are from Friedman, "McMahon-Hussein Correspondence," p. 87: Clayton to Jacob, 11 March 1916; Clayton to Beach, 17 April 1916. I do not recall coming across these letters in the Clayton papers at Durham University. Possibly they are part of a further collection not yet committed to a public repository. For evidence of this, see separate appreciations expressed by Friedman, p. 87, n. 12, and p. 93, n. 28.

[23] See note 21.

[24] Samuel, *Memoirs*, pp. 140–42.

[25] Earl of Oxford and Asquith, *Memories and Reflections*, vol. 2 (London: Cassell, 1928), 59. Samuel had also circulated memoranda on the "Future of Palestine" to the Cabinet, where they had served the purpose of acquainting that body with Zionist views. According to Israel M. Sieff, from 1915 to 1920 an associate and personal assistant to Weizmann, Samuel's ideas were largely formulated by Weizmann. Jon Kimche, *There Could Have Been Peace* (New York: Dial Press, 1973), pp. 106–07,

[26] Monroe, *Britain's Moment*, p. 39.

[28] Dr. Chaim Weizmann (1874–1952): reader in Biochemistry, University of

Manchester; director of Admiralty Laboratories, 1916–1919; president, World Zionist Organization and Jewish Agency for Palestine, 1921–31 and 1935–46; first president of the State of Israel, 1949–52.

28 Charles Webster, *The Art and Practice of Diplomacy* (London: Chatto and Windus, 1961), pp. 5–6. Leonard Stein, a former aide of Weizmann's, in his masterful study of the Balfour Declaration, described him thus: "[He was] not only a dexterous and resourceful advocate—flexible, sure-footed, highly sensitive to atmosphere, and with an unerring instinct for timing; he possessed in a high degree the power to kindle the imagination and to import to others some of his own mystical faith in the destiny of his people and the significance of its survival." Leonard Stein, *The Balfour Declaration*, p. 126.

29 On this question Mayir Verete has concluded in convincing perspective: "To my mind it calls the story of the lady who—as the saying goes—was willing, and only wanted to be seduced. Britain likewise willed Palestine, wanted the Zionists and courted them. Weizmann happened to come her way, talked to her to have the Zionists and go with them to Palestine, as only her they desired and to her they would be faithful. Britain was seduced. She was ready to be seduced by any Zionist of stature." "The Balfour Declaration and Its Makers," *Middle Eastern Studies* 6 (January 1970), 67.

30 Cab. 24/9.

31 Article 8 of Sykes' instructions read: "With regard to the BROWN area [internationally administered Palestine under the Sykes-Picot Agreement], no political negotiations shall be directly entered into with native elements in this area until it is actually occupied," meaning that the British were determined to keep a free hand in the disposal of Palestine [and?] its "native elements." These instructions support my contention that Palestine was not pledged to the Arabs. It is highly doubtful that Lloyd George would have issued them were he aware of a directly contradictory promise.

32 Stein, *Balfour Declaration*, p. 336.

33 DNME, pp. 23–25. The treaty was never brought into force because the Russians failed to ratify it.

34 "Report on the Committee on Terms of Peace," 28 April 1917. Cab. 21/71.

35 See Nevakivi, *Britain, France*, p. 48. The Arab Bureau was a Foreign Office institution acting as a branch of the Department of Military Intelligence in Egypt. See chapter 3.

36 DBFP, vol. 4, pp. 245–47.

37 Nevakivi, *Britain, France*, p. 52.

38 For the various drafts, see Stein, *Balfour Declaration*, p. 664.

39 DNME, p. 26. The strongest objections to the statement came from a Jewish cabinet member, Sir Edwin Montague.

40 Cab. 23/4, 261(12).

41 Meinertzhagen, *Middle East Diary, 1917–1956* (London: Cresset Press, 1959), p. 9.

42 Quoted in Stein, *Balfour Declaration*, p. 555.

43 *Is It Peace?* (London: Hodder and Stoughton, 1923), p. 251.

44 "Synopsis of Our Obligations to Our Allies and Others"; Cab. 24/45.

45 Stein, *Balfour Declaration*, p. 549.

[46] Sir Ronald Graham was head of the Foreign Office's Eastern Department. FO 371/3054, 207945/84173.

[47] Stein, *Balfour Declaration,* pp. 533–42, 550.

[48] "The Future of Palestine," by Lord Curzon, 26 October 1917. FO 371/ 3083, 207407/143082. Also see War Cabinet meeting, 4 October 1917; Cab. 23/4, 245 (18).

[49] FO 371/3061, 234467/214354.

Chapter 3: The Invasion of Palestine, 1917

[1] John Marlowe, *Late Victorian* (London: Cresset Press, 1967), p. 114. According to Ronald Storrs, Cox was looking for a successor and Wilson heartily concurred with the choice of Clayton as Cox's nominal deputy. Cox was tired and frustrated and thought he would do well to resign and "let Clayton begin with a clear slate." However, Clayton turned down the offer early in May 1917. *Orientations,* pp. 247, 255.

[2] *Seven Pillars of Wisdom* (Garden City, N.Y.: Doubleday, Doran & Co., 1935), p. 57.

[3]. Anonymous correspondent to *The Times* (London), 12 September 1929, p. 14.

[4] To *The Near East and India,* 26 September 1929, p. 335.

[5] Anonymous correspondent to *The Times* (London), 12 September 1929, p. 14.

[6] Clayton, *Arabian Diary,* p. 64.

[7] See note 5.

[8] To *The Times* (London), 13 September 1929, p. 14.

[9] *Colonel Lawrence* (New York: Dodd, Mead & Co., 1934), p. 67.

[10] *Orientations,* pp. 172–73.

[11] Gladys Bendit [John Presland], *Deedes Bey* (London: Macmillan & Co., 1942), p. 263.

[12] To *The Times* (London), 17 September 1929, p. 17.

[13] To Clayton, 15 November 1915; Wingate papers, 135/5. Cited in Kedourie, "Cairo and Khartoum," pp. 18–19.

[14] Clayton to Wingate, 6 January 1916. Wingate papers. Quoted in Briton Cooper Busch, *Britain, India and the Arabs, 1914–1921* (Berkeley and Los Angeles: University of California Press, 1971), p. 91.

[15] W.J. Childs, "Memorandum on the Arab Bureau, Its Purposes and Services," 19 April 1923. FO 406/51, no. 26, pp. 66–67.

[16] Clayton, *Arabian Diary,* p. 63.

[17] Ibid., p. 65.

[18] Clayton papers, 139/5.

[19] Lt. Col. Cyril Wilson to Clayton, January and 20 March 1917; Clayton papers. Quoted in Clayton, *Arabian Diary,* p. 68. Wilson was Wingate's representative in Jiddah.

[20] On 28 December 1916, according to the War Cabinet notes of a conference at 10 Downing Street on 3 April 1917. Cab. 24/9, pp. 306–10.

[21] Viscount Wavell, *Allenby* (London: George G. Harrap & Co., 1946), pp. 154–55.

[22] Clayton, *Arabian Diary,* pp. 68–69.

[23] 22 July 1917. Sykes papers.

[24] Mark Sykes in War Cabinet meeting, 17 August 1917. Cab. 23/3. 217 (17). The Cabinet's discussion was in response to a telegram from Allenby requesting to be "clearly informed as to the policy of His Majesty's Government in regard to Palestine."

[25] To Clayton, 31 December 1917; Clayton papers. Cited in Clayton, *Arabian Diary,* p. 69. Major General Sir Lee Stack, K.B.E., 1918.

[26] War Cabinet notes, 3 April 1917. Cab. 24/9 (G.T. 372), pp. 306–10.

[27] 22 July 1917. Sykes papers.

[28] "Note by Brigadier General Clayton on the Future Political Status of Egypt," appendix to ch. 17 in Lord Lloyd, *Egypt Since Cromer,* vol. 1 (London: Macmillan & Co., 1933), pp. 262–63.

[29] Clayton to Wingate, 9 October 1915; Clayton papers 135/4. Cited in Kedourie, "Cairo and Khartoum," p. 19. The article contains Kedourie's argument regarding the strength of the on-the-spot officials.

[30] *England and the Middle East,* p. 42.

[31] Ibid., p. 66.

[32] Ibid., p. 213.

[33] "Cairo and Khartoum," p. 28.

[34] *An Introduction to Contemporary History* (1964; reprint ed., Baltimore: Penguin Books, 1967), p. 169.

[35] 20 August 1917. Sykes papers.

[36] Sykes papers in the possession of Sir Richard Sykes, Bart., at Sledmere, Yorkshire. Quoted in Stein, *Balfour Declaration,* p. 629.

[37] Shane Leslie, *Mark Sykes* (London: Cassell, 1923), p. 272. He spoke at Manchester on 7 December 1917.

[38] *Orientations,* p. 336.

[39] To Sykes, 15 December 1917. Clayton papers.

[40] FO 371/3061, 236700/214354.

[41] Storrs, *Orientations,* p. 348.

[42] 15 December 1917. Clayton papers.

[43] *Orientations,* p. 342.

[44] Ibid., p. 336.

[45] Ibid., pp. 338–45.

[46] Bendit, *Deedes Bey,* pp. 280–81.

[47] Weizmann to Sir Ronald Graham, 17 December 1917. FO 371/3054, 239129/84173.

[48] 11 December 1917. FO 317/3054, 235200/84173.

[49] 14 December 1917. FO 371/3054, 237384/84173.

[50] Sykes to Clayton, 11 December 1917; FO 371/3061, 235199/214354. Clayton to Sykes, 14 December 1917; FO 371/3061, 237239/214354.

[51] 12 December 1917. Clayton papers (copy of FO telegram 1181).

[52] Sometime during 1917 Sykes had conceived the idea of an Arab-Jewish-Armenian combination of buffer states across the Middle East, with each nation contributing its peculiar genius and all serving British interests. Sykes's letter to Lord Robert Cecil on 13 October 1917 is printed in Leslie, *Mark Sykes,* pp. 272–75.

[53] *Britain, France,* p. 51. Sir Stewart Symes, a member of the Arab Bureau and later governor-general of the Sudan, told in his autobiography of the time Sykes visited the East "complete with quip and caricature ... [f]ollowed [by] George (the late Lord) Lloyd, anxious 'lest Mark in a gust of mirth should let slip a British interest.'" *Tour of Duty* (London: Collins, 1946), p. 33.

[54] 15 December 1917. Clayton papers.

[55] According to Elizabeth Monroe, Clayton showed less prescience than did the American observer William Yale. "Clayton expressed misgiving," she said, "but, being by nature both moderate and detached, and by profession an intelligence officer, he couched his reports as information, and not as warnings." *Britain's Moment,* p. 45.

[56] See note 54.

[57] 17 December 1917. Clayton papers.

[58] Clayton papers.

[59] Clayton papers 147/3. Deedes had handled the Zionist question for the Arab Bureau from early 1917 and in Palestine organized the initial relief for the Jewish colonies. Bendit, *Deedes Bey,* p. 285. Also, for an appreciation of Deedes's Zionism, see Eliahu Elath, ed., *Memories of Sir Wyndham Deedes* (London: Victor Gollancz, 1958).

[60] 30 December 1917. FO 371/3061, 245447/214354.

[61] Wavell, *Allenby,* p. 198. Allenby considered Clayton "one of the ablest men of the day." Quoted in *The Times* (London), 12 September 1929, p. 14.

Chapter 4: Palestine Conquered, Early 1918

[1] P. 58.

[2] Hurewitz, *Diplomacy,* p. 29.

[3] *Great Britain and Palestine, 1915–1945* (London: Oxford Univ. Press, 1946), pp. 147–48. See also "British Commitments to King Hussein," memorandum by the Political Intelligence Department of the Foreign Office, 5 November 1918. FO 371/3384, 183770/747. The department introduced the discussion of the Hogarth commitments with two illuminating sentences: "With regard to Palestine, His Majesty's Government are committed by Sir H. McMahon's letter to the Sharif on the 24th October, 1915, to *its inclusion in the boundaries of Arab independence.* But they have stated their policy regarding the Palestinian Holy Places and Zionist colonisation in their message to him of the 4th January, 1918." The first sentence may be erroneous in conception, but it shows clearly the department's perception of the limited nature of the commitment to Zionism. The second sentence is equally clear on the limited burden of the Hogarth message regarding Zionism. Emphasis added.

[4] DNME, pp. 27–28.

[5] *Wilson vs. Lenin* (Cleveland and New York: World Publishing Co., 1959), p. 310.

[6] David Lloyd George, *War Memoirs,* vol. 5: *1917–1918* (Boston. Little, Brown and Co., 1936), pp. 63–73.

[7] Ray Stannard Baker, *Woodrow Wilson and World Settlement*, vol. 3, (New York: Doubleday, Page & Co., 1922), pp. 42–45.

[8] *United States Policy and the Partition of Turkey, 1914–1924* (Baltimore: John Hopkins Press, 1965), p. 80.

[9] Population statistics taken from William R. Polk, David M. Stamler, and Edmund Asfour, *Backdrop to Tragedy* (Boston: Beacon Press, 1957), pp. 318–19. For discussion on the status of the Arabs under the Ottomans, see pp. 34–64, 225–65.

[10] Allenby to secretary of state for war, 2 March 1918. FO 371/3389, 77141/2070.

[11] *The Times* (London), 12 September 1929, p. 14.

[12] Clayton, *Arabian Diary*, p. 70.

[13] "The Palestine and West Arabian Situation," 1 January 1918. FO 371/3388, 3767/2070.

[14] 7 January 1918. FO 371/3388, 3767/2070.

[15] Foreign Office to Wingate, 12 January 1918. FO 371/3388, 3767/2070. Wingate to Foreign Office, 15 January 1918. FO 371/3388, 9811, 2070.

[16] 16 January 1918 supplement to 1 January memorandum by Sykes with Hardinge's minutes. See note 13.

[17] Clayton to Sykes, 4 February 1918. FO 371/3398, 36757/28547.

[18] *Orientations*, pp. 371–72.

[19] FO 371/3394, 21931/11053.

[20] FO 371/3394, 14214/11053. For the original list of commission objectives, see chapter 3. Graham had invited Weizmann for a discussion of the commission's objectives with Balfour on 26 December 1917. Graham to Weizmann, 26 December 1917. FO 371/3054, 239129/84173.

[21] FO 371/3394, 14519/11053. Ormsby-Gore was also to be given the temporary and local rank of major to raise him to the necessary status to carry out his duties.

[22] FO 371/3388, 14557/2070.

[23] 26 January 1918. FO 371/3398, 28547.

[24] 2 February 1918. FO 800/221.

[25] FO 371/3398, 28547.

[26] FO 371/3398, 36757/28547.

[27] FO 882/7, cited in Phillip Knightley and Colin Simpson, *The Secret Lives of Lawrence of Arabia* (New York: Bantam, 1969), p. 118.

[28] 8 February 1918. Clayton Papers 148/4. Some British officials were shocked by news of the commission's coming. See Storrs, *Orientations*, p. 399.

[29] A copy of the Foreign Office telegram is in the Clayton papers.

[30] "Synopsis of Our Obligations to Our Allies and Others," February 1918. Cab. 24/45 (3917).

[31] 15 February 1918. FO 371/3398, 27647.

[32] 2 February 1918. Wingate papers 148/5.

[33] FO 800/221.

[34] 3 March 1918. Ibid.

[35] Chaim Weizmann, *Trial and Error* (1949; reprinted., New York: Schocken Books, 1966), pp. 212–14.

[36] 14 March 1918. FO 371/3391, 48034/4079.

[37] Clayton papers.

[38] *Trial and Error*, p. 215.

[39] Sir Ronald Wingate, *Wingate of the Sudan* (London: John Murray, 1955), pp. 225–26.

[40] 31 March 1918. FO 371/3383, 81519/747.

[41] *Trial and Error,* p. 216.

[42] See note 40.

Chapter 5: The Zionist Commission in Palestine, April-June 1918

[1] For Weizmann's account, see *Trial and Error,* pp. 216ff.

[2] Philip Graves, member of the Arab section of headquarters staff in Palestine and journalist and author, has written of "hearing the Declaration discussed by the Military Governor of Jerusalem with a representative of the Hejaz Government and several prominent citizens of Jerusalem in January, 1918." News of the declaration was widespread, even among the inhabitants of Palestine. According to Graves, it was not made public in the form of an official proclamation, "since such publication was deemed unnecessary and also somewhat presumptuous." *Palestine* (New York: George H. Doran Co., 1923), pp. 47–48.

[3] 4 April 1918. FO 371/3391.

[4] See Norman Cohn, *Warrant for Genocide* (New York: Harper & Row, 1966). Deedes was Clayton's deputy chief political officer.

[5] *Trial and Error,* pp. 217–18. Weizmann did not identify the person or group who he thought had done the selecting. Nothing about the conversation or the *Protocols* is to be found in Bendit, *Deedes Bey.* Also see Jon Kimche, *The Second Arab Awakening,* p. 181.

[6] *Trial and Error,* p. 218.

[7] Ibid., pp. 219–20.

[8] To Sykes, 9 April 1918. Sykes papers.

[9] 18 April 1918. Clayton papers

[10] In this connection it is worth noting that in his autobiography, Sir Reader Bullard told why he thought he had been lucky to become involved in the administration of Iraq instead of Palestine: "Vagueness of policy created difficulties in Iraq, but the vagueness in Palestine was more dangerous, because it was deliberate . . . the Balfour Declaration . . . accepted an ambiguous formula—a National Home for the Jewish people—which might mean anything . . . . I thought myself fortunate that I was not one of those who had to try to administer Palestine under a shifting, ambiguous policy without enjoying the sympathy of either of the two parties concerned." *The Camels Must Go* (London: Faber & Faber, 1961), p. 123

[11] Kimche, *There Could Have Been Peace,* pp. 140–41.

[12] Storrs to Clayton, 22 April 1918. FO 371/3398.

[13] Weizmann to Ormsby-Gore, 16 April 1918. FO 371/3398, 92392/28547.

[14] To Clayton, 22 April 1918. FO 371/3398.

[15] *Trial and Error,* p. 220.

[16] *Seven Pillars,* p. 57.

[17] *Cross Roads to Israel* (London: Collins, 1965), pp. 39–40.

18 18 April 1918. FO 371/3394, 85908/11053.
19 FO 371/3395, 86912/11053. His first report had been dispatched early and
contained little of value. See FO 371/3394, 83691/11053.
20 A mufti is an Islamic religious official and community leader who issues
legal opinions on points of Islamic law. A qadi is a judge of Islamic law.
Kamal al-Husayni lived until 1921, when he was succeeded by Hajj Muhammad Amin al-Husayni.
21 See chapter 4. Clayton to Sykes, 26 January 1918. FO 371/3398; Wingate
to *FO,*27 January 1918. FO 371/3388.
22 *Seven Pillars,* p. 58.
23 To Symes, 20 April 1918. FO 371/3394, 851/11053.
24 Weizmann noted that British officials "had only a vague notion about the
aim of our movement, and the spirit of the Declaration, and have been
awaiting our explanations before themselves coming to a definite conclusion." Letter to Brandeis, 25 April 1918. FO 371/3395, 98469/11053.
25 *The Seat of Pilate* (London: Cresset Press, 1959), p. 76.
26 The guest list included Sylvain Levi, the mufti, Musa Kazim al-Husayni
(mayor of Jerusalem), Ismail al-Husayni (director of education), Arif Pasha
Daudi; Porphyrios II (archbishop of Mount Sinai) and D. G. Salama (vice
mayor), representing the Greek Orthodox patriarchate and community;
the Armenian bishop of Cairo, representing the Armenian patriarchate
and community; Abu Suan, representing the Latin Catholic patriarchate;
Lieutenant-Colonel Lord William Percy, Major James Rothschild, and Major Ormsby-Gore. Copy of speech enclosed with letter from Storrs to Clayton, 30 April 1918, FO 371/3395, and report by Clayton to Foreign Office,
1 May 1918, FO 371/3394. Also see Storrs, *Orientations,* p. 400.
27 FO 371/3395, 98469/11053.
28 War Office, General Staff, "Notes on Zionism," 20 May 1919, FO 371/
4171. Also see undated Israel Sieff letter to Jon Kimche in Kimche, *There
Could Have Been Peace,* pp. 126–27: "For I had come to understand from
what [Weizmann] told me that not only the fate of the Balfour Declaration
but also the prospect of a Jewish state would depend largely on what the
Zionist Commission would be able to achieve. We were, in fact, to lay the
practical foundations of our state while war was still raging, and the future
uncertain. It was to be our act of faith and to this now I devoted all my
efforts. For we were to create the fait accompli that might well be decisive
in the negotiations at the Peace Conference."
29 FO 371/3395, 98469/11053.
30 Clayton to Foreign Office, 24 May 1918. FO 371/3391, 92609/4079.
31 Antonius, *Arab Awakening,* pp. 229–30.
32 Details for this meeting and Lawrence's remarks come from Kimche, *Second Arab Awakening,* pp. 179–83, and *There Could Have Been Peace,* pp. 170–
73, citing the private papers and diaries of Palestinian historian Arif al-
Arif. I could trace no record of this meeting in the Foreign Office files or
among the Clayton papers. Kimche could find no corroborating evidence
in the Zionist records, either; nor is the episode mentioned in Weizmann's
autobiography. There is some slight evidence in Antonius, *Arab Awakening,*
pp. 269–70, where meetings between Zionist and Arab leaders are acknowledged, apparently in the presence of Dr. Faris Nimr Pasha. Significantly, at this time a group of Syrian nationalists of the Syrian Unity Party

was also troubled by the future ambitions of the Sharifians and British. See chapter 6.

[33] FO 371/3395, 125475/11053.

[34] 30 April 1918, quoted in Kimche, *There Could Have Been Peace*, pp. 144–45.

[35] Clayton to Foreign Office, 7 June 1918. FO 371/3391.

[36] Memorandum on Ormsby-Gore report, 18 May 1918. Quoted in Kimche, *There Could Have Been Peace*, p. 52.

[37] On 26 May 1918, Clayton cabled the Foreign Office: "Discussions between Weizmann and Feisal can do no harm and may be productive of excellent results. The present time is particularly favourable as Feisal is proceeding shortly to Jeddah to see his father with whom he will be able to discuss the result of his meeting with Weizmann. Sympathetic attitude of the King of the Hejaz and of Feisal will go far towards a [co-ordination?] of Zionist and Arab policies. FO 371. 27647/94197. Also Clayton to Symes, 13 June 1918; Clayton papers.

Chapter 6: Weizmann, Faysal, and Ottoman Defeat, Summer 1918

[1] 3 March 1918. FO 800/221.

[2] Clayton to Symes, 13 June 1918. Clayton papers.

[3] Clayton to Foreign Office, 7 June 1918. FO 371/3391, 102630/4079.

[4] For a colorful account of the trip and talks, see Weizmann, *Trial and Error*, pp. 232–35.

[5] Clayton to Foreign Office, 12 June 1918. FO 371/3398, 105824/27647.

[6] According to C. P. Scott, Weizmann said that "Damascus, Baghdad, and Medina were three necessary pillars of the Arab State and must be preserved for it." *Political Diaries of C. P. Scott, 1911–1928,* ed. Trevor Wilson (Ithaca, N.Y.: Cornell University Press, 1970), pp. 360–61.

[7] See note 5. Sykes and Hardinge's comments were added in minutes to Clayton's report.

[8] *Trial and Error*, p. 235.

[9] Scott, *Political Diaries*, p. 360.

[10] Clayton papers 148/10. From 1917 to 1919 Symes was an intelligence officer attached to the high commissioner's staff in Egypt. He later held administrative posts in Egypt, Palestine, Aden, and Tanganyika, and from 1934 to 1940 was governor-general of the Anglo-Egyptian Sudan.

[11] Clayton to Foreign Office, 11 July 1918. FO 371/3395, 137853. Clayton objected to Ormsby-Gore's statements being included in the minutes of the Zionist Commission's 17th meeting.

[12] See note 10 for source of Weizmann's plans. Emphasis in original.

[13] 16 June 1918. FO 371/3395, 130342/11053.

[14] The mufti of Jerusalem had already been approached on the subject by Ronald Storrs and had expressed total opposition to the project. Clayton to Balfour, 16 June 1918. FO 371/3395, 130342/11053. In 1919 the Zionists offered the Arabs eighty thousand pounds for the Wall, but the

Arabs refused to sell then, too. Vincent Sheean, *Personal History* (Garden City, N.Y.: Doubleday, Doran & CO., 1934), p. 350.

[15] Material on the land problems encountered by OETA is adapted from Polk, Stamler, and Asfour, *Backdrop to Tragedy,* pp. 70–71, 233–40.

[16] Ibid., p. 235.

[17] 18 June 1918. FO 800/221.

[18] See chapter 5.

[19] Clayton papers 148/10. Most of this memorandum is printed in Symes, *Tour of Duty,* pp. 30–33. According to C. P. Scott, Weizmann said Faysal "was largely under the influence of an Englishman, T. E. Lawrence, one of those extraordinary adventurous travellers who assimilate themselves wholly to the people of strange lands and acquire ascendancy over them. It was he who had started the whole Arab movement of revolt and created the new Kingdom of the Hedjaz." *Political Diaries,* p. 360. In his autobiography, Weizmann paid tribute to the services T. E. Lawrence rendered Zionism. He considered Lawrence's relationship to the Zionist movement to be "a very positive one." *Trial and Error,* p. 236.

[20] The memorial was sent from Cairo on 7 May 1918. Clayton to Balfour, 21 September 1918. FO 371/3384, 171829/74. It is interesting to note that this memorial was formulated at nearly the same time that the Palestinian leaders were talking with the Zionists in secret about the same problems.

[21] The Syrians were nationalists of the Party of Syrian Unity, according to Nevakivi, *Britain, France,* p. 61. Antonius names them in *Arab Awakening,* p. 433. In the judgment of Elizabeth Monroe, it was Walrond's "perceptive reporting about the worries of sophisticated Arabs" that helped account for this fresh British promise. *Britain's Moment,* p. 48.

[22] Great Britain, *Parliamentary Papers,* 1939, Cmd. 5974, p. 49. According to Elizabeth Monroe, both contemporary explanations for the release of this document seem to be right. One was that a revived Turkish propaganda needed countering, and the second was that the British government wanted to give "would-be federalists . . . some guarantee of immunity from the vagaries of the Sharif." *Britain's Moment,* p. 48.

[23] *Arab Awakening,* p. 273. In Curzon's view, the declaration would still not be inconsistent with annexation, since no explicit disclaimer of that action had been made. Cab. 27/24 EC 20th meeting, 15 July 1918, 2nd minute.

[24] Nahum Sokolow, *History of Zionism,* vol. 2 (New York: KTAV Publishing House, 1919), pp. 142–45.

[25] FO 371/3388, 115336/1495.

[26] FO 371/3398, 123904/27647.

[27] Kimche, *There Could Have Been Peace,* pp. 56–57.

[28] FO 371/3398, 138908/27647. Weizmann also suggested diffidently that greater efficiency would result from General Clayton's being put in total charge of British policy in the Middle East, instead of having to share responsibility with the Arab Bureau and residency in Cairo.

[29] Clayton papers.

[30] Cab. 23/7, 457 (7). On 11 July 1918, Balfour had mentioned in a meeting of the Eastern Committee that "our object apparently now was to destroy the Sykes-Picot Agreement." Cab. 27/24, EC 19th meeting. The Eastern Committee had superseded and absorbed the functions of the Persia and Middle East Committees and held forty-two meetings from 28 March to

7 January 1919, with Lord Curzon as chairman. See War Cabinet decision, 21 March 1918. Cab. 23/5, 369 (11). Its full records are in Cab. 27/24. The committee was supposed to coordinate policy at the Cabinet level but was unable to achieve full harmony among the many departments involved with the Middle East. See Nevakivi, *Britain, France,* pp. 66–67. Weizmann's 17 July 1918 letter to Balfour, in which he criticized the 1916 agreement, was received on 12 August.

[31] Sykes to Eastern Committee, 18 July 1918. Cab. 27/24, EC 21st meeting.

[32] Cab. 23/7, 457 (7).

[33] Cab. 23/7, 459 (9).

[34] 18 July 1918. Cab. 27/24, EC 21st meeting.

[35] 14 August 1918. Hogarth papers, file three.

[36] "Report on the Existing Political Situation in Palestine and Contiguous Areas by the Political Officer in Charge of the Zionist Commission, August 1919," 22 August 1919. FO 371/3395, 152266/11053 and FO 371/3389, 147225/2070. Among those present at the meeting were Achad Ha'am, Leon Simon, Joseph Cowen, Albert Hyamson, Norman Bentwich, A. Aaronsohn, Leonard Stein, S. Marks, S. Landman, and Nahum Sokolow, chairman.

[37] Weizmann, *Trial and Error,* pp. 227–28. Jabotinsky was a right-wing extremist who became impatient with Weizmann's more moderate, pro-British stance. In 1925 he founded the World Union of Zionist Revisionists.

[38] 5 September 1918. FO 371/3389, 152846/2070.

[39] Clayton to Ormsby-Gore, 13 September 1918. FO 800/221.

[40] 19 September 1918. FO 800/210.

[41] *Democratic Ideals and Reality* (New York: Henry Holt & Co., 1919), p. 154.

Chapter 7: Between War and Peace

[1] Wingate to Clayton, 3 October 1918. Clayton papers 150/2.

[2] 18 July 1918. Cab. 27/24, EC 21st meeting.

[3] 23 September 1918. FO 371/3383, 162968/747.

[4] 3 October 1918. Cab. 27/34, EC 34th meeting, appendix A. The 30 September agreement at the Foreign Office was formally approved in a letter from Balfour to Cambon on 19 October 1918. FO 371/3384, 172890/747.

[5] 3 October 1918. Cab. 27/24, EC 34th meeting.

[6] See Nevakivi, *Britain, France,* p. 76.

[7] FO 371/3384, 170193/747. The Cabinet approved the memorandum on 14 October 1918. Cab. 23/8, 485 (9 and appendix).

[8] 10 October 1918. Clayton papers.

[9] Hogarth papers.

[10] See Nevakivi, *Britain, France,* p. 264 (appendix B).

[11] According to Briton Cooper Busch, "The declaration had actually been meant more as a whip with which to flog the French from Syria." *Britain, India, and the Arabs, 1914–1921,* p. 276.

[12] *The Independent Arab* (London: John Murray, 1933), p. 280. Curzon later admitted that the British had not understood the "full purport and bear-

ing" of the joint declaration. 5 December 1918. Cab. 27/24, EC 41st meeting.

[13] 16 November 1918. FO 371/3385, 189886/747.

[14] FO 371/3385, 199355/747.

[15] "The Political Future of Iraq," 22 November 1918. Wingate papers 150/5.

[16] Cambon to Foreign Office, 22 October 1918. FO 371/3384, 176523/747.

[17] FO 371/3384, 176523/747.

[18] See Norman and Helen Bentwich, *Mandate Memories, 1918–1948* (London: Hogarth Press, 1965), p. 27.

[19] Eder to Weizmann. FO 371/3398, 178952/27647.

[20] Ibid., minutes by Kidston and Ormsby-Gore.

[21] 29 October 1918. Cab. 27/24, E.C. 37th meeting.

[22] See Nevakivi, *Britain, France,* pp. 68–88.

[23] 1 November 1918. Hogarth papers.

[24] Clayton papers. Weizmann had been disappointed by his reception in London. C.P. Scott noted in his diary for 25 and 26 October that Weizmann had been in England three weeks "and found no one to whom he could report. Balfour had seen him for twenty-five minutes, tired and half asleep, but had taken no step and would take none. His report had simply been pigeonholed." *Political Diaries,* pp. 360–61.

[25] "Reconstruction of Arabia" in *Letters of T.E. Lawrence,* ed. David Garnett (London: Jonathan Cape, 1938), pp. 265–69. Lawrence ridiculed the 1916 agreement: "The geographical absurdities of the present Agreement will laugh it out of Court, and it would be perhaps as well if we spared ourselves a second effort on the same lines."

[26] 5 November 1918. Clayton papers.

[27] FO 371/3395, 182887/11053.

[28] FO 371/3395, 191998/11053.

[29] Storrs to Headquarters, OETA, 4 November 1918. FO 371/3385, 747.

[30] 8 November 1918. FO 371/3385, 198575/747.

[31] 15 November 1918, enclosed in Clayton to Balfour, 6 December 1918, FO 371/3386, 213403/747.

[32] *Palestine* was published in London by the British Palestine Committee beginning in January 1917. On its front page it carried two mottoes. One advocated a British dominion in Palestine for the Jewish nation, and the second quoted the *Spectator:* "If [Disraeli] had freed the Holy Land, and restored the Jews, as he might have done, instead of pottering about with Roumelia and Afghanistan, he would have died Dictator."

[33] Sykes to Ormsby-Gore, 17 November 1918. FO 371/3398, 199447/27647.

[34] Weizmann to Ormsby-Gore, 19 November 1918. Ibid. The letter was merely for the record. Ormsby-Gore had already responded to Weizmann's suggestion.

[35] Ormsby-Gore minute, 18 November 1918. Ibid. For Allenby's reaction, see Allenby to Foreign Office, 25 November 1918. FO 371/3385, 195250/747.

[36] Toynbee minute, 2 December 1918. Ibid. On 28 October 1918, the British had handed over the area of Transjordan to an Arab governor. Ormsby-Gore had noted at the time that this action recognized Transjordan as an Arab country, and the Jordan River as the boundary of Palestine. Sooner or later, he said, this would involve "our telling the Zionists that the ancient

territory of Reuben, Gilead and Manasseh is not to form part of the 'national home.'" Ormsby-Gore minute to Clayton to Foreign Office, 31 October 1918. FO 371/3384, 181689/747.

[37] Emphasis in original.

[38] Sykes to Ormsby-Gore, 20 November 1918. FO 371/3385, 192446/747.

[39] To Foreign Office, 20 November 1918. FO 371/3385, 192763/747.

[40] Clayton to Foreign Office, 21 November 1918, FO 371/3385, 193411/747; Allenby to Foreign Office, 25 November 1918, FO 371l/3385, 195250/747. Lawrence also thought there would be no difficulty in reconciling Zionists and Arabs in Palestine provided the administration remained in British hands. 21 November 1918. Cab. 27/24, EC 38th meeting.

[41] "Proposals Relating to the Establishment of a Jewish National Home in Palestine," 20 November 1918. FO 371/3385, 191828/747.

[42] 18 November 1918. FO 371/3385, 191229/747.

[43] "French and Arab Claims in the Middle East in Relation to British Interests," 19 December 1918. FO 371/3385, pp.183–86.

[44] Weizmann, "Note on the Interview with Mr. Balfour," 4 December 1918. FO 371/3385, 203091/747.

[45] Balfour to Weizmann, 18 December 1918. FO 371/3385, 203091/747. Weizmann had written Sir Eyre Crowe on 9 December about using the interview.

[46] See above.

[47] Weizmann to Eder, 28 November 1918. FO 371/3385, 201968/747.

[48] Clayton to Foreign Office, 5 December 1918. Ibid.

[49] Ibid.

[50] 6 December 1918, with Enclosures: Money to General Staff, 20 November 1918; and Colonel John E. Hubbard to OETA(S) Headquarters, Jerusalem, 20 November 1918. FO 371/3386, 213403/747. Weizmann thought that Colonel Hubbard went beyond his duty to encourage Arabs and discourage Jews. *Trial and Error*, p. 220.

[51] Minute to Clayton to Foreign Office, 5 December 1918. FO 371/3385, 201968/747.

[52] 5 December 1918. Cab. 27/24, EC 41st meeting, and annex.

[53] "The Strategic Importance of Syria to the British Empire," 9 December 1918. FO 371/3385, 202919/747. The memorandum was written by Field-Marshal Sir Henry Wilson, according to Nevakivi, *Britain, France*, pp. 98–99. Only a few days earlier, Balfour had told the Eastern Committee: "I never quite understood the inception of the Sykes-Picot Agreement, I never thoroughly understood it, and do not understand it to this day." 5 December 1918. Cab. 27/24, EC 41st meeting.

[54] 16 December 1918. Cab. 27/24, EC 43rd meeting. Also see David Lloyd George, *Memoirs of the Peace Conference*, vol. 2 (New Haven: Yale University Press, 1939), pp. 744–46.

[55] In Weizmann Archives, Israel. Cited by Knightley and Simpson, *Secret Lives of Lawrence of Arabia*, pp. 130–31.

[56] 17 December 1918. FO 371/4153, 13534/275.

[57] Ibid.

[58] Clayton to Foreign Office, 31 December 1918. FO 371/4170, 1051.

[59] *Arab Awakening*, p. 284.

[60] For the text of the agreement, see ibid., pp. 437–39. Also see Knightley

and Simpson, *Secret Lives of Lawrence of Arabia*, pp. 131–32. The original is in St. Antony's College, Oxford.

[61] See Aharon Cohen, *Israel and the Arab World* (New York: Funk & Wagnalls, 1970), pp. 141–43, for a discussion of the agreement and Arab attempts to explain it away.

[62] David Lloyd George, *The Truth About the Peace Treaties*, vol. 2 (London: Victor Gollancz, 1938), p. 1038.

[63] "French and Arab Claims." See note 41.

[64] Nevakivi, *Britain, France*, pp. 91–93.

[65] 16 January 1919. FO 800/215.

[66] Ibid.

[67] See Nevakivi, *Britain, France*, p. 102. According to the author, Balfour, Milner, and Chamberlain, in addition to the Canadian prime minister, Sir Robert Borden, all wished U.S. participation in Palestine.

Chapter 8: Palestine in the Peace

[1] DNME, pp. 61–62.

[2] See Zeine, *Struggle*, p. 32.

[3] DNME, pp. 38–39.

[4] Lloyd George, *Peace Conference*, vol. 2, 676–77.

[5] Nevakivi, *Britain, France*, p. 110.

[6] *Letters*, p. 273.

[7] Faysal, accompanied by Lawrence, had visited Balfour in London on 11 December. Balfour noted that Faysal's conversation had been "as violently anti-French as it was undisguisedly pro-British." FO 371/3386, 205516/747.

[8] Kidston memorandum, 25 January 1919; Graham minute, same date; Curzon minute, 26 January. FO 371/4153, 18816/275.

[9] 26 January 1919. FO 800/215.

[10] DNME, pp. 45–50.

[11] Lloyd George, *Peace Conference*, vol. 2, 748. The presentation took place on 27 February, not 23 February as Weizmann has it in *Trial and Error*, p. 243.

[12] *Trial and Error*, pp. 247–48.

[13] Alpheus Thomas Mason, *Brandeis* (New York: Viking Press, 1946), p. 455. Mason notes that Brandeis and Wise were advocating support for British trusteeship and that Wilson, who strongly approved of Zionism, had met with Weizmann on 15 January 1919. Weizmann may also have been informed of the report made by the intelligence section of the American delegation on 21 January 1919. The report recommended that Palestine be made a separate state and asserted that "It is right that Palestine should become a Jewish state, if the Jews, being given the full opportunity, make it such." DNME, pp. 40–45.

[14] Weizmann, *Trial and Error*, p. 243.

[15] Mason, *Brandeis*, p. 455.

[16] FRUS, vol. 4, 166–69.
[17] Weizmann, *Trial and Error*, pp. 243–45.
[18] Leslie, *Mark Sykes*, p. 282.
[19] Ibid., p. 284.
[20] Ibid., pp. 287–88.
[21] Nevakivi, *Britain, France*, p. 116.
[22] Ibid., pp. 116–18.
[23] Lloyd George, *Peace Conference*, vol. 2, 678. Milner to Lloyd George, 6 March 1919.
[24] Nevakivi, *Britain, France*, pp. 119–23.
[25] Ibid., pp. 126–27.
[26] FRUS, vol. 3, 1024–38. According to Zeine, Ghanim's speech defeated its own purpose. It was too long and too obviously French-inspired for Wilson's taste. *Struggle*, pp. 72–73.
[27] FO 800/215.
[28] On 27 August 1918, Lloyd George had written to Balfour reassuring him of his strong support for his policy on Zionism. Lloyd George papers, F/3/3/30.
[29] 18 February 1919. FO 800/215.
[30] To Lloyd George, 19 February 1919. FO 800/215.
[31] Meinertzhagen said Weizmann agreed with him about the identity of Zionism and Bolshevism, and when he asked Weizmann for his frank view of Bolshevism, he was answered: "If Christ were to come to Paris now, he would preach Bolshevism." Meinertzhagen then commented, and in so doing revealed his bitter attitude: "Do you think any Christian nation would now give Christ a passport to travel freely in Europe? Even he would be refused." *Diary*, p. 14.
[32] Meinertzhagen liked Weizmann, but was annoyed that he was a Jew. ". . . it annoys me," he said, "that he should be so far ahead of Christians in intelligence and general purity of mind, and it annoys me that such a continent of knowledge should be combating Christians for principles which are Christian, and which are as pure and progressive as any principles since the day of Christ." *Diary*, p. 67.
[33] Ibid., pp. 88–89.
[34] Ibid., p. 14.
[35] Ibid., p. 15.
[36] Quoted in Cohen, *Israel*, pp. 143–44.
[37] Ibid., p. 144. Zangwill's proposal was known in Palestine and discussed there by a Jewish diarist early in 1919. See Redcliffe N. Salaman, *Palestine Reclaimed* (London: George Routledge & Sons, 1920), pp. 175–76.
[38] *Trial and Error*, p. 245.
[39] Esco Foundation for Palestine, *Palestine* (New Haven: Yale University Press, 1947), p. 142.
[40] Cohen, *Israel*, p. 144.
[41] Esco, *Palestine*, p. 142.
[42] Cohen, *Israel*, pp. 144–45; Meinertzhagen, *Diary*, pp. 15–16. According to Meinertzhagen, he, Lawrence, Faysal, Frankfurter, and Weizmann had drafted the letter.
[43] *Israel*, pp. 147–48. Taken from the Zionist Central Archives.
[44] 11 March 1919. Lloyd George papers. F205/3/9.
[45] December 1918. Cab. 27/24, EC 41st meeting.

[46] To Lloyd George, 8 March 1919. Lloyd George, *Peace Conference,* vol. 2, 678–80.

[47] Ibid., pp. 695–96.

[48] Ibid., p. 696. "Syrian tangle" was Milner's phrase.

[49] FRUS, vol. 5, 1–14.

[50] Nevakivi has suggested that Clemenceau agreed because he wanted to avoid controversy with his allies until he had obtained the proposed Anglo-American guarantees to France in case of German attack. *Britain, France,* p. 129.

[51] FO 800/215.

[52] "A Note of Warning About the Middle East," 25 March 1919. FO 406/41, 46887.

[53] See note 51.

[54] See note 52.

[55] See note 51.

[56] Meinertzhagen, Diary, p. 17.

[57] Ibid., pp. 17–19.

[58] Ibid., pp. 19–20.

[59] The memorandum is summarized in W. K. Hancock, *Smuts* (Cambridge, Eng.: Cambridge University Press, 1962), p. 514.

[60] Weizmann, "Note on the Interview with Mr. Balfour," 4 December 1918. FO 371/3385, 747. In June 1919, Balfour voiced his conviction that the revolutionary movement was largely Jewish-led, that in fact Lenin was a Jew, and that Jewish revolutionary fervor could be constructively diverted by Zionism. See note 64.

[61] FO 271/4153, 49607/275.

[63] Curzon minute, ibid.

[63] 30 March 1919. Clayton papers. General Archibald Perceival Wavell was at the time BGGS with the EEF.

[64] Frankfurter, "Memorandum of Interview in Mr. Balfour's Apartment, 23 Rue Nitot, on Tuesday, June 24th at 4:45 p.m." FO 800/217. Also DBFP, vol. 4, 1276–78.

[65] FO 800/215.

[66] FO 800/216.

[67] 7 April 1919. FO 800/216.

[68] 9 April 1919. FO 800/216.

[69] "The Present Position of the Middle Eastern Question," 18 April 1919. FO 406/41.

[70] "Review of the Situation in the Middle East, with Special Reference to the Danger of Delay in Reaching a General Settlement," 18 April 1919. FO 406/41.

[71] The British were represented by Lawrence, Gertrude Bell, and Sir Valentine Chirol of the Foreign Office, who was also connected with *The Times;* and the French by Robert de Caix (afterwards French commissioner in Syria), Philippe Millet (foreign editor of *Le Temps),* Henri Brenier (director-general of the Marseilles chamber of commerce and a Syrian expert), Sabatier d'Espeyran (French Foreign Office), and Auguste Gauvain (foreign editor of the *Journal des Debats).* Henry Wickham Steed, *Through Thirty Years, 1892–1922,* vol. 2 (London: William Heinemann, 1924), p. 300.

[72] The staff included Professor Albert Howe Lybyer of the University of

Illinois; Captain William Yale, a State Department special agent in the Middle East and an official observer of the EEF in Palestine; and Dr. G. R. Montgomery, who had long been associated with Ottoman affairs and in 1916 was appointed special asisstant to Ambassador Morgenthau at Constantinople. Harry N. Howard, *The King-Crane Commission* (Beirut: Khayats, 1963), p. 38, 39–41.

[73] Ibid., p. 47n.

[74] DBFP, vol. 4, 252–53.

[75] Clayton to Foreign Office, 21 May 1919. DBFP, vol. 4, 265. Clayton reported that Faysal told him during an interview that he never had any intention of carrying out an agreement with the French and that Syria was bitterly opposed to any form of French penetration.

[76] Lawrence, *Letters*, pp. 276–79.

[77] DBFP, vol. 4, 272.

[78] FRUS, vol. 5, 466–72.

[79] DBFP, vol. 4, 260–61.

[80] Ibid., 261–62.

[81] DBFP, vol. 4, 281 n.4

[82] The U.S. government had *not* officially approved the declaration. Wilson had only given his personal approval. See Lansing to Wilson, 28 February 1918. FRUS, *The Lansing Papers, 1914–1920*, vol. 2, 107–08.

[83] Frankfurter did not request permission to show Wilson's letter "to all those who are interested—not to be published of course" until 20 May. It may be that this request was at Balfour's behest for the purpose of informing the British Foreign Office of Wilson's official position. At any rate clearance was given immediately by Gilbert F. Close, confidential secretary to Wilson. See DBFP, vol. 4, 260–62. Also see Nevakivi, *Britain, France*, pp. 160–61, on the linking of Wilson's assurance and Balfour's cable to Curzon.

[84] DBFP, vol. 4, 311n.

[85] FRUS, vol. 5, 616.

[86] DBFP, vol. 4, 578–79. Also FRUS, vol. 5, 808.

[87] FRUS, vol. 5, 760–62.

[88] Ibid., 766.

[89] Ibid., 807–12.

[90] Ibid., p. 760. Wilson said he could not keep his commissioners in Paris any longer.

[91] Nevakivi, *Britain, France*, p. 163.

[92] Ibid.

[93] Hogarth papers.

[94] To Derby, 30 May 1919. DBFP, vol. 4, 254–55.

[95] To Balfour, 30 May 1919. Telegrams from Faysal, the Hijaz representatives in Paris, and the British political officer were enclosed. DBFP, vol. 4, 256–57.

[96] FRUS, vol. 6, 132.

[97] 31 May 1919. DBFP, vol. 4, 259.

[98] Clayton to Curzon, 1 June 1919. DBFP, vol. 4, p. 263.

[99] *Israel*, p. 151.

[100] Ibid., p. 157.

[101] Ibid., p. 145.

[102] DBFP, vol. 4, 273n.
[103] To Curzon. Ibid., 277.
[104] To Curzon. Ibid., 272–74.
[105] Howard, *King-Crane*, pp. 91–92.
[106] To Curzon. DBFP, vol. 4, 281–82.
[107] Ibid., 282.
[108] To Tyrrell, 5 June 1919, enclosed in Curzon to Balfour, 19 June 1919. Ibid., 283–85.
[109] To Curzon. Ibid., 300–01.
[110] See note 64.
[111] "Note by Sir R. Graham of conversations with Mr. Samuel and Dr. Weizmann," 2 July 1919. DBFP, vol. 4, 307–08.
[112] *The Israelis* (New York: Holt, Rinehart & Winston, 1971), p. 152.
[113] *Trial and Error*, p. 258.
[114] Elon, *Israelis*, p. 173.
[115] Minute to "Note by Sir R. Graham," 3 July 1919. DBFP, vol. 4, 308.
[116] Minutes of meeting enclosed in Curzon to Balfour, 8 August 1919. DBFP, vol. 4, 330–35. Present were Weizmann, Clayton, Lord Rothschild, Sir Alfred Mond, James de Rothschild, Dr. Levin, and Messrs. Berligne, Dizengoff, Goldberg, Landman, Naiditch, Sacher, Simon, Slatopolsky, Ussishkin, Wilkansky.
[117] Weizmann to Balfour, 23 July 1919. DBFP, vol. 4, 326.
[118] O. A. Scott minute, 6 August 1919. FO 371/4233, 112379/112061.
[119] DBFP, vol. 4, 326–27.
[120] "A.C.H." minute, 6 August 1919. FO 371/4233, 111235/111235.
[121] Esco, *Palestine*, p. 169.
[122] To Forbes Adam, 24 July 1919. DBFP, vol. 4, 317–18.
[123] Minute, 28 July 1919. Ibid.
[124] Ibid. Also see Forbes Adam memorandum, 26 September 1919. Ibid., 428.
[125] Ibid., 329.
[126] See Balfour to Curzon, 11 September 1919. Ibid., 381–82; see also 355.
[127] Vansittart, Crowe, and Balfour minutes to Curzon to Balfour, 5 August 1919. Ibid., 329–30.
[128] Meinertzhagen, *Diary*, pp. 24–27.
[129] DBFP, vol. 4, 340–49.
[130] Earl of Ronaldshay, *Life of Lord Curzon*, vol. 3 (London: Ernest Benn, 1928), 203.
[131] Scott, *Diaries*, p. 376.
[132] Allenby to Churchill, 6 August 1919. DBFP, vol. 4, 338–39.
[133] Bentwich, *Mandate*, pp. 45–46.
[134] 6 August 1919. DBFP, vol. 4, 338–39.
[135] 30 August 1919. Ibid., 367–69.
[136] "Arab Movement and Zionism," 12 August 1919. Ibid., 360–65.
[137] FO 371/4171, 1051.
[138] *Cross Roads*, p. 33.
[139] 13 September 1919. FO 406/41. Also see Nevakivi, *Britain, France*, pp. 265–66. Lloyd George was at Deauville at the time. Hence the Anglo-French agreement is sometimes referred to as the Deauville Agreement.
[140] Howard, *King-Crane*, p. 258.

[141] See excerpts from the commission's report in ibid., pp. 345–61. When the text of the report was published, Moody of the Colonial Office minuted that its authors had failed "to realize that questions of politics are questions of power." 1 January 1923. CO 732/11, 276.

[142] Howard, *King-Crane*, pp. 320–21. Howard also notes (p. 262) that when Crane came to London in the autumn of 1919, he showed the report to Lord Allenby (who had been made a field marshal and a peer for his wartime exploits) and his aides, and to Hogarth. According to a memorandum supplied by Captain Donald M. Brodie, U.S. Army, secretary and treasurer of the commission, they "all approved it. Mr. Hogarth said that he would have been proud to have had his name attached to it."

[143] Elizabeth Monroe's judgment about the Balfour Declaration policy is inescapable: "Measured by Britain's interests alone, it was one of the greatest mistakes in our imperial history." *Britain's Moment*, p. 43.

[144] Lloyd George's ignorance of foreign affairs and his belief in his own intuition were perhaps best illustrated by this affair. Desmond Stewart has summarized it well: "Unluckily for Greece, the British prime minister was still the Lloyd George whose political astuteness was neatly balanced by ignorance of the world. He considered Venizelos the greatest Greek statesman since Pericles; he was undisturbed by the fact that the Greeks were a minority both in Pontus and western Anatolia. The Greeks, Lloyd George was certain, were the coming people in the eastern Mediterranean; the Turks it was needless to take into account." *The Middle East* (Garden City, N.Y.: Doubleday & Co., 1971), p. 230.

Chapter 9: Palestine after Versailles

[1] P. 177–78.

[2] 17 September 1919. DBFP, vol. 4, 391.

[3] 26 September 1919. Ibid., 425–28.

[4] Meinertzhagen to Curzon, 2 December 1919. Ibid., 565.

[5] Curzon to Bayley, 27 December 1919, ibid., 605; Samuel, *Memoirs*, p. 148; Meinertzhagen to Curzon, 13 January 1920, DBFP, vol. 4, 613–17.

[6] Allenby to Lloyd George, 24 December 1919, and Bols to chief of the imperial general staff, 21 December 1919, FO 406/43, enclosures 2 and 3 in 56. Bols promised a "country of milk and honey in ten years" and no anti-Zionist activities if Weizmann were there, if Samuel would visit, and if he could have a "big financial fellow" and consideration for a loan. For the report on the Palestine Congress of 27 February 1920 in Damascus, see FO 406/43, enclosures in 168. See Howard M. Sachar, *The Emergence of the Middle East, 1914–1924* (New York: Alfred A. Knopf, 1969), p. 274.

[7] 2 April 1920. FO 406/43, 173.

[8] Robert John and Sami Hadawi, *The Palestine Diary*, vol. 1: 1914–1945 (Beirut: Palestine Research Center, 1970), 158.

[9] *Diary*, pp. 55–56. See pp. 78–79 for more details on this incident, which led to Meinertzhagen's losing his appointment. On 6 June, Walford Har-

mood Montague Selby, first secretary, the residency, Cairo, and later principal private secretary to the foreign secretary, 1924–32, and envoy and ambassador to Vienna and Lisbon, 1933–40, wrote to Sir William Tyrrell refuting Zionist accusations against Allenby and the military administration and giving the direct lie to charges of anti-Semitism on the part of British officers in Palestine. FO 371/5114, 7095/61. Selby was a good friend of Clayton's.

10 Sachar, *Emergence*, pp. 391–94. See also Storrs, *Orientations*, pp. 386–88.
11 H.W.V. Temperley, ed., *A History of the Peace Conference of Paris*, vol. 6 (London: Henry Frowde and Hodder & Stoughton, 1924), 175.
12 Scott, *Political Diaries*, pp. 384–85. The Zionists, Scott said, were in "terror" of Palestine being turned over to Faysal's Syria. The Foreign Office, too, was in the dark about policy at the time. Hubert Young asked: "Is it possible for us to define exactly what our Zionist policy is, and to inform all concerned?" Lord Hardinge replied that they had better wait until after San Remo, "where we may hope for developments. In the meantime our policy is based on Mr. Balfour's Declaration. It is no use to try to force the pace at San Remo." FO 371/5118, 3478/85.
13 Samuel, *Memoirs*, p. 150; John and Hadawi, *Palestine Diary*, pp. 157–58n; Sykes, *Cross Roads*, p. 54.
14 Samuel, *Memoirs*, p. 150.
15 Sachar, *Emergence*, p. 394.
16 Samuel, *Memoirs*, pp. 151–52; Samuel to Curzon, 14 May 1920; FO 800/156.
17 29 October 1920. FO 800/156.
18 *Bible and Sword* (1956; reprint ed., New York: Minerva Books, 1968), p. 341.
19 Zeine, *Struggle*, pp. 138, 183–88.
20 Storrs, *Orientations*, pp. 505–06. See also Samuel, *Memoirs*, pp. 157–58.
21 *Israel*, p. 162.
22 Samuel, *Memoirs*, pp. 154–57; FO 406/44, enclosure 1 in 222.
23 10 October 1920. FO 406/44, enclosure in 83. See Samuel, *Memoirs*, pp. 159–60, for his letter to the king, 12 September 1920.
24 Klieman, *Foundations*, pp. 68–76.
25 Ibid., p. 72; Samuel, *Memoirs*, pp. 159–60.
26 Sir Alec Seath Kirkbride, *A Crackle of Thorns* (London: John Murray, 1956), p. 25. Sir Alec at the time was one of the few roving British officers commissioned to maintain order in Transjordan. According to him, the mandated area east of the Jordan was "intended to serve as a reserve of land for use in the resettlement of Arabs once the National Home for the Jews . . . became an accomplished fact" (pp. 19–20). It was not at that time intended to be an independent state.
27 FO 406/45, enclosures in no. 78.
28 Monroe, *Britain's Moment*, p. 68. In titling her third chapter, Ms. Monroe describes 1922 to 1945 as the "years of good management." Also see Meinertzhagen, *Diary* pp. 94–96,
29 See Klieman, *Foundations*, pp. 105–38, for an excellent discussion of the Cairo conference. Lawrence thought that Churchill had "made straight all the tangle, finding solutions fulfilling (I think) our promises in letter and spirit (where humanly possible) without sacrificing any interest of our

Empire or any interest of the peoples concerned. So we were quit of the war-time Eastern adventure, with clean hands, but three years too late to earn the gratitude which peoples, if not states, can pay." *Seven Pillars*, p. 276n.

[30] For Abdullah's version of the story, see Abdullah, King of Jordan, *Memoirs*, tr. G. Khuri and ed. Philip P. Graves (London: Jonathan Cape, 1950), pp. 190–205.

[31] Klieman, *Foundations*, pp. 127–28, 259–73; John and Hadawi, *Palestine Diary*, p. 169.

[32] For a recent treatment of the appointment of the new mufti, see Kedourie, "Sir Herbert Samuel and the Government of Palestine," in *Chatham House Version*, pp. 52–81.

[33] Presented to the Cabinet by Churchill on 9 June 1921. Cab. 24/125.

[34] *Memoirs*, p. 168.

[35] John and Hadawi, *Palestine Diary*, p. 172. Samuel had already ordered a temporary halt to immigration on 14 May. Klieman, *Foundations*, p. 175.

[36] "Notes on Conversation Held at Mr. Balfour's House on July 22nd, 1921," in Meinertzhagen, *Diary*, pp. 103–06.

[37] Klieman, *Foundations*, pp. 187–88.

[38] *Cross Roads*, pp. 76–78.

[39] See note 36.

[40] Cab. 24/127, C.P. 3213. Much of the memorandum was a result of Churchill's taking Meinertzhagen's advice. See Meinertzhagen, *Diary*, pp. 106–09.

[41] Meinertzhagen, *Diary*, pp. 111–12.

[42] Cmd. 1540. See John and Hadawi, *Palestine Diary*, p. 176; Klieman, *Foundations*, p. 176.

[43] Cmd. 1540.

[44] Graves, *Palestine*, pp. 103–04. In a more recently published book, Howard Sachar described the Arab-Zionist dynamic in the following way: "During the course of the 1919, an authentically Palestinian Arab nationalism began to develop slowly among the younger elements in the towns and cities. Religious emotionalism played a role. So did outrage—at the dynamic, secularized, 'insolent' Zionist youth, with their Western clothing, their higher wages, their free and cocksure assumption that someday they would govern their own Jewish state in Palestine. The Zionists and their supporters did not take Arab unrest, or even Arab sensitivities, quite seriously at first." *Emergence*, p. 391.

[45] Klieman, *Foundations*, pp. 191–92, citing Samuel to Churchill, 18 July 1921, Lloyd George papers F/9/3/72.

[46] Sykes, *Cross Roads*, pp. 82–83.

[47] Klieman, *Foundations*, p. 197n, citing letter in Weizmann Archives, Rehovot, Israel. Musa Alami described the delegation as a "pathetic body. Apart from their secretary, who was a tourist agent and spoke some English, none of them had had any contact with the West, or spoke a word of any language other than Arabic and Turkish; they were living in another world." Geoffrey Furlonge, *Palestine Is My Country* (London: John Murray, 1969), p. 80.

[48] Sykes, *Cross Roads*, p. 83.

[49] DNME, pp. 103–06.

[50] Sykes, *Cross Roads*, p. 88.

[51] Weizmann, *Trial and Error*, p. 290.
[52] Ibid., 290–91.
[53] Ibid. The phrase was Balfour's. See also Sykes, *Cross Roads*, pp. 90–91; John and Hadawi, *Palestine Diary*, pp. 184–85. The white paper had undoubtedly swung many Arab sympathizers over to the government.
[54] 5 July 1922. FO 406/50, 38.
[55] Weizmann, *Trial and Error*, pp. 291–93.
[56] Bendit, *Deedes Bey*, p. 349; Samuel, *Memoirs*, p. 172.
[57] Samuel to Shuckburgh, 20 July 1922. CO 733/39, 3796C.
[58] 4 July 1922. Samuel papers, Oxford University.
[59] Churchill to Samuel, 5 August 1922; Young minute, 2 August 1922. CO 733/39, 37960.
[60] Elizabeth Burgoyne, ed., *Gertrude Bell: From Her Personal Papers, 1914–1926* (London: Ernest Benn, 1961), vol. 2, 112–13.
[61] Clayton, *Arabian Diary*, p. 73
[62] Ibid., pp. 74–75.
[63] Holt, *Egypt, and the Fertile Crescent*, p. 298; DNME, p. 102.
[64] 16 February 1923. Cab. 24/159, CP 106 (23).
[65] Arnold J. Toynbee, *Survey of International Affairs, 1925*, vol. 1: *The Islamic World Since the Peace Settlement* (London: Oxford University Press, 1927), p. 362. Also see Abdullah, *Memoirs*, pp. 207–11.
[66] Clayton, *Arabian Diary*, p. 76 and passim.
[67] To Duke of Devonshire, 8 December 1922. FO 371/8998, 206; CP 4379. The ninth duke of Devonshire, Victor Christian William Cavendish, was governor-general of Canada, 1916–21, and colonial secretary, 1922–24.
[68] Esco, *Palestine*, p. 288; Hanna, *British Policy*, p. 84.
[69] Cab. 24/159, CP 106 (23).
[70] Continuation of 17 February memorandum above, 13 March 1923. FO 371/8998, 301, CP 149 (23).
[71] "Palestine," *Journal of the Royal Central Asian Society* 10, pt. 4 (1923), 279.
[72] Cab. 24/160, CP 293 (23).
[73] 27 July 1923. Cab. 24/161, CP 351 (23).
[74] *Diary*, p. 135. At the same time that Meinertzhagen was accusing Clayton of a lapse of taste, he was talking to Weizmann on his own authority, inquiring "whether, when and if Palestine becomes a Jewish Sovereign State, Great Britain would be granted air, naval and military bases in Palestine in perpetuity." After a few days' consideration, Weizmann proposed the use of Haifa as a naval base, airfields in Gaza and Jaffa, and military bases on the coast between Gaza and Haifa. Shuckburgh was "furious" over his subordinate's indiscretions, but Churchill merely advised him not to bring it up before the Committee on Palestine as it would receive a "hostile reception." Meinertzhagen fulminated, "Appeasement again. We are backing the wrong horse, and, my God, we shall suffer for it if and when another war is sprung on us" (pp. 131–33).
[75] Quoted in Thomas Jones, *Whitehall Diary*, ed. Keith Middlemas, vol. 1: *1916–1925* (London: Oxford University Press, 1969), 246.
[76] Ibid.
[77] *British Policy*, p. 85.
[78] See Devonshire, "Future of Palestine," 27 October 1923. Cab. 24/162, CP 433 (23).
[79] 25 January 1924. Cab. 24/165, CP 136 (24).

[80] CO 733/78, CP 121 (24). Enclosed was a memorandum by the Middle East Department of the Colonial Office, "Palestine," 12 February 1924. Also in Cab. 24/165.

[81] Thomas to Samuel, 22 February 1924; Shuckburgh minute, undated. CO 733/78, 18161.

[82] Furlonge, *Palestine Is My Country*, p. 88.

[83] P. 168.

[84] Kedourie, "Sir Herbert Samuel," pp. 52–81.

[85] Furlonge, *Palestine Is My Country*, p. 89.

[86] *Diary*, p. 134. The quoted apology was inserted editorially; it was not part of the original diary. It should be noted that Christopher Sykes, no enemy of Zionism, has described Meinertzhagen as a "Zionist extremist." *Cross Roads*, p. 79.

[87] Furlonge, *Palestine Is My Country*, pp. 89–90.

[88] Ibid., pp. 90–91.

[89] *England in Palestine* (London: Kegan Paul, 1932), pp. 40–41.

[90] Clayton to Shuckburgh, 3 August 1923. CO 783/60, 40373.

[91] See Kedourie, "Sir Herbert Samuel," pp. 63–69.

[92] To Colonial Office, 6 July 1923, CO 733/47. Cited in Kedourie, "Sir Herbert Samuel," pp. 64–65.

[93] *A Palestine Notebook, 1918–1923* (Garden City, N.Y.: Doubleday, Page & Co., 1923), pp. 238–39.

[94] 13 March 1924. Samuel papers.

[95] "Sir Herbert Samuel," p. 65.

[96] 3 March 1924. FO 800/156.

[97] 19 March 1924. FO 800/156.

[98] *Palestine Diary* (London: Victor Gollancz, 1938), p. 35.

[99] Ibid., p. 104.

[100] Wiezmann, *Trial and Error*, pp. 295–97. Kisch had been picked because of his attractiveness to both British and Jews. As Weizmann said: "we needed a man belonging to both worlds, English as well as Jewish." He was not picked for any special ability with Arabs. See also Bentwich, *Mandate*, pp. 93–95.

[101] *Palestine Diary*, p. 134.

[102] Ibid., p. 143.

[103] *Mandate*, p. 34.

[104] *Orientations*, p. 506.

[105] Ibid., p. 507.

[106] Sykes, *Cross Roads*, p. 97.

[107] Toynbee, *Survey*, p. 395.

[108] Letter to *The Near East and India*, 26 September 1929, p. 355.

[109] Clayton, *Arabian Diary*, p. 77. Keith-Roach, Clayton's first assistant secretary, who worked in a room adjoining his, summarized in 1929 Sir Gilbert's personality and attitudes in the midst of Palestine's peculiar trials. "Clayton's outstanding characteristic was his sincerity; a sincerity firmly fixed on deep religious conviction, his honesty of purpose was so apparent that no man, Moslem, Jew, Agnostic, or Christian, could be long in his presence without being awed by it. I have known persons come in and begin to make the most scandalous statements to gain their own ends, but, after a few minutes with Clayton, his quiet smile and steady gaze had quite disarmed them, and they left his presence abashed at their own

baseness. During our two years of daily contact, I never knew him to lose his temper. He never let a colleague down. He never gave a promise to anyone he did not keep. Whether in the office dealing with some difficult problem, playing tennis, or singing hymns with his wife—to whom he owes so much—and his children on Sunday evenings, he was always the same— an ambassador of what is best in English life." Letter to *The Times* (London), 4 October 1929, p. 10.

[110] Clayton, *Arabian Diary*, p. 150.

[111] Stein to Toynbee, 25 November 1926. Quoted in Toynbee, *Survey*, p. 392.

[112] Cohen, *Israel*, p. 171.

[113] Toynbee, *Survey*, pp. 395–96.

[114] Cohen, *Israel*, p. 170.

[115] 1 July 1922. DNME, p. 102.

[116] "Policy in Palestine," 17 February 1923. Cab. 24/159, CP 106 (23), p. 12.

[117] See note 80.

[118] 21 April 1925. CO 733/102.

[119] Hogarth to Gertrude Bell, 11 April 1920. Cited in Klieman, *Foundations*, p. 28.

[120] Ronald Robinson, John Gallagher, and Alice Denny, *Africa and the Victorians* (London: Macmillan & Co., 1961), p. 470. See also William Roger Louis, *Great Britain and Germany's Lost Colonies, 1914–1919* (London: Oxford University Press, Clarendon Press, 1967).

[121] *The Western Question in Greece and Turkey* (London: Constable & Co., 1923), p. 45.

[122] *Democratic Ideals*, pp. 89–90.

[123] Sachar, *Emergence*, p. 44.

[124] Halford L. Hoskins, *British Routes to India* (London: Longmans, Green & Co., 1966), p. 452.

[125] *Palestine Diary*, p. 19.

[126] *Israel*, pp. 165–66.

[127] *Trial and Error*, p. 216. Weizmann's attitude toward Arabs is not difficult to document, but the following incident and observation are worthy of notice. On 29 November 1921, Weizmann met with the Palestinian Arab delegation at the Colonial Office. A British observer, E. Mills, a Palestinian government officer at the Colonial Office, blamed the failure of the meeting on Weizmann's presentation. "Dr. Weizmann, while his speech was conciliatory, adopted an unfortunate manner in delivering it. His attitude was of the nature of a conqueror handing to beaten foes the terms of peace. Also I think he despises the members of the Delegation as not worthy protagonists—that it is a little derogatory to him to expect him to meet them on the same ground." "Note on a Meeting Between the Arab Delegation and the Zionist Organization"; CO 537/855; cited in Klieman, *Foundations*, pp. 196–97.

[128] "Whose Country Is Palestine?" *Times Literary Supplement*, 23 October 1970, pp. 1209–11.

[129] For details, see Cohen, *Israel*, pp. 153–60. Cohen cites a work by Chaim Kalvarisky originally published in Hebrew: "Plans and Speeches," *At the Parting of Our Ways* (1939), pp. 25–26. Also see Esco, *Palestine*, vol. 1, 562–64.

[130] Ibid.,

[131] Ibid.,

[132] *British Policy*, p. 86.

Index